The Bowery Savings Bank of New York

Oct 12th 1857

The Bowery
Savings Bank
of New York

A Social
and Financial History

Oscar Schisgall

amacom
American Management Associations

Library of Congress Cataloging in Publication Data
Schisgall, Oscar, 1901–
    The Bowery Savings Bank of New York.

    Rev. ed. of: Out of one small chest. 1975.
    Includes index.
    1. Bowery Savings Bank of New York—History.
I. Schisgall, Oscar, 1901–   Out of one small chest.
II. Title.
HG2613.N54B675   1984   332.2'1'097471   84-6335
ISBN 0-8144-5788-6

Printing number

10 9 8 7 6 5 4 3 2 1

Preface

As the bank marks its 150th anniversary year and the second edition of this book goes to press I want to express my gratitude to all who so generously shared with me their knowledge of banking and of the glowing history of The Bowery Savings Bank. Former Chairman Earl B. Schwulst, former Chairman Morris D. Crawford, Jr., former President John W. Larsen, and former General Counsel Jack Older were unstinting in the time and help they gave me in recording the events of their administrations.

With equal enthusiasm, Chairman Ellis T. Gravette, Jr. has guided me through the developments of the present administration. The knowledge I gained from him was augmented in meetings with Vice Chairman Stuart D. Root, President Jerald C. Newman, Executive Vice President Alan R. Cohen, Senior Vice President Gary Brody, Treasurer Dolores J. Morrissey, General Counsel Leonard S. Rassnick, Senior Vice President Diane A. Tracy, Vice Presidents Barbara Edler and Grace Pichardo, and Recorder of the trustees' meetings Veronica Kuckel.

And I owe many more ideas than they realize to my frequent luncheon companions, Frederick H. Brackett, Victor Elias, and John P. Williams.

The assistance and information all these officers gave me, as did at least forty other people, proved invaluable. I would wish the readers of this account to know how great my indebtedness is to every one of them.

Oscar Schisgall

Contents

THE CITY OF NEW YORK
OFFICE OF THE MAYOR
NEW YORK, N.Y. 10007

December 19, 1983

The Bowery Savings Bank
110 East 42nd Street
New York, New York 10017

Dear Friends:

Throughout 1984, The Bowery will celebrate its 150th year by continuing its time-honored tradition of civic participation in the most constructive and innovative sense of that term.

There are 150 years of banking history at The Bowery from which to draw examples, but by keeping within the parameters of current times, the list of The Bowery's contributions to the quality of life in our City merits the appreciative recognition of all New Yorkers.

Here are just a few of The Bowery's many vital undertakings: active involvement in the renovation of Times Square, 42nd Street; participation in Fordham Plaza; sponsorship of a summer athletic program for City children with the Police Athletic League; an active community development program and initiation of creative financing concepts which have resulted in the construction and rehabilitation of thousands of modern apartment facilities.

Community and housing redevelopment projects include the Bedford-Stuyvesant Restoration, the Albee Square Shopping Mall, the 145th Street and St. Nicholas Avenues housing and business complex....and the list goes on.

Here's to The Bowery and the next 150 years!

Sincerely,

Edward I. Koch
Mayor

It gives me great pleasure to extend my
sincere congratulations to The Bowery Savings Bank
on its 150th anniversary.

The Bowery's pervasive role in the growth of
the entire metropolitan area is indeed noteworthy.
It is through The Bowery that so many people first
obtained professional financial advice, that so many
business people started their careers, and that so
many civic organizations found support for worthy
endeavors.

The Bowery has been a community leader in the
truest sense of the word. Over the past 150 years,
The Bowery has helped to marshal the resources that
have enabled the State and the City to grow and
prosper.

The Bowery Savings Bank has given solid and
lasting support to New York, and I applaud the Bank
on behalf of all New Yorkers on the occasion of its
150th anniversary.

Mario M. Cuomo

November 30, 1983

PART ONE

~

The Decades
of Growth
(1834 - 1974)

1

EVERYBODY WANTS YOUR MONEY

In 1974, when the first edition of this history appeared, it reported:

More than 25 million American families, almost half the country's population, maintain accounts in savings banks—and they now find themselves exhorted on all sides to move their funds elsewhere. Everybody wants the total of more than $100 billion these people have managed to accumulate in their savings accounts. Commercial banks, mutual funds, savings and loan associations, municipalities, even the federal government—all are engaged in publicity campaigns to attract those funds. Each offers its own glittering inducements, generally in the form of high interest rates. The commercial banks stress the convenience of the "full service" they can give—checking privileges, personal loans, credit cards, and other consumer services that in most states have so far not been permitted to savings banks.

One can hardly blame the average citizen for being confused. Where is it wisest to keep his money? Should he withdraw it from a thrift institution and put it into a commercial bank? Should he use it to buy tax-exempt municipal bonds? Ought he to invest it in U.S. Treasury obligations or maybe in a mutual fund that will invade the stock market? Is it better to buy gold?

The most insistent beckonings come from commercial banks, of which there are some 13,500 in the United States. By comparison the savings banks are few in number—486 at the latest count. In any struggle between the two types of banks the mutual savings banks seem like a David confronting an army of Goliaths.

Yet the competition between them has been severe and often dramatic. There was a day a few years ago when the president of a large Eastern commercial bank, the Franklin National, rose with grim purpose at a convention of the American Bankers Association. He pointed at the representatives of the nation's savings banks and demanded that all such institutions be expelled from the parent organization.

If many at the meeting were shocked and embarrassed, it was because the savings banks, almost a century earlier, had helped to found the American Bankers Association. They had been its constant supporters. And so the motion for expulsion was defeated. But this incident emphasized the tensions and the bitter competition that have arisen between the commercial banks and the mutual savings institutions.

The difference between them lies largely in the fact that mutual savings banks have never enjoyed the same freedom of operation as commercial banks. There is a

2

simple reason. Commercial banks are owned by stockholders to whom management is accountable. If management is inefficient or corrupt, it can be dismissed by the share-holding owners. They are the bosses.

The mutuals, on the other hand, are not owned by anybody. They have no stockholders. Operated for the benefit of their depositors—under the scrutiny of unsalaried, public-spirited trustees—they are answerable only to state Banking Departments. Therefore the Banking Departments have been extremely zealous in protecting depositors' savings. They have limited the investment of such funds to areas that present the least risk: mortgages soundly secured by real estate, government and other high-quality bonds, a restricted amount of corporate stock. The Superintendents of Banks have also insisted that thrift institutions at all times retain sufficient liquid assets to meet all normal withdrawals on demand.

Such stringent regulations may have had drawbacks, but they also had beneficial effects. They assured the safety of money entrusted to savings banks, and its ready availability.

As for the present intensification of inter-bank competition, its primary cause is clear. In a period of inflation everybody needs more money. The commercial banks are beleaguered with applications for loans. They have been empowered to charge borrowers interest rates of more than 11 percent. That means they can earn enormous profits—*provided they have the money to lend*. Where can they get the money? As they consider their options, their eyes turn to the billions of dollars in the country's thrift institutions. It is an alluring sight.

As if the competition of commercial banks were not enough to bewilder a depositor, he now sees mutual savings banks competing *among themselves*. Every thrift institution promises him "the highest interest rates." In addition they dangle free gifts before his eyes as a reward for new deposits. A person can withdraw money from one bank, spread it among several others, and without any loss of interest he can walk off with a clock, or dishes, or an electric blanket, or any of a hundred other enticements. A Southern bank offered feminine depositors free wigs. One in Pennsylvania made it possible for new clients to purchase synthetic diamonds at half price.

Clearly this kind of competition does nothing to increase the total resources of the nation's banks. It merely redistributes funds. "The only real beneficiaries of the give-away orgy," one banker observed, "were the advertising agencies that publicized them and the sellers of the merchandise which banks were giving away." The Banking Department of New York State, finally recognizing the absurdity of give-aways, ended their use on July 1, 1973—except to feature the opening of a new branch.

One of the most outspoken opponents of free gifts was The Bowery Savings Bank of New York. And yet in time The Bowery itself yielded to the policy. "We had to do it as a defensive measure," said the bank's chairman, Morris D. Crawford, Jr. "In a competitive period no bank can afford to let others draw away its depositors. The same reason applied to our advertising of the highest interest rates. If we didn't do it people would ask, 'Doesn't The Bowery pay the highest rates?' We do, of course, as do most savings banks. But we had to *say* so."

By 1974 competition for deposits had become so severe, especially on the part of commercial banks, that The Bowery's chairman, speaking on behalf of the entire savings bank industry, protested before the Senate Banking Committee in Washington. "In the past many of the commercial banks would not even accept savings deposits," he said. "But today commercial banks have turned increasingly to savings and time deposits as a major source of lendable funds." He called this "a revolutionary departure from tradition."

Revolutionary or evolutionary, it has resulted in sapping so much money out of the thrift institutions that the 1973 Annual Report of the National Association of Mutual Savings Banks began with the statement: "For the mutual savings bank industry, 1973 and early 1974 was one of the most difficult periods in history." All savings banks, it went on, were struck by "disintermediation (the withdrawal of funds for investment elsewhere) of devastating proportions."

There was a psychological cause, too, for the drain on savings deposits: the pressures of inflation. One could not help wondering if the dollar being preserved in a savings account would continue to become less and less valuable with every passing month. Should it not be withdrawn now to purchase some necessity or comfort which might be much more costly in the future?

Depositors, however, are not the only ones concerned about the condition of savings banks. There are also the people who seek mortgage loans. For generations the thrift institutions have been one of the principal sources of such loans. They have helped build millions of American homes. Almost 70 percent of their assets lie in home-loan mortgages. So one may well ask: Why has it become so difficult in the mid-1970s to obtain a mortgage from a thrift institution? Is it because so much money has been transferred from savings accounts to other forms of investment?

One of the primary purposes of this book is to examine all such problems as they pertain to depositors, to borrowers, and to the banks themselves.

This can best be done, I feel, by considering the experiences of the biggest—and one of the oldest—of all American thrift institutions, The Bowery Savings Bank. With assets of over $4 billion it has long been a leader in its industry. Its history, spanning almost a century and a half, reflects the history of the United States itself.

5

Since 1834 it has endured and survived—and helped countless of its depositors to survive—wars, panics, depressions, inflations, bank closings, and all the other hardships man has managed to heap upon himself.

Apart from that, its annals present a remarkable story of enterprise and innovation, of constant growth achieved in spite of economic, social, and political obstacles. Over the years it has dealt in the savings of every ethnic, racial, and religious group that has come across the seas: Jews from Russia, Poland, and Germany; Catholics from Ireland and Italy; Protestants from Scandinavia; Buddhists from China; blacks and whites. All were served by the bank. Yet I know of no institution that is more typically American.

Its trustees have included scores of citizens distinguished in industry, the professions, the arts, education, and government. Since they have from the start been forbidden by law to profit in any way from their association with the bank, their presence on the board has always been an expression of public service. Some of them, in accepting their positions, have actually had to sacrifice doing business with The Bowery.

Possibly we can learn to cope more intelligently with today's economic challenges by glancing back to see how these men dealt with similar challenges in the past. Earl B. Schwulst, former chairman of The Bowery, may have been right when he said, "The trouble is that each generation seems to have to learn from its own mistakes instead of learning from the mistakes of preceding generations." And yet, by studying the events of the past century and a half, by seeing them through the eyes of the savings bankers who have had the responsibility of managing the funds of millions of people, we may conceivably gain the kind of sophistication we need today to see us through our contemporary trials.

6

2

THE CHEST

It is hard to realize that the modern Bowery Savings Bank, with its 700,000 accounts, was launched as a sort of philanthropic enterprise for underprivileged "little people." It is equally hard to realize that this institution, whose mortgage loans have helped construct thousands of American homes, was at the outset forbidden to make any mortgage loans at all.

To understand the growth of The Bowery—and of similar thrift institutions—and to appreciate the struggles that preceded every change in its operations, one must begin by considering the motivations of its founders.

Forty-one of them, all New York businessmen, were convened late in 1833 in the offices of the Butchers and Drovers Bank at number 128 on the Bowery. No doubt they were puzzled by the purpose of the gathering. There are no minutes to indicate who made the initial speech of clarification, but it may be assumed it came from Benjamin M. Brown, president of the Butchers and Drovers Bank, host of the occasion.

These men were here, they were told, because hundreds of their neighbors needed help. The majority of such neighbors were immigrants: Irish, Poles, Germans, Italians, Englishmen. They had been pouring into the New World as into a haven, fleeing from the cholera epidemics, the famines and depressions that were ravaging Europe.

For the most part they were diligent and readily found work. Yet their assets were generally too meager to merit the notice of commercial banks. What then were they to do with the few dollars they could save? Where would such funds be secure?

As long as these "little people"—maids, coachmen, laborers, and such—had no convenient way to lay money aside, it often happened that when they lost their jobs they were penniless. Many became public charges. Others—those immigrants who found it difficult to adjust to the new life in America—had likewise to be supported by public charity. And public charity had become so heavy a burden for the New York community that Governor DeWitt Clinton bitterly complained, "The fruits of industry are applied to the wants of idleness; a laborious poor man is taxed for the support of an idle beggar."

The governor conceded that no human being ought to be left to starve. But he insisted that society must provide something better than a system of doles. With remarkable foresight he warned that "Pauperism increases with the augmentation of the funds applied to its relief."

The men at the meeting solemnly agreed that a more intelligent solution than charity had to be devised. There *ought* to be a savings institution for the "little people" of the Bowery area. Thomas Jeremiah, a well-to-do grocer, expressed his own philosophy in a few simple words: "When you help a man to save his first dollar you have started him on the road to self-respect and self-reliance."

So worthy a proposal could not be opposed. The business group voted unanimously to seek the right to establish a thrift institution. A committee of distinguished citizens, including Hamilton Fish, Peter C. Stuyvesant, and Anson G. Phelps, was sent to request the state legislature to charter the bank. After obtaining the consent of Assemblyman Peter S. Titus to be their spokesman, they had to wait from January to May for a decision; but in the end they won legislative assent. The Bowery Savings Bank became a reality.

Among the charter's seventeen stipulations was one which ruled: "The Trustees of the said corporation shall not, directly or indirectly, receive any pay or emolument for their services." (In more recent years this was amended to conform with general corporate practice: Trustees may now receive a modest fee for attending board meetings or for engaging in special committee activities.)

Another section read: "The amount of deposits received by said corporation shall not exceed five hundred thousand dollars." Probably the founders anticipated that so huge a total would never be reached, for they offered no immediate objection to the clause. Besides, the other thrift institutions operated under similar strictures.

Accepting the charter, the founders plunged into the details of organization. For guidance they could look at the Philadelphia Savings Fund Society and the Provident Institution for Savings in Boston, the first two savings banks in the United States. Moreover, the City of New York (then limited to Manhattan) already had three such institutions—the Bank for Savings, founded in 1819; the Seamen's, in 1824; and the Greenwich, in 1833. But each of these was located at a considerable distance from the heavily populated neighborhood around the Bowery. People who lived on Grand, Hester, Mulberry, Broome, and other nearby streets would have to travel long distances to deposit money in the existing banks. It was too much to expect.

The matter of quarters for the new institution might have presented a serious problem, since it had no funds. Happily, the officers of the Butchers and Drovers were generous and altruistic. They offered the new bank free space to set up a counter and receive deposits.

And so The Bowery Savings Bank was able to open for business on the evening of June 2, 1834—a rent-free tenant in the Butchers and Drovers' premises.

The first time the doors were unlocked five depositors were waiting on the steps. These were two brothers, Ernest and William Aims, both butchers; Sheperd Devcau, a household servant; a woman named Mary St. Clair Forde, who said she had no occupation she wished noted in the books; and Silvanus Bedell, who described himself simply as "a gentleman."

Their names were still being inscribed in the first red-covered ledger when other depositors entered the dimly lit bank. The line that formed included a carpenter, a shoemaker, a baker, a tailor, a mason, several seamstresses—fifty people in all, and every one of humble means. The bank was fulfilling its purpose.

The New York Times editorially said:

This is the Poor Man's Bank . . . to enable him to save the earnings of his honest industry, to promote economy, temperance, and enterprise, to raise him in the world, to provide for his old age. Let the friends of the poor, who cry out against the monopolies of the rich, give the poor their iron chest, where they too may get interest on their money no matter how small the sum may be.

Essentially, that objective has never changed. Only recently John W. Larsen, then The Bowery's president, defined the purposes of the institution this way: "A mutual savings bank exists for the benefit of its depositors. It devotes itself to the ideal of enabling men and women and their families to enjoy a large measure of economic security through their own efforts; and pledges itself to help them achieve these goals."

So some things are constant.

Fortunately The Bowery's operations in no way conflicted with those of the Butchers and Drovers. Nor was there any infringement on the commercial bank's time, since the new institution was open only Mondays and Saturdays from five o'clock in the evening to eight. Its "tellers" were not tellers. Teller duties were performed by volunteers among the founders. Though they were surely well-intentioned, most of them knew nothing whatever about the job they were undertaking. David Cotheal was a merchant. Eleutheros D. Comstock was a ship-carpenter. Frederick R. Lee dealt in hardware. So it went.

Before long these novices were visited by Daniel C. Tylee, the chief accountant of the older Bank for Savings, and Mr. Tylee amicably gave them a crash course in bank management. Whether he was motivated by compassion or simple amusement at the neophytes' ineptitude, no one ever knew.

At any rate, the amateur tellers did exceedingly well. During the first year they enrolled 531 depositors who entrusted them with a total of $72,742. The expenses they incurred as organizing costs throughout that first year—principally "for procuring a set of books and other necessities"—came to a total of $459.93. (By 1974 the annual operating expenses of the bank were almost $30,000,000!)

As might have been foreseen, with more and more people bringing in deposits the volunteers soon found they needed assistance. Again they received it from the Butchers and Drovers. The volunteers were joined by employees of the Butchers and Drovers who likewise, for a long time, worked without pay.

Obviously there was more to banking than collecting money, more than finding investments for it. There were the ledgers to be kept, and these were written with such meticulous Spencerian calligraphy that every entry became a work of artistry. One has only to see these notations in the old books to understand the hours of painstaking labor they consumed—and to realize how the invention of the typewriter has destroyed a fine art.

The lack of sophistication of early depositors was demonstrated by the questions they asked and by the answers they received:

"Do I really get *paid* for leaving my money here?"

"Yes, indeed. You will receive dividends."

"How much?"

"That will depend on how much we can earn by investing our funds."

"What if I don't want to wait till you earn money? What if I want my money back quick?"

"You may have it whenever you like. Here are the regulations."

Each depositor was given a paper on which the bank's founders had written instructions, by hand, for methods of withdrawal; these documents generally soothed doubts.

Since the fledgling bank had no vaults, money and

papers were kept in a small, leather-bound chest 14 inches wide and 7 inches high. It lay under the counter. When business increased to a point which warranted the added expenditure, the trustees voted to purchase a second chest. Every night these two repositories of the bank's total assets were placed for safekeeping in the vaults of the Butchers and Drovers. On any Monday or Saturday evening the bank's entire wealth could have been carried off by armed bandits. Yet this never happened. One of the chests still exists, a treasured relic of the institution.

ᘛᐧᘚ

Despite the absence of thieves, there were other dangers to worry the trustees. Time after time they had to rush to bolt the doors against possible violence and intrusion.

For these were days of historic riots and gang battles in New York. When drunken mobs clashed in combat, as they often did, no one could foretell what would happen. On one memorable night a crowd of Irish Americans decided to gather in nearby Chatham Square for the purpose of organizing an all-Irish regiment to protect America. Other citizens felt such a project ought to be scotched. They marched to break up the meeting of the Irish, and the ensuing bloody battle raged within earshot of the bank until the militia arrived.

Even more threatening was the disastrous conflagration of 1835 which destroyed more than 700 homes. That night several trustees of the bank stood in front of their wooden building, terrified and irresolute. Looking southward, hardly more than a mile away, they could see lurid walls of flame rising into the skies from the area around Wall Street. Fire-fighters were there, working desperately, but this was an icy mid-winter night, and water froze in the hoses.

The trustees must have been close to panic. Ought they to remove the two chests and carry them to the farmlands north of 14th Street? Would the coffers be safe there?

Before they could reach a decision, a series of blasts roared out of the smoke and flames. The fire-fighters had turned to explosives in the form of gunpowder. They were blasting a chasm some two hundred yards wide in the path of the oncoming blaze. They had to destroy scores of buildings, but they created a gap across which the fire would not easily spread to devour all of New York. In that way the great conflagration was brought under control, and The Bowery remained untouched.

But it faced its first real problem.

Its original charter had permitted its funds to be invested only in the bonds of Pennsylvania, Ohio, New York State, and the City of New York. Presumably these were the best and safest securities obtainable. Indeed, they were so good that *everybody* wanted them, and their price soared to record heights. In ratio to their cost, returns on them would be so low as to make it almost impossible for the bank to pay depositors any dividends.

Benjamin M. Brown had been chosen to be The Bowery's first president, largely because of his experience in being also head of the Butchers and Drovers. In early 1835 he called an emergency meeting of the trustees. The issue that confronted them was clear: Another way of investing the bank's funds had to be found, a way that would yield sufficient revenue to make the distribution of dividends possible.

The specific questions Brown posed to the trustees were these: *What was the most logical area for investment in a rapidly growing city? Where was money most urgently needed?*

There was but one intelligent answer: for the construction of homes and business buildings. New York desperately needed both after the tragic fire.

Benjamin Brown dispatched a committee to present the bank's case to the state legislature. The committee's argument was sensible and persuasive. Even so, several lawmakers demurred on the grounds that the lending of money in large sums had traditionally been a function of commercial banks. Why disrupt the established order?

Fortunately, such objections did not sway the majority of legislators. In 1835 The Bowery was empowered to lend its money on real estate mortgages—provided it lent no more than 50 percent of any property's value.

So successful did this area of investment prove to be that by the end of the first year of mortgage operations the depositors were able to collect $1,730 in dividends. This may not seem much in our day, but for most small savers it was the first time they had experienced the excitement of earning anything at all without having to do extra work. Certainly it must have been an exhilarating occasion.

Ever since the 1835 change in charter provisions, mortgage loans have remained the mainstay of the bank's investment policies. And depositors have been collecting dividends without interruption in amounts that varied between 1½ percent (1 percent on larger balances) in depression years to 7¾ percent (on long-term deposits) in the 1970s.

Nor was the right to make real estate loans the only early change of regulations the bank had to request. Its second president, David Cotheal, had to send another committee of trustees to the legislature. This delegation pointed out that the charter allowed the bank to accept no more than total deposits of $500,000. The limitation had been designed to prevent thrift institutions from enticing big deposits away from commercial banks. Now experience was proving that such a limitation was wholly inadequate and unreasonable.

"After The Bowery's coffers contain $500,000," the committee chairman demanded of the lawmakers, "should the bank then be closed to all prudent people who wish to accumulate further savings?"

Not only was such an idea retrogressive; it was patently unsocial and unfair.

"As you well know," the committee's spokesman argued, "every month brings additional immigrants into New York. Every month new wage earners seek to open savings accounts. Every month older depositors wish to add to their savings. Must all such good people be turned away, discouraged from providing for their future, because an arbitrary limit has been placed on the total amount the bank may accept? We should never be afraid to correct errors. Even the Constitution provides for amendments."

Again a few legislators protested. "It was never intended," they argued once more, "that thrift institutions should achieve a size that would compete with commercial banks."

Happily, a majority of the legislature again overrode such arguments. They favored the social considerations The Bowery supported, and the limiting ceiling was removed.

Why was it necessary to dispatch committees to the state legislature whenever any change of policy or activity was deemed essential? Why was it still necessary after 140-odd years? The primary reason, perhaps, is that the writers of the U.S. Constitution made no specific provisions to govern the conduct of banks. Was this an oversight? A deliberate omission? Or was it—as is much more likely—that the various Colonies, unwilling to surrender local privileges, were already espousing the cause of states' rights? Whatever the answer, mutual savings banks have been chartered and supervised at the state level. Thus every reform desired by The Bowery Savings Bank and its sister banks had to be sought from the political administration of the state.

Because the changes they needed were often viewed by commercial banks as infringements on their own prerogatives, almost every advance has plunged the savings banks into legal controversy. For more than a hundred years The Bowery in these matters has received the counsel, guidance, and cooperation of one of the country's most venerable law firms, Cadwalader, Wickersham, and Taft. But no lawyers could rescue the savings banks from the calamitous events of 1837.

3

THE

LOCOFOCO ERA

A former aide of Franklin Delano Roosevelt once told me that after the President had declared the bank holiday of 1933 he remarked, "Everything the banks of this nation have ever learned had to be learned the hard way—hard for them and hard for the country." The President might have made the same comment a century earlier during the administration of Andrew Jackson.

In 1833, only a few months before the founding of The Bowery, a feud between Jackson and Nicholas

Biddle, head of the Bank of the United States, had threatened to wreck the entire monetary system of the country.

As every historian of the period has recorded, President Jackson was convinced that the Bank of the United States, the principal repository of government funds, was misusing its powers. Not only was Nicholas Biddle dominating other banks because of the loans he had granted them—loans made possible through the use of federal deposits; but also, as "Old Hickory" bitterly told his Cabinet, Biddle had amassed tremendous legislative power by lending money to scores of political leaders. Because these men were heavily in his debt, the President charged, they were doing "Biddle's bidding."

Even as distinguished a patriot as Daniel Webster had made stirring speeches in Biddle's defense. Now it appeared that the illustrious Webster had actually been selling his talents to the banker. This became a shocking revelation with the disclosure of a letter sent to Biddle on December 21, 1833 in which Webster wrote:

> I believe my retainer has not been renewed
> or refreshed as usual. If it be wished that
> my relation to the Bank should be continued
> it may be well to send me the usual retainers.
>
> Yours with regard,
>
> *Dan'l Webster.*

Jackson was outraged. Described by an English observer as "vigorous, brusque, uncouth, relentless, straightforward, and open," he determined to wrest the unconscionable powers out of Biddle's hands. This could be done only by withdrawing all government funds from the Bank of the United States and by refusing to renew its charter. Defying furious opposition by political giants like Clay and Calhoun, Old Hickory had his way.

Jackson ordered the withdrawal of every dollar the

government had deposited in the Bank of the United States. He distributed these funds to a number of state banks. The managers of some local institutions, as if intoxicated by the unexpected influx of wealth, lent their newly obtained money with a recklessness and profligacy which could lead only to disaster. In fact, the countless bad debts that were incurred by these banks became one of the causes of the financial panic that eventually shook the country.

And though the organizers of The Bowery were living through these hazardous days, they apparently gave scant attention to what was happening. Instead, they continued with cheerful innocence to serve the "little people" of their community.

More dangerous than anything else at the time was the fact that everywhere state-chartered commercial banks were printing their own banknotes. This meant, of course, that these institutions were assuming heavy obligations. Few of them seemed to reflect that an expansion of debt which is not solidly based on assets must inevitably result in catastrophe.

But why should anyone have had such morbid thoughts? Paper money was plentiful. Business was good. For the first and last time in history, the federal government had paid all its debts and had actually distributed a surplus of $37 million to the states. So the banks in those states continued issuing their own banknotes—with little gold, silver, or anything else to support their generosity. And nobody cared. What did anything matter? Entrepreneurs were making fortunes. On paper.

Bankers were equally paper-happy, and one must include those of The Bowery Savings Bank. More and more homes had to be built. The Bowery was being overrun by mortgage seekers. Every dollar it could muster found eager applicants for loans.

Yes, the spirit of nothing-can-stop-the-good-old-U.S.A.

was on the land. The glory of the future was as limitless as sunshine. At The Bowery and at the Butchers and Drovers, business thrived so well that by 1836 both institutions felt their quarters had become too constricted to house such successful ventures.

So the Butchers and Drovers, its eyes fixed on larger premises, was delighted to accept The Bowery's offer to purchase its site near the corner of Grand Street. Here was testimony to the incredible pace of the American economy: After less than two years of existence the savings bank was able to acquire its own building.

In January of 1836 a new sign rose over the entrance. Trustees could stand in front of it, rub their hands in satisfaction, and congratulate themselves.

In committing their institution to the expenditure of $23,500 for the property, the trustees were expressing unbounded confidence in the future. Indeed, they felt so prosperous that within a few months they authorized salaries of $300 a year for each of the clerks, $50 a year for a porter, and a munificent $1,000 a year for a Mr. Giles H. Coggeshall, who was given the title of Secretary.

No doubt the trustees felt entitled to indulge such evidences of success. In two years they had attracted 2,166 depositors and had all of $311,595 in their till. And since The Bowery now owned the vaults of the Butchers and Drovers, the two leather-bound chests, in which all assets had been kept, were at last put aside.

❧

If there were scattered flashes of discontent in the American economy, recurrent riots against one thing or another, anybody with sense knew such demonstrations were sponsored by irresponsible radicals. These protesters were nothing but locofocos.

22

(The word "locofoco" has all but vanished from the language. Its original definition was a match that could be struck against any rough surface. On a night when a group of radicals met in New York, someone tried to disrupt their gathering by turning off all the gas lights. The radicals countered by striking locofocos, and the meeting continued by match-light. Thereafter people with radical ideas were scoffed at as locofocos.)

More than anything else, the housing boom seemed to corroborate the conviction that this was America's endless golden age of opportunity. Inspired speculators were buying public lands with such abandon that in two brief years, from 1834 to 1836, their purchases leaped from 4 million acres to 20 million. Many of these acquisitions were being paid for with banknotes issued by commercial banks.

How much of such dubious paper currency could the nation absorb? No one knew—until a warning clap of thunder sounded out of Washington. The value of the banknotes had become so questionable that in July the Secretary of the Treasury, in a "Specie Circular," notified the nation of a drastic decision: Henceforth the government would accept no banknotes at all in payment for public lands, taxes, or other sums due the Treasury, *but only gold and silver.*

The Secretary might as well have proclaimed a revolution.

At The Bowery Savings Bank harried depositors rushed in with questions. Did the government's edict mean that all banknotes were now worthless? If so, could depositors retrieve their savings in gold or silver?

The fear reached its wild climax in 1837. This happened when the United States was confronted by a shortage of farm products as abruptly, as unexpectedly, as a hundred and forty years later it would face an oil shortage. The cost of food became terrifying. Flour at

$15 a barrel was so unbelievable that New York witnessed a new kind of riot—"flour riots"—with thousands milling and shouting in the streets because dealers wanted gold, not paper.

That ended the spurious boom. Everybody knew that if he was to survive he had to follow the government's example and rely on gold and silver only, not on bank-notes.

People rushed to The Bowery Savings Bank as they were rushing to all banks. They demanded their money—"In specie! In specie!" But no bank had enough gold and silver to meet so overwhelming a demand. Helpless, commercial banks in every state began to close their doors.

At The Bowery the lines stretched out into the street. These people were as frantic as everybody else. What most pressingly threatened the institution was the fact that almost all its money was now tied up in long-term mortgages. There was no way of converting these to immediate cash. The one thing the trustees had failed to do, because they had not foreseen a crisis, was to retain sufficient liquid reserves for meeting an emergency like this.

Benjamin Brown had just yielded the bank's presidency to David Cotheal; Brown himself had assumed the title of Chairman of the Executive Committee. President Cotheal promptly called a meeting of the board of trustees and its newly appointed legal counsel, Henry J. Feltus.

The bank, he told the men, was in desperate straits. Mortgage-poor, it could not meet depositors' demands. He turned to the lawyer. "How," he asked, "shall we proceed in case it should be necessary to wind up our affairs?"

Before Feltus could answer, President Cotheal made one last plea. "Let me talk to the people at the Bank for Savings. They have been in existence much longer than we have. Perhaps they can offer advice or help us out. They must realize that if *we* go under, it will undermine confidence in all savings banks, including their own."

The worried trustees gladly postponed any decision until Cotheal could talk to the men at the Bank for Savings. Cotheal was right in assuming the older institution would not wish to see a sister enterprise fail. Out of its liquid assets it now gave The Bowery $40,000 of marketable New York City bonds (called "stocks") in exchange for $50,000 in mortgage assets.

Such a bonanza at once enabled the bank to pay those depositors who clamored for their money. Others, seeing that payments were being made on demand, went home reassured, leaving their savings intact. Thus The Bowery Savings Bank survived its first ordeal—something it could not have done without the aid of the Bank for Savings.

Survival, however, could not obliterate the loss of deposits during the critical days. These had dropped from $311,000 to $191,000, a decline of $120,000. At the next meeting of the trustees, held in a grim mood, President Cotheal gave solemn expression to the lesson to be derived from the experience:

For the safety of depositors and for the solvency of the bank, he warned, *investments in long-term mortgage loans must never again comprise all of The Bowery's assets. The bank must at all times maintain adequate cash reserves—or reserves in the form of assets that could easily be converted to cash.*

Thus the panic of 1837 confirmed Tom Paine's classic prediction that out of every panic something new and useful can be learned. This crisis taught ensuing generations of Bowery trustees the importance of keeping reserves healthy enough to meet any emergency, something they have never forgotten.

In our time one seldom hears of a depositor who asks

a savings bank officer about the institution's ability to cope with emergencies. With federally insured deposits, it seems unnecessary to worry about a bank's solvency. We tend to take that for granted. But we can take it for granted only because events like those of 1837 have taught all thrift institutions and the government itself a few major principles of sound banking.

4

LANDMARK
FOR THE AGES

The modern branch of The Bowery, the third on the original site, stands at number 130 on the Bowery—a branch built late in the 1890s. It is so impressive that it has been declared one of New York's historic landmarks. This insures its permanence as a metropolitan attraction and as a monument to its architects, a firm headed by Stanford White. With stately Greek columns rising to a frieze of sculptured figures, it has all the dignity and majesty of an Hellenic temple. One mounts a few steps to enter, and the hushed, shadowy interior, under a ceiling that seems a hundred feet high, is downright breathtaking. One is tempted to talk in whispers; the presence of a chapel, though unexpected, seems wholly fitting.

Yet the first time I was driven there my taxi driver shook his head in pity as he contemplated the building. "A cathedral in the slums," he said.

In some ways his comment was apt. If you visit the street called the Bowery in our time, its deterioration is one of the saddest of the city's sights. Its buildings appear to be sagging with age. One of them, recently painted white with lurid scarlet trimmings around its windows, resembles (in the words of the same taxi-driving poet) "an old whore among sisters too tired to put on their paint."

This air of decay can hardly be blamed on today's generation. It began shortly after the Civil War and gathered momentum all too swiftly. By 1879 a journalist named Paul Prowler wrote of the Bowery:

> It is a place of cheap lodging houses, saloons, dime museums, pawn shops, second-hand clothing stores, lottery shops, shooting galleries and the like. The museums have a frontage that is made up with gaudily painted figures on canvas which are supposed to represent the attractions within. Abandoned frowsy females accost on every side as you make your way up from Chatham Square. And should they entice you within, certain of the resorts will fleece you. Your watch and other valuables will disappear. You will be surrounded by sporting men, crooks, gamblers, sailors, out-of-towners with a streak of degenerate curiosity, tramps, bar-flies.

What Paul Prowler did not see in his era is a common enough sight in ours: derelicts, stupefied by liquor, sprawling asleep on the sidewalk. Policemen are so accustomed to this sort of thing that they stroll past without even glancing at the crumpled figures. It is not merely an ugly spectacle; it goes far beyond ugliness to a symbol of human degradation—and worse, of human *indifference* to degradation.

In spite of this social decay, records and prints remind us that in its prime, during the 1830s when The Bowery Savings Bank was young, the Bowery was the most fashionable and most celebrated shopping avenue in America. To the United States it was what the Rue de la Paix was to Paris, Piccadilly to London, Unter den Linden to Berlin. Here exquisitely gowned women in their carriages came to patronize New York's most elegant shops. Here, before fire destroyed it, stood the imposing Bowery Theatre. Here were the exclusive North American and New England hotels as well as the Apollo Museum. Jewelers, drapers, furriers, restaurants—more than 240 thriving enterprises lined the street. People who rode by in the evenings on the city's first horse-drawn cars could hear music blaring out of German beer halls, and with the music flowed the smells of kraut and wurst.

❧

A century later, one of The Bowery's most distinguished presidents, Henry Bruère, told his trustees: "Hope of America's future lies in the capacities of its people to show a resourceful, independent initiative, and in their willingness to cooperate whole-heartedly for the common good."

Certainly this was the characteristic the American people demonstrated after the panic of 1837. The dollar simply had to be made viable again. The country could not function without an acceptable medium of exchange. What was it to be?

"If the Indians got along by paying in wampum, if other peoples got along by paying in sea shells," one commentator observed, "I guess we can manage with the paper dollars we're swapping."

The nation had just elected Martin Van Buren to its Presidency, a man who was precisely what the United States needed though admittedly colorless in contrast to Andrew Jackson.

"Martin Van Buren's main concern," according to historian Henry B. Parkes, "was to put the finances of the Government on a sound footing. The widespread failures of the State banks had shown the dangers of entrusting them with government money, so Van Buren decided that henceforth there would be a complete divorce between government and private banking. The government would keep its money in its own Independent Treasury. Vaults known as 'sub-treasuries' would be constructed in various cities, where government officials would receive and pay out funds on a strictly specie basis."

Whether the President's actions would in themselves have restored national solvency is debatable. They were loudly supported by the radical locofocos; they were bitterly opposed by those who resented federal interference.

In the midst of this controversy the economy found leadership in an unexpected quarter. One of New York's ablest bankers, James G. King, stepped into the fiscal arena.

"This country is dedicated to private enterprise," he maintained, "and private enterprise must act in its own behalf."

Thereupon he invited a group of the city's leading businessmen to his office.

"Gentlemen," he told them, "we may not like the banknotes that are in circulation. We may not have much faith in their value. But at present they are the only medium of monetary exchange we have. Until federally guaranteed banknotes appear to replace them we have the choice of closing all our factories and offices while we wait for the new money to arrive—which may take years. Or else we can *accept* the currency we now have.

"I say to you, gentlemen, that it would be fatal to our economy to suspend trade while we wait for the new money. We must keep America alive by using whatever banknotes *are* available to us. As long as the workingman can, through them, obtain food and lodging and clothing in exchange for his labor, nothing can destroy our nation. I ask you to join me in the course I propose to follow. *We must continue to honor the present banknotes until a new form of currency arrives.*"

If there had been a choice, King's argument might have been vigorously challenged. As one of his supporters put it, "When all you've got is rubber money I guess you have to deal in rubber money."

The Bowery Savings Bank had adopted James King's philosophy even before he had expressed it. The bank had never refused to accept the current banknotes.

King himself did something else for America's recovery. He sailed to Britain and managed to persuade the Bank of England that the United States had taken a firm grip on its future. The personal respect he commanded must have swayed the British, for they soon renewed credit to American firms "to strengthen our customers." Beyond that, they shipped to New York several million dollars' worth of gold and silver specie for distribution to banks at the lowest possible interest rates. One is tempted to describe the act as the precursor, in reverse, of the Marshall Plan.

And so, within a couple of years after the panic of 1837, America regained its economic health.

So did The Bowery Savings Bank. Once more its trustees could relax. Once more they could demonstrate their optimism with investments in the future. In February of 1838 the bank's third president, James Mills, presented, at a candlelit meeting in his office, a resolution which his board enthusiastically adopted. It read: *Resolved that arrangements be made with the Manhattan Gas Light Company for the introduction of gas into the Banking room.*

What better testimony of affluence could the institution provide? It had recouped the deposits it had lost in 1837; it had added to them in gratifying volume. By 1840 its 3,215 customers were entrusting it with the record amount of $623,984. In return they were collecting dividends of $21,661.

Such constant expansion further encouraged the trustees. Now they purchased the property adjacent to their first home. Here, at number 130, they erected a new building complete with residential quarters for the secretary and his family. The new building immediately attracted new depositors, for it seemed a monument to success. In fact, money began to flow in so fast that unexpectedly, in 1853, the trustees faced an embarrassment of riches.

President Mills called a hasty meeting.

"We now have deposits of over $3,000,000," he announced, speaking with uneasiness rather than pride. "We are committed to paying out $175,693 in dividends. The problem is that new deposits are pouring in faster than they can prudently be invested. That means our income is not keeping pace with these new deposits. We may, therefore, have to reduce dividends for everybody. I see but one means of avoiding this."

The means he urged was a *curb* on deposits. The trustees somewhat hesitantly concurred. Of course the law itself had long been regulating ceilings on deposits. (Over the years these limits have varied from a low of $500 to $7,500 by 1936, and then to $10,000, and finally to $20,000. Now the ceilings have been completely removed.) The trustees' action in 1853, however, was the first time they had themselves fixed a limit on deposits. With the power granted them by their charter they voted to keep deposits down to a maximum of $1,000 per account.

In the minutes of that meeting, those present were quoted as being "of the opinion that in consenting to receive large sums on deposit, subject to be withdrawn at a moment's notice, we depart from our primary object." That primary object was described as "keeping safely the small surplus earnings of the faithful domestic worker and frugal mechanic and laborer, and collaterally paying them such interest as a careful investment of the funds would warrant."

By limiting deposits to $1,000, the bank obviously reduced its obligation with regard to the amount it had to pay out in dividends. This procedure, while temporary, allowed an opportunity to build up reserves. It was, of course, putting into effect that primary lesson of 1837. How important the lesson was became clear in 1854.

That was when the Knickerbocker Savings Bank of New York ran into trouble which compelled it to suspend all business. The event stunned depositors of all savings banks. Immediately runs began. The Bowery did not escape. Within a week it lost over $168,000 in withdrawals. Yet the reserves it had so prudently amassed made it easy to meet the new challenge, and it suffered hardly any difficulties in what came to be known as the panic of 1854.

Limiting the size of deposits was by no means a measure taken only by James Mills. It has been a Bowery safeguard invoked again and again over the years. John W. Larsen, the bank's former president, defined it as "a breathing spell to allow the ratio of reserves to deposits to catch up to a prudent level."

A century ago not all savings banks took such precautions. In consequence the nation suffered the failures of the Taunton Institution for Savings, the Gloucester Institute for Savings, and the People's Five Cents Savings Bank, all in Massachusetts; later the failures of the Six Penny Savings Bank of Rochester, the Guardian Savings Institute, and the Bowling Green Savings Bank in New York.

In other words, not every mutual savings bank has always operated by the same safety rules.

I realize how contradictory it must seem, in a time of fierce inter-bank competition for funds, to suggest that any particular bank does not always welcome deposits. Yet it is true. The very *size* of a deposit is a factor.

As an illustration, consider an event that occurred during the administration of Earl Schwulst as The Bowery's chairman. He was visited by the treasurer of the Ford Foundation, who had come to deposit $10 million in The Bowery.

One would have imagined that Mr. Schwulst would have accepted the money with alacrity. Instead he asked, "*Why* do you want to do this?"

"Frankly," the Ford Foundation representative said, "our experts tell me there is no better investment in today's market."

Was Mr. Schwulst flattered? To a degree. At the same time he shook his head. "I appreciate the offer," he said, "but I can't accept it."

The Ford Foundation's treasurer was amazed. "Can't accept ten million dollars? Why on earth not?"

"If we pay you our current dividend rate of 5 percent," the chairman explained, "we have to give you $500,000 a year. That means we have to invest the money at *more* than 5 percent. If we don't, we can take a serious loss on the deposit. But you say your experts have already combed the market. I regard them as being as good as our own investment officers. If *they* haven't been able to find an investment that will pay more than 5 percent, where shall we find one?

"And there's a second reason," the chairman continued. "Let's say that during the course of the year your men find an investment that does pay 6 or 7 or 8 percent. They'll want to withdraw the ten million from us and place it elsewhere. Isn't that so?"

"Naturally. It's their job."

"That means we've got to keep ten million dollars always liquid on the chance that you may at any moment want to withdraw it—and we can lose money that way, too. If we needed to borrow ten million dollars desperately, which we don't, we'd do better to borrow it from a commercial bank. There, when the loan became due, we might hope for an extension or a renewal if we desired it. But in your case there would be no chance of an extension. You might want or have to have the money at once. So you see, don't you, why we can't take the ten million?"

I recount his decision—which, incidentally, was repeated when Harvard University wanted to deposit $5 million at The Bowery—because it indicates that being money-hungry must have its limitations. In banking as in eating, it is better to be a gourmet than a glutton.

ᢙᢆ᠊ᡋᢀ

How the American dollar ever managed to become the most stable medium of exchange in the world is a mystery when one remembers its periods of extreme volatility. In one such period, 1857—with the troubles of 1854 not yet forgotten—the trustees of The Bowery once more were drawn into the country's financial turmoil. This time, to rescue themselves, they had to take action which for them was as drastic as it was novel.

Again the cause lay in the irrepressible optimism of the American people. Everybody knew the country's future had to be glorious. Commercial banks were lending money with a generosity that matched the recklessness of earlier days. The most speculative ventures were made to appear gilt-edged. And it was easy to do. With railroads being built toward the Far West, was it not logical to acquire land along the rights-of-way? (Few promoters suggested that one might have to wait several generations before realizing a profit.) With the nation's population increasing by the hundreds of thousands and daily requiring more and more food, was it not intelligent to invest in agricultural projects? (Nobody talked about possible crop failures or about the voracious destructiveness of seven-year locusts.) As for the residents of New York, to see for themselves that prosperity was at hand they had only to look at their harbor, crowded with sails and steamships and ferries headed for more than a hundred docks. They had only to stare at the scores upon scores of buildings being constructed in every direction.

It was all exciting—and deceptive. Too many loans and projects had been ill advised. Too many investments were yielding nothing but disappointment.

When borrowers found it impossible to meet their obligations, fear set in, even at banks; and fear, as always, was the forerunner of panic. Bankers hastily called in loans; and the lack of response frightened them all the more. Then, as securities plunged, there came a signal of what was to happen next: The Ohio Life Insurance and Trust Company of Cincinnati suspended business. The country's telegraph wires, some newly installed, flashed the news everywhere.

That was the catalyst. With panicky creditors still insisting on the immediate payment of debts, more than 1,200 New York firms went into bankruptcy. As one historian put it, "Throughout the country bank after bank closed its doors. Old, established commercial houses were wrecked, and business came almost to a standstill."

As in a former year, long lines of worried depositors besieged the tellers' cages of The Bowery. In four days they withdrew more than $500,000, draining away half of the $1,022,883 the bank had available in cash reserves. At this rate the reserves would soon be gone.

Those trustees who could leave their own threatened businesses answered the call of the bank's president, James Mills. They were harried when they gathered in his office. Mills himself was the most distraught of them all. The anxieties of that day may well have contributed to his death within a few months. He was a proud man, proud of the way he had served his depositors without ever accepting compensation. Once, when offered a salary by his board, he had retorted, "Gentlemen, if you insist that I accept pay you may have my resignation."

In spite of his present agitation, Mills was the only one who offered a way of dealing with the panic-stricken depositors. "We must not deprive them of the right to draw what moneys they may require for their immediate livelihood," he said. "But we must at the same time, for their security and ours, protect the bank."

The plan he proposed was adopted. Before the bank opened for business the next morning, the waiting lines of depositors saw a sign go up on the doors. It announced that every depositor could until further notice withdraw *a percentage* of his funds. The percentage would apply equally to everybody.

One might have supposed this would rouse cries of

37

protest. It did not. "As long as everybody knew that no single depositor would be favored by 'getting there first,'" one observer reported, "the sense of panic ceased. People were no longer worried about losing all their savings." The wild run on the bank stopped, and a number of depositors, not knowing what to do with the cash they had already withdrawn, brought it back. Within a couple of days $50,000 was redeposited.

And soon thereafter an unanticipated thing happened: Since many clients had closed their accounts during the panic, those who remained now received extra dividends! It was a case of fewer mouths being present to share the pie; so there were bigger slices for those who remained at the table.

It seems paradoxical to say that the bank actually profited from the panic of 1857. Yet it is true. When people learned that depositors of The Bowery were receiving extra dividends, amounting to 50 percent of their regular dividends, they rushed in with their money. This was too good a thing to be missed. By 1858 all withdrawals had been regained, and a quarter of a million dollars in new deposits had flowed into the bank.

When James Mills died in February, it must have been with the satisfaction of knowing he had left a strong and solvent institution to his successor in the presidency, Thomas Jeremiah. The Bowery's growth now continued so vigorously that by 1860 it had 41,692 depositors and total assets of well over $10 million.

As they administered this wealth, the trustees must surely have heard what historians have called "the distant rumblings of war." They must have known something was going to happen. But what? Not being certain, they looked toward Washington, waiting to see what that lanky, newly elected occupant of the White House intended to do.

5

ONE NATION INDIVISIBLE

I once asked a veteran of The Bowery how a man like Thomas Jeremiah, formerly a grocer, had managed to become so able a bank president, serving through fourteen critical years that included the Civil War. Nothing in his early life could have prepared him for such responsibility.

"To begin with," my informant said, "you must remember that he had been one of the bank's founders. For twenty-eight years he had also been a trustee. In that capacity he had been familiar with every operation of the bank. No man understood its problems better than he did."

So there he was, Thomas Jeremiah, former grocer, heading a great institution in what had become the financial capital of the nation. It was clear that he would have to give the bank his full time. Its head was certainly entitled to a salary commensurate with the dignity and responsibility of the position. The trustees unanimously voted Mr. Jeremiah a salary of $3,000 a year.

A meticulous man reared in the strict discipline of Quakerism, he insisted on an almost religious devotion to integrity and efficiency. The state had appointed three commissioners to inspect the accounts of mutual savings banks, and these men invariably found Jeremiah's records thorough, accurate, and up-to-date.

They made a point of reporting this because it was unusual. In one document the commissioners wrote: "In our examinations we have often found the books of a Savings Bank sadly in arrear, because the treasurer had been too much occupied with his duties as cashier to keep them written up."

Precise and businesslike, Thomas Jeremiah could never tolerate such dereliction. Even in the worst years of the Civil War he wanted every transaction to be correctly recorded every day. The trouble—revealed years later—was that some of the bank's clerks were far less meticulous than their boss.

As a Quaker dedicated to peace, Jeremiah could not espouse war, but he believed firmly in the sanctity of the Union. In this he differed sharply with New York's Mayor Fernando Wood. As history has almost forgotten, the mayor wanted New York to secede from the nation.

"Why should not New York City," he wrote in 1861, "instead of supporting by her contributions in revenues two-thirds of the expenses of the United States, become also equally independent? As a free city, with but nominal duty imports, her local government could be supported without taxation upon her people. Thus we could live free from taxes, and have cheap goods nearly duty free."

The citizens of New York not only rejected this idea. They also—after a great patriotic mass meeting in Union Square, immediately following the firing on Fort Sumter—forced the City Council to throw Fernando Wood out of office, and elected George Opdyke to replace him.

Thomas Jeremiah must have been pleased by this show of patriotic fervor. He joined the other bankers of the city in a common purpose and reported to his trustees that the group had agreed "to band themselves together, putting their coin into a common fund and otherwise aiding one another, so as to enable them to sustain their leaders and by joint action to relieve the wants of the Government."

This consortium of bankers undertook to provide $150 million in gold—a truly fantastic sum—to the United States Treasury. In exchange, the banks would receive Treasury notes bearing 7.3 percent interest. If The Bowery originally contributed only $50,000 to this pool, it was because Jeremiah and his board felt they had no right to commit more than a prudent amount of depositors' funds to any venture without their approval.

In this, however, he underestimated the patriotism and the desires of "little people."

I know of no written record of what any depositors may have said to him. Yet I do recall what was once told me by the late Reverend Mr. James Bradley of Lee, Massachusetts, who traced his ancestry back to the Pilgrims.

"My grandfather was employed in New York," he said. "He was a man of modest means, but he wanted desperately to aid the government. With the four or five dollars he could save every month he could hardly buy government bonds. But when he heard that savings banks were buying those bonds he recognized the possibilities of cooperative action. He realized that when thousands of people like himself brought their five-dollar bills to a savings bank, these deposits added up to considerable sums which could be of tremendous help to the government. So he took his savings to the bank as his own best way of investing in the government's cause."

Thousands of others must have been moved by the same impulse, and their deposits were used as they would have wished—"to preserve the Union." The Bowery's holdings of government bonds rose from $2,673,000 in the first year of the war to $7,212,000 by 1865. Before all else, the Union had to be made strong. Nobody's future—not even a bank's—would be secure in a weak nation.

ᘒᔆᘎ

There were two principal New York streets along which troops marched off to war. One was Broadway, the other the Bowery. Whenever regiments went by, work inside the bank stopped. Thomas Jeremiah and his staff, dutifully pressing hands to their hearts as flags were carried past them, watched men and caissons and mounted officers start southward.

Jeremiah must have had conflicting emotions as he viewed the marchers. Deeply as he and his trustees believed in keeping the union of the states inviolate, his Quakerism could not condone people killing one another. He deplored seeing boys go off to die. But how might he have felt about those young men so "indifferent" to the future of the United States that they remained deaf to repeated calls for volunteers?

The necessity of passing the Draft Act of 1863 indicated that there were a great many such Northerners who had no desire to fight. And the Act, affecting all men between the ages of 18 and 45, made a sad mistake. Instead of honorably exempting those who had families to support, or other good reason not to enter the armed services, the legislation stipulated that draftees could pay substitutes to serve for them. The legal fee was $300.

Some young men eagerly accepted the $300, joined regiments, and promptly deserted to flee to another state. Known as "bounty jumpers," they could easily have repeated the process elsewhere—as many did.

The most obvious inequity of the Draft Act was that a wealthy man could afford to hire a substitute while a poor man was at a helpless disadvantage. Once the unfairness of this became manifest—and again it required wild street rioting to make the government see the unfairness—the legislature of New York responded. It authorized a $2 million bond issue whose funds would be earmarked for loans to deserving poor people who could not afford to pay the $300 fee. The law stipulated that such loans must go only to men whose support was urgently needed at home.

As an institution which was dealing so intimately with the needs of people in modest circumstances, The Bowery Savings Bank could certainly sympathize with the intent of the bond issue. It bought 10 percent of the entire offering, far more than duty or even patriotism demanded.

This in no way precluded the bank's increasing purchases of federal securities. Secretary of the Treasury Salmon P. Chase had called upon the country's 1,400 banks, savings as well as commercial, to set an example of confidence in the nation's future, and this they did by buying federal notes.

One serious circumstance, however, worried the trustees of The Bowery as it must have troubled every other thoughtful person. *More than 7,000 different issues of banknotes, all printed by local banks, were now in circulation.* If such currency became valueless, how much confidence could one have in any of America's paper indebtedness?

Still, despite obvious dangers, The Bowery kept buying more and more government bonds. One can well imagine the apprehensions of its less venturesome trustees. Was it *wise* to sink half of the bank's assets in government paper? Not that anyone doubted the necessity of such funding, or doubted that Mr. Lincoln needed such help if he was to safeguard the Union. But how fair was it to "little people" to plant so large a part of their savings in the wastelands of war?

Conversely, there was the argument: "If we allow the Union to collapse for want of support, the savings of 'little people' could be entirely wiped out."

So the bank's purchases of government paper continued. In the minutes of one trustee meeting there is the prediction: "The world will recall with wonder and astonishment the trials and losses sustained by the people to preserve the life of the Nation."

Secretary of the Treasury Salmon P. Chase was as troubled as everyone else by the dubious value of the banknotes that were sustaining the war effort. It was this concern among others that prompted him in 1863 to champion the issuance of a national currency. In this he succeeded. When the National Currency and Banking System became a reality, the strength of the entire United States lay behind the monetary commitments of the land.

The trustees of The Bowery, like the directors of all banks, had some reason to be reassured. But reassurance never had a chance to drift into euphoria, for soon the board was summoned by President Jeremiah to confront a new problem—that of depositors who had disappeared.

44

When a depositor has died in battle or anywhere else, Jeremiah reminded his associates, it is the duty of the bank, by law and as a matter of ethics, to seek out his heirs. The Bowery had no right to keep his savings forever.

There had in the past always been a few accounts left untouched for years, often by people who had moved to other regions. Now, because of war casualties, such accounts were becoming more numerous. Something would have to be done about them.

One trustee asked, "We add dividends to these deposits, do we not?"

"For twenty years, yes. That is the law. After twenty years of inactivity they are listed as dormant. But paying dividends does not absolve us from making every possible effort to locate a depositor if he is alive—or his heirs if he is dead."

The problem involved all banks, of course, as it still does. (Legislation requires the periodic publication of names of those who are being sought as the owners of neglected accounts. When New York State revised its law in 1937, it specified that such accounts would be placed in the "dormant" category after 15 years of inactivity. It is now 10 years. At that time, 1937, The Bowery had 1,908 such accounts on its books, their balances totaling over $302,000. According to the law, when search for a missing depositor or his heirs is abandoned, the money at issue escheats to the state.)

After the Civil War, however, The Bowery Savings Bank, like its sister institutions, had to pursue its own methods of tracing vanished clients. It sent a representative to Washington to search the files of the War Department. It sought the aid of the Grand Army of the Republic. It asked the help of foreign consulates on the chance that people might have gone abroad. It made exhaustive inquiries in every state capital. It invoked the assistance of churches. It even scrutinized lists of prison inmates.

By such diverse means, many owners of dormant accounts were indeed located. Some were astonished and delighted, having completely forgotten the funds they had saved. Others with personal reasons for disappearing—reasons like a lady with whom they chose to live in secret—were embarrassed and even resentful when found. I once consulted a Bowery officer on the matter of dormant accounts, and he sighed like a man sadly contemplating human frailty.

"The cause?" he said. "There are as many reasons as there are people. Most of them simply forget. But many wives hold out money from their household expenses and deposit it in secret savings accounts. Similarly, husbands hold out money from pay envelopes and deposit it without letting their wives know. Both refuse to let the banks send any communications to their homes. A few move away and in time abandon their funds, or else they die without having told anyone about a deposit. By the time we try to locate these persons, after fifteen years of account inactivity, most traces of them have disappeared. Fortunately, their balances are generally small."

But not always. One woman who had left $7,500 in The Bowery had left money in other thrift institutions, too, for a total exceeding $60,000! Though she had long since died, a searcher located her family through the records of a mortician, and the heirs received a windfall. In another case a deposit which The Bowery sent to the State Escheat Department in 1967 amounted to over $10,000. That same year the Department's assets rose to more than $115 million—and that was in one state only.

One might regard all this as incredible evidence of

46

carelessness or forgetfulness. Is it unusual? A sign of congenitally erratic memory? Not necessarily.

Robert W. Sparks, a very level-headed man who retired after serving as executive vice president of The Bowery Savings Bank, confessed that he himself had for many years forgotten funds he had left, before going off to World War I, in the Irving Savings Bank. A friend chanced to see his name in a published list of those "missing." In that way Mr. Sparks, professionally interested in locating owners of dormant Bowery accounts, unexpectedly located himself. When I commented on the doubtful quality of his memory, he answered with a chuckle:

"Show me any human frailty, and I'll show you a banker who has it."

ᘓᔍᘒ

During the 1860s, so unprecedented a number of savings banks appeared that one might have imagined a new fad had seized the nation's financiers. In New York State 78 were opened in that decade. On a countrywide basis the number leaped from 278 in 1860 to 517 in 1870, and they had 1,630,846 accounts. (In other words, more savings banks were in existence then than make up the roster of the National Association of Mutual Savings Banks in our time.)

It would be naive to suppose that every one of them immediately prospered. Some opened in the wrong place at the wrong time. The original Rockland County Savings Bank—not the one in existence today—received in its first full year of operations 23 deposits totaling $54.50. Of this amount, $26.50 was withdrawn. One can see why the bank suspended business. Eight additional savings institutions in the state also had to close their doors, usually for causes attributable to poor or inexperienced management. But those banks which failed were in the minority. In almost every case their depositors retrieved their money. Seventy-odd years later, when the Commissioner of Banks in Massachusetts surveyed the entire history of savings banks failures, he reported:

> A careful examination of all available records indicates that the aggregate of all depositor losses during the past century and a quarter amounted approximately to $\frac{1}{40}$ of 1 percent of the total deposits during that period. That record of safety has probably never been equalled by any system of financial institutions in history. This record becomes even more impressive when it is realized that the depositors received last year (1940) in interest or dividends on their accounts *more than nine times as much as the aggregate of all losses sustained during the past one hundred and twenty-five years.*

For the most part, however, American savings banks did well during this decade of war and reconstruction, and The Bowery was among them. It even purchased adjacent property in order to expand its space to accommodate growing needs. For its home town was thriving. As the country's financial capital, New York was backing—and reaping profits from—almost every aspect of reconstruction. Prices and wages were rising, buildings were going up, plants were expanding and producing more goods than ever, national and international commerce was booming. The street called the Bowery became noisy with more beer halls and more roisterers. Business was good.

"All this activity offered a two-fold benefit to the savings banks," wrote one historian. "It attracted increased deposits from workers who were earning more than ever, and it offered increased employment for funds in mortgages."

And yet thrift institutions had to cope with the competition (then as now) of other attractions in the money market. Government and corporate securities were tempting people with interest rates and dividends which savings banks could not match. Opposed to this, fortunately, was the advantage The Bowery, the Greenwich, the Bank for Savings, the Seamen's, the Emigrant, and other thrift institutions had in a reputation for safety. For years they had proved themselves reliable. Accounts in such institutions did not fluctuate in value as did the prices of securities. If you wanted to be sure of having your savings intact when you needed them, the answer lay in savings banks.

So it was that by the end of the Civil War decade The Bowery had more depositors than ever—53,000 "little people" whose individual savings averaged about $340. In total they ran to well over $18 million.

Again one might have asked: What could possibly happen to shake so big, strong, and reliable an institution? What now?

6

THE GET-RICH-QUICK CROWD

The story of The Bowery Savings Bank, or of any long-established financial institution, suggests a sobering lesson to be learned from the economic history of the United States: Its citizens have always managed to turn periods of prosperity into depressions. Conversely, being a remarkably resilient people, they have always managed to rise out of their own ashes to create a new era of good times. In retrospect these cycles of boom, bust, boom seem to have occurred as predictably as the comings and goings of the seasons.

The cause? There is seldom agreement. I recall the tirade of an angry speaker who stood on a platform in front of Trinity Church, at the corner of Broadway and Wall Street in New York, and shook an accusing finger at the entire financial district. He harangued a noon-hour audience with the details of the huge profits some corporations were earning while their stockholders watched the value of their securities sink lower and lower.

"Why do we trust these Wall Street money-manipulators with our investments?" he cried. "Why do we listen to what they say? I ask you why? *Why?*"

A voice in the crowd called, "Don't ask! Tell!"

Glaring at the heckler, the speaker retorted, "All right, I'll tell you! It's because we're stupid enough to think a man who makes a fortune for himself is interested in making a fortune for us too! It's because we're foolish enough to *respect* the guy who feathers his nest at our expense!"

It occurred to me that, in spite of all his bombast, the man had touched upon one element of truth. We Americans do respect financial success. We *want* to believe that our most eminent men of wealth are too wise and able to be dishonest. When one of them proves us wrong, the revelation is tragic. It has always been so.

In the 1870s the conservative trustees of The Bowery must have groaned when so distinguished and respected a financier as Jay Gould, the railroad titan, was arrested on criminal charges. People used to buy securities on the proudly stated theory: "If it's good enough for Jay Gould it's good enough for me!" Now he was accused of cheating thousands of investors, large and small, by selling them $5 million worth of fraudulent stock.

Though some Bowery trustees may have bought Gould's offerings, few of the bank's modest depositors were among the victims. They were not the kind of people who carried their money to Wall Street. Frugal and hard-working, they preferred the security of savings accounts to the lure of the stock market. Yet they suffered a setback of a different kind.

In 1872 a general strike of the building trades crippled New York and ended the income of many workingmen. For sustenance they had to fall back on their savings, and some of the bank's smallest accounts became even smaller.

Seeing this erosion of finances, Bowery tellers would often plead with depositors to withdraw less every week; to make their money last as long as possible. No doubt this was done in the true spirit of a family thrift institution. And when the strike finally ended one newspaper editorial commented: "If this ordeal has taught the workingman anything at all, it is the importance of having substantial savings for emergencies."

Apparently many laboring people had the same thought. After the strike, the deposits they brought to The Bowery and to other savings banks were larger than ever. One of The Bowery's employees wrote that on paydays working-men, still in their overalls, would line up at the tellers' cages. The overalls had long cuffs that rose almost to the knees. Men would dip their hands deep into the cuffs and bring up crumpled bills. At one point the bank had to issue a request that people "please lay their bills out flat in their passbooks when making deposits."

Crumpled or flat, the bills poured in, and deposits constantly increased. Thus when Thomas Jeremiah died and Samuel T. Brown succeeded him as The Bowery's president, Brown discovered that deposits had soared from $10 million in 1869 to $27 million by 1873. Many small depositors had become *large* depositors with several thousands of dollars in their accounts. Faced with this, the new president called in his trustees. As always, his manner was that of a church deacon dealing in matters of morality.

"The bank was founded," he reminded his associates,

"to benefit the small, thrifty investor rather than serve as a depository for well-to-do persons. Our earnings were intended to be divided among *little* people. I intend to ask that big deposits be withdrawn or left with us at a smaller rate of interest."

"What if depositors refuse to meet such terms?" he was asked.

"Then I propose to request of the state legislature the right to reduce dividends on all deposits above one thousand dollars."

This Samuel Brown eventually did, and the legislature responded by amending Section 13 of the bank's charter to read: "The Board of Trustees may from time to time regulate the rate of interest to be allowed to depositors." It stipulated that "the interest on deposits exceeding one thousand dollars shall be at least *one percent less* than the interest allowed to others."

This restored what President Brown considered the essential character of the bank. But almost simultaneously another challenging situation developed, one of a nationwide nature. As the Manhattan Company described the event in one of its publications:

A predatory Wall Street group had conceived the idea of cornering the gold market and quietly began buying up all specie. The price of gold was being forced up to giddy, dangerous heights.

And then suddenly, between 11:50 A.M. and 12:11 P.M. on September 24, 1869, an interval of only 21 minutes, prices crashed amid the wildest confusion. This disastrous day on which thousands of speculators were ruined became known as "Black Friday."

It was not learned until years later that Henry Clews (a conservative financier), alarmed at the reckless actions of the gold-hoarding pool, had sent a telegram to President Grant, asking him to act. The President's response had been the release of five million dollars in gold, an amount sufficient to smash the pool.

It was as if the bullion of Fort Knox had been offered to the public on a "name your own terms" basis. This instantly caused the inflated price of gold to collapse. Those who *had* bought it with their savings or with borrowed funds were virtually wiped out.

Critics later maintained that the President could have avoided the national hysteria by *gradually* releasing gold. But this did not happen, and those who were caught that "Black Friday" were already on their way to the panic of 1873. This ultimate disaster was precipitated when the bank of Jay Cooke and Company failed. Abruptly, millions of people feared all banks might fail. Millions ran to get their money out of these institutions before it was too late.

Before The Bowery opened next morning, so great a mob thronged around the bank (by this time it had well over 53,000 depositors) that harried trustees needed police help to force their way into the building. Breathless and disheveled when at last they gathered in President Brown's office, they took decisive action. First they authorized the immediate sale of $2 million in government securities. This would provide cash for emergency demands at teller cages.

Next the board resorted to a clause in the charter it had never before been forced to invoke. When its resolution was adopted, President Brown went out to address the crowds in the street. Standing on the top step of the entrance, he raised his arms for attention and waited until the throng became silent. Then his deep voice rolled across the Bowery.

Henceforth, he announced, all depositors would be required to give sixty days' notice of their intention to withdraw their funds. Only emergency family needs in small amounts—as for medical expenses—would be honored without such notice. This step was being taken, he asserted, as protection for every depositor's savings. It was a safeguard that would be maintained as long as the national crisis made it necessary.

The effect of the announcement was magical. People realized that nobody could deplete the bank's resources that day or for weeks to come. And as long as nobody else could withdraw funds, there was no need for immediate fear that one's own savings would vanish. Thousands of reassured depositors went home. Their money was safe. Throughout the country almost 20 other savings bank failed during the crisis, but at The Bowery the 1873 panic was under control.

❧

Despite his bank's dignity and solidity, it must have been disheartening for a man like President Samuel Brown to walk along the Bowery during the latter years of the 1870s. Day by day the street was changing its character. For one thing, an elevated railway had been built along its length. Whenever a train thundered overhead, terrified horses reared. Some broke free and bolted, endangering everyone in their path.

"Instead of the expected blessing," wrote Alvin F. Harlow in *Old Bowery Days,* "the new railroad proved a curse. Overhanging the sidewalks, it shut out as much light from the buildings as possible and gave them the maximum noise. How anyone sleeps upstairs on such a street on a summer night, with windows open and those rambling earthquakes roaring by almost within arms' length, belching smoke and cinders into the room, is beyond the comprehension of anyone who has not become inured to it."

Within the wooden structure that housed The Bowery Savings Bank, the floors and walls trembled every time a train passed. And mingled with the shouts of street hawkers, there were other noises almost as bad. Near City Hall, work was in progress on the Brooklyn Bridge, soon to be the longest span in the world; all day heavy trucks rumbled by the bank, carrying materials to the construction gangs.

Even more dispiriting was the metamorphosis in the appearance of the Bowery. What had been so elegant a shopping avenue a few years ago was dotted with saloons and shooting galleries and seven-cent lodging houses; with dime museums and "Cheap John" auction rooms and pleasure palaces to lure seamen as they came off their ships. A block or two from the bank the Bowery Mission was welcoming vagrants, and Salvation Army girls wandered into every shop, rattling their tambourines in quest of coins.

It was true that Tony Pastor's Theatre was showing the plays of Shakespeare and, at the northern end of the street, Cooper Union was offering free education. But in most other aspects the Bowery was sinking into a mire of honky-tonks.

That the bank could maintain its quiet dignity in such an atmosphere was something of a paradox. And yet, to accommodate its ever expanding business, it once more had to renovate and expand its quarters.

Some people might have balked at spending $63,574 to improve an old building while real estate values all around the place were crumbling. The president's answer to such doubts was firm: "We are obligated by our charter and by our word to serve the people of this community; and to serve them properly where they live, we need adequate space."

By contrast with the notorious costs of some other buildings, The Bowery's expenditures for renovation were small. Only recently, Boss Tweed of Tammany Hall had "supervised" the construction of the new County Court House a few minutes' walk from the bank. At Tweed's direction the city had been charged $641,000 for carpets in the building, $1,973,545 for plastering, and $2,960,187 for furniture and cabinet work. It was outrageous. Yet it was among the smallest of Tweed's operations. By the time he was sent to prison he had, according to reports, drained the city of more than $100 million.

To the bank's trustees, who had been chosen for their integrity and adherence to high ethical principles, this must have seemed an age of moral collapse. The disintegration of the street was merely a reflection of a general spiritual disintegration.

Already some of the Bowery's older residents were sadly trying to find ways of commemorating the more noteworthy aspects of past years. One day three women, led by a Mrs. Parkhurst Duer who worked in a nearby music store, went from door to door, appealing for contributions so that they might place a plaque on the building at number 15 on the Bowery. When they came to the bank, they explained to President Brown that the tablet was intended for the 25-cents-a-night lodging house in which a sick, disillusioned, and broken-spirited man had died a few years ago at the age of 38. "He was different from most down-and-outers," Mrs. Duer said. "He was a gentle kind of a man, and he did a lot of good things before he slid downhill. We think the Bowery ought to remember him."

What sort of things did he do?

"Oh, he wrote songs."

What songs?

"Well, there was *Suwanee River* and *Oh, Suzanna* and *My Old Kentucky Home* and *Old Black Joe* and *Camptown Races* and *Come Where My Love Lies Dreaming* and *Massa's in the Cold, Cold Ground* and—oh, lots of songs. We want to put up a plaque at number 15 that says 'The Last Home of Stephen Collins Foster.' "

℮✦☉

When his health began to fail, Samuel Brown relinquished the presidency of the bank to Henry Lyles, Jr. Lyles served only from 1878 to 1880, yet he distinguished himself in two ways.

First, he established a leadership among bankers which gave The Bowery new prestige. The opportunity rose out of national dissension over the place of silver in the federal currency. While California and the Klondike were producing gold, many other regions were mining silver. Understandably, the owners of these mines were doing their utmost to have silver accepted as legal tender. Their spokesmen in Congress were eloquent. Their appeal to the nation was vigorous.

The trustees of The Bowery were among those who sternly objected to such glorification of silver. Speaking for them, Lyles was vehement. He declared that the acceptance of silver currency would "debase the gold standard, would tend to compromise the national credit and to create distrust in the minds of the people." His outspoken convictions, gaining wide publicity, focused a good deal of attention on The Bowery Savings Bank itself.

Lyles' second act of importance was, unfortunately, one which caused profound embarrassment for him, for his staff, for the board of trustees, and for everyone connected with the management of the bank. He ordered an audit of the books.

The accountants quickly discovered that the ledgers were not only out of date but utterly inaccurate and in hopeless disarray. Worse, they had been that way ever since 1852—*a period of 27 years!*

One can imagine the horror of the trustees, demanding to know how such a thing could have happened. The cause lay in the ancient system of bookkeeping. Still using handwritten notations as they had in the early days, the overworked tellers and clerks had been unable to keep pace with growth. They were trying to record the transactions of 70,000 depositors in the same way they had dealt with a few hundred. It was impossible. One could visualize a harried teller writing $5.23 in a passbook and entering $5.32 in a ledger—or, at the end of an exhausting day, altogether forgetting to post some small entry. Human errors had multiplied to such proportions that the auditors reported: "The more rapidly the business grew, the more the antiquated system interfered with itself. It is practically impossible to trace an error through the mass of detail."

Henry Lyles, Jr. took prompt remedial action. He "sectionalized" the system. Hiring more bookkeepers, he entrusted each man with a manageable number of accounts. Responsibility for accuracy was now pinpointed, and nobody had more work than he could handle.

Though by no means perfect, the new system was surely an improvement on the old. When Lyles resigned, he could point to the sectionalized practice as a monument to his administration. But it was a monument destined to have only a brief existence. The bookkeeper's quill pen was on its way to becoming a museum piece, swept into disuse by the advent of a mechanized age.

7

THE GOOD
OLD DAYS?

"All institutions of civilization must pass through New York before they are accepted elsewhere in America." So, in 1896, wrote Mrs. Burton Harrison, a scholarly authority on Americana. Had she been a Brahmin she would probably have said the same thing about Boston. In either case she would have been wrong.

Things were happening in the United States which Mrs. Harrison may not even have noticed. For example, financial circles had recently witnessed, without much interest, the birth of a new type of thrift institution. This was called a building and loan association; later it would be known as a savings and loan association.

Until the first of these was organized in Philadelphia, the savings banks' only competitor for people's deposits had been a very few commercial banks. Now this third entity was rising. The trustees of The Bowery were as remiss as everyone else in granting it scant attention. It was too small to be worrisome. Besides, in a geographical sense it lay outside the bank's range of operations. What if a few dozen such companies were being organized in remote areas? Why be concerned?

Generally these building and loan associations took root in states which lacked savings banks. Yet the people in these regions needed mortgage assistance if they were to build homes. By cooperative efforts they created their own means of obtaining funds. Month by month the members of each organization deposited small sums until enough money lay in the common pool to make a loan feasible. Then, in an auction, a mortgage loan went to the highest bidder. The rest of the contributors had to wait until another adequate amount had been accumulated.

Gradually this concept broadened to allow outsiders to invest in the associations. The new class of members sought no mortgages. They asked only to share in profits. Obviously they were welcomed, because they made mortgage money more quickly available.

It must be said that most of these associations were managed with integrity. But the scent of quick profits invariably attracts charlatans. Quite a few of them rushed into this developing new business. By 1888 there were more than 3,000 building and loan associations in the United States; by 1893 there were 5,600. Among so many there were bound to be some dishonest men.

Historians credit Herbert Hoover with the ultimate

clean-up process. "By one of the more fortunate strokes of chance," wrote J. E. Ewalt, "Hoover was President of the United States when savings and loan leaders saw that something had to be done, and done right away, to assure any real future for their institutions." Once the federal government stepped into the picture through the agency of the Federal Home Loan Bank System, the charlatans fled.

Thereupon the savings and loan associations began to flourish as never before. In time they attracted more deposits than the savings banks themselves. By 1974 their assets exceeded $294 billion.

Why, I once asked an officer of the National Association of Mutual Savings Banks, have the savings and loan associations been able to outdistance the savings banks in growth?

"Primarily," he said, "because in the past the savings banks were afraid of federal interference and preferred to remain state-chartered. And only seventeen states, plus Puerto Rico, have chartered savings banks. The savings and loan associations, on the other hand, have long been both state- and federally chartered. That meant they could spring up everywhere. They now have fifty states in which to operate as opposed to our seventeen."

Have these associations complained about what mutual savings banks feared—undue federal interference?

"If *you* had been able to amass $294 billion," he asked, "would you complain?"

இ~௦

In these days of highly complicated, competitive banking maneuvers, the procedures of a century ago tend to seem simple. "Apart from keeping their records straight," one modern young banker told me, "all they had to worry about was the type of mortgage loans they made and maybe keeping their inkwells filled."

Clearly he had not troubled to examine the past. Nor had he read Earl B. Schwulst's observation that "the savings bank business is not always routine but, on the contrary, it often is involved with the comedies and tragedies in the lives of many everyday people." Had he looked back he would have learned that The Bowery Savings Bank had causes for distress which are unknown today. As one example, it had to contend with babies.

For no reason anyone can now explain, The Bowery's policy, like that of other banks, had long been to segregate men and women depositors. Males went to one teller, females to another. They waited in lines at opposite sides of the banking room.

In general, people who came to *make* deposits could complete the transaction within a few minutes. But those who wished to withdraw funds, especially on crowded days, could anticipate long delays.

That was because withdrawals followed an ancient system. Once you had made out a withdrawal slip, you stood in line, awaiting your chance to present it to a teller. He copied it in his own records and gave you a numbered card. While you sat down to wait (provided you had the good fortune to find an empty seat), your withdrawal slip went to one clerk for the verification of your signature; to another who checked your balance; to a third who studied and initialed the transaction; to a fourth, the cashier, who would in time pay out the money. With scores of people ahead of you, this process might well consume an hour or two before a floorman's stentorian voice called your number. As a result, women who could not leave their children behind for prolonged periods took them along to the bank. Some even brought lunch.

Edward Wood, who had become president of The Bowery upon the resignation of Henry Lyles, Jr., fretted over the fact that the children often became noisy. Not understanding why they had to remain inactive, the youngsters protested by wailing. President Wood's nerves were assailed by the cries. So were his sensibilities. The sounds destroyed the dignity of the bank.

One morning he summoned a brass-buttoned floorman to his office. "Let's not keep those women with noisy children waiting," he said. "Call their numbers and get them to the cashier's window ahead of the others. The sooner we speed them out of the bank, the quieter it will be."

The floorman assured the president this could be managed. For a few days it worked well. Mr. Wood, however, had not counted on the wit of his female clients. As soon as they observed that women with screaming children received preferential treatment, they *all* brought their children. Some even pinched their little ones to induce howls. Within a week Mr. Wood's fine plan caused pandemonium. When he could no longer endure it he resorted to new strategy.

"We'll handle this a different way," he told the floorman. "Run out and buy chocolate wafers and hard candies."

Fifteen minutes later the tall president of The Bowery Savings Bank was handing out candy and cookies to youngsters. When the little ones began giving attention to these goodies, they stopped crying. Mr. Wood had bribed his way to dignified silence.

There was another difficulty to be overcome, one of a different nature. This had to do with the sentimentality of trustees.

A few years earlier, in 1875, Trustee William Dennistoun had died while in office. The minutes of the next board meeting show that one man said: "Would it not be well that each member should have his particular chair, and when he is called away by death let it remain empty for a time to remind us of the uncertainty of life?"

It was meant to be a reverential gesture. The trustees adopted the resolution without question. What went wrong was that empty chairs soon cast a pall over board meetings. Men hesitated to raise their voices. Uneasy glances went to the unoccupied seats. It was as if a ghost were in attendance.

Without comment and without asking anyone's approval, President Wood had the empty chairs removed. They remained out of sight until replacements had been elected for the departed trustees. Then the chairs were brought back. Thereafter the meetings resumed their customary fervor. Mr. Wood had achieved another diplomatic success.

⌾⌾

On October 13, 1884—while the financial world was still trying to recover from its latest panic—The Bowery Savings Bank made history. It granted the largest mortgage loan ever made up to that time by an American savings bank. This went to the New York Produce Exchange for the building it planned to erect on Broadway, facing Bowling Green. The amount involved was $1.5 million, at an interest rate of 4½ percent.

So enormous a transaction on the part of a thrift institution naturally merited comment in business publications; it caused considerable conversation in financial circles; and it brought to the bank a new aura of importance and prestige. This was indeed Big Business—in 1884. (Not long ago, in the 1970s, the bank granted a mortgage loan of $33 million without eliciting any particular notice!)

After the news of the $1.5 million mortgage had spread, the parade to The Bowery of mortgage seekers grew longer every day. It was clear that if you wanted a sizable mortgage The Bowery was the place to go. Whereas the bank's outstanding loans in 1883 had amounted to only $7 million, the figure leaped to almost $10.5 million by 1885.

Experienced applicants learned to stay away on days when semiannual dividends were distributed. Those were days of chaos. Thousands of people crowded the premises, passbooks in hand, elbowing one another aside in their eagerness to have their new assets inscribed in their books. *Harper's Weekly* published a woodcut of the scene, a picture that could easily have been mistaken for an indoor riot. In an effort to avoid such periodic uprisings, the bank eventually adopted a new system. On the front cover of every passbook it pasted the notation:

> Books left to have the interest put
> on must be left for that purpose *one*
> *week*, and called for during the hours
> of business. Interest can not be
> drawn until it is written up.

This measure helped to end the riotous aspects of Dividend Days. Nevertheless, those who wished to do mortgage business still found it wise to come on less crowded occasions.

People must have marveled at the incredible location of this great financial institution among so many odd neighbors. At number 105 was Owney Geoghegan's Saloon, featuring daily bare-knuckled prizefights in a cleared area among the tables. Owney Geoghegan had been the leader of the Gas House Gang, and he had never lost his love of a good fracas. Nearer to Chatham Square and to Chinatown, Paddy Martin's Saloon offered a different kind of attraction—opium pipes in its cellar. And just beyond the bank, at number 138, the Gaiety Musée presented Bosco the Snake Eater and also the Brooklyn Lion Tamer. These two were the rivals of Ludwig the Bloodsucker, the human vampire advertised by another nearby museum.

On a somewhat higher cultural level was Callahan's Cafe. Almost any evening you could hear the voices of Irish tenors floating out of Callahan's, singing "Just Break the News to Mother," "A Violet from His Mother's Grave," "Just Tell Them That You Saw Me," "She May Have Seen Better Days," and similar classics which often caused heart-broken men to weep in their beer.

And yet, out of these cheap resorts emerged people like Irving Berlin, Al Jolson, and scores of others who contributed to American entertainment history. Here they had their chance to be heard, to be encouraged and inspired by audience reaction.

It would be wrong, however, to regard the activities of this street as a measure of New York's cultural interests. During these teeming 1880s the Metropolitan Opera House, in its elegant uptown location, inaugurated its programs with a stirring performance of *Faust*. Its artistry matched that of any opera company in Europe, if you could accept the judgment of critics. At the Met, Leopold Damrosch and Anton Seidl were conducting the works of the world's greatest composers, while stars like Lili Lehmann repeatedly crossed the ocean to sing for Americans. And Americans loved music. The Philharmonic Orchestra was constantly filling the hall Andrew Carnegie had given to the city; Theodore Thomas was drawing crowds to his own orchestra; and when Madison Square Garden opened —"the eighth wonder of the world," as one writer described it—17,000 people crowded into the place to hear Edouard Strauss lead his musicians.

There is little doubt that The Bowery Savings Bank

was, like others, being asked to contribute funds for the city's cultural activities, and such requests were endless. At the Academy of Music on 14th Street, there were benefit performances to raise money for a pedestal that would be ready when the Statue of Liberty arrived; elsewhere funds were being raised to erect a monument of General Washington on the steps of the Sub-Treasury Building. But as one of The Bowery's officers explained: "The money in this bank, as in all mutual savings banks, does not belong to the officers or to the trustees. It belongs to the depositors. Therefore the law prohibits us from giving it away."

Of course, nothing prevented the trustees from making *personal* contributions to good causes, and this, it may be assumed, they did generously. (It was more than half a century later that legislation was finally enacted which permitted mutual savings banks to support worthy community causes.)

Meanwhile the bank was becoming an international institution. Many of its depositors who returned to the lands of their origins, or went west, trusted The Bowery so implicitly that they left their savings in its vaults. Deposits were arriving from places as distant as California and Ireland and Germany. As in so many times of the past, American prosperity seemed certain to be permanent. And so it might well have been—except for what happened in India.

8

THE IMPORTANCE OF SILVER

How could an act of the British government in India affect the savings of people in the United States? If the question puzzled the average citizen, he could hardly be blamed. It bewildered many a sophisticated businessman. It brought confusion even to Wall Street.

What made matters incomprehensible to ,most Americans was the fact that the economy of the United States was flourishing. One commentator wrote that "business transactions in 1892 went beyond that of any other year in the history of the country. All records were broken in trade." The Bowery Savings Bank, like many of its sister banks, was prospering as the nation itself prospered.

Once more it outgrew its quarters. This time no amount of renovation of the old building could fill its needs. What it required was far more space, and the trustees voted to construct a new bank that would extend from their present site to adjoining property on Grand Street, which they purchased for $155,500.

When the architectural firm of McKim, Mead, and White was retained to design the L-shaped structure, the bank won the services of the city's most distinguished architect, Stanford White. The trustees and President Wood were justifiably proud. They may have lost a few nights' sleep, however, when they learned that the cost of the new building would exceed $570,000. As one of the bank's later officers put it, "Perhaps they would not have ventured upon such elaborate plans could they have foreseen the great distress which was to overwhelm the entire financial world during 1893."

The trouble in 1893 once more had its roots in the demands of mine owners and their supporters to have silver become an accredited part of the country's currency. The Bowery's opposition to this was as firm as ever. Its president invited the heads of New York's leading banks to a conference in his office. They passed a resolution condemning such recognition of silver, dispatched the message to Washington, and saw in chagrin that it had no effect. The proponents of silver won their battle. Now $222 million in silver bullion came to federal vaults.

How could such wealth cause problems?

It happened that India too had a silver currency. Moreover, India—with its enormous population—accounted for fully one-third of the world's use of silver. Therefore, when the British government abruptly suspended India's coinage of the metal, one-third of the world's market for silver evaporated. As silver lost its market, its value dropped.

In the United States the price fell within a few days from 78 cents to 65 cents an ounce. This caused a depreciation of $37 million in the value of the Treasury's silver bullion. It also reduced, by some 16⅔ percent, the value of the silver the *banks* were holding.

With the metal's price so low and its future so uncertain, there was a rush to the banks and to the Sub-Treasuries. People demanded to have their silver exchanged for gold or gold certificates. This happened at a most unfortunate moment. Within two months the Treasury would have to meet huge interest payments, and almost overnight it saw its gold reserves whittled down to about $100 million. With this demand continuing, the supply could soon be depleted to a point which would leave the government in an untenable position. Such danger induced the Secretary of the Treasury, with scarcely any warning, to suspend all further issuance of gold certificates.

To the holders of depreciated silver, this was appalling. Was the federal government bent on ruining them? Floods of protesting letters inundated the Congress; editorials cried of injustice; telegrams went to the White House.

President Grover Cleveland, trying to reassure the nation, issued a statement promising "to keep the public faith and to preserve the parity between gold and silver." The promise sounded meaningless. *How* did the President propose to "preserve parity" between silver, which had lost much of its value, and gold, which was being made unobtainable? Was the White House preoccupied with words and abandoning its common sense?

People continued to assail the banks, insisting on getting gold certificates in exchange for their silver holdings. Unable to comply, a number of commercial banks began to close their doors. In such a crisis it was inevitable that the stock market too should be undermined. On July 26th the market crashed.

Even then the public's demand for gold did not abate. On a single day in New York, long lines of people presented to the Sub-Treasury over $7 million in silver currency for which they demanded gold certificates—at a time when the Sub-Treasury found itself with gold resources amounting to less than $10 million.

Something had to be done. The deeply distraught President Cleveland summoned banker J. Pierpont Morgan to the White House for consultation and advice. They talked for hours. Afterwards Morgan went home to confer with other bankers. Within a few days the private banking houses of Morgan, Belmont, and Rothschild agreed to supply the American government with 3,400,000 ounces of gold taken from their holdings abroad as well as in the United States. In exchange they received thirty-year federal bonds bearing interest of 4½ percent.

The arrangement, replenishing the Treasury's gold supply, did much to relieve the American crisis. Yet it was not a gesture of generosity on the part of the international financiers. It was, as much as anything else, a matter of self-protection. These men knew they could not do business in a bankrupt United States.

How did The Bowery Savings Bank and other thrift institutions fare throughout this national turmoil? They survived largely because of their reputation for safeguarding the funds of depositors. Once again The Bowery had resorted to demanding sixty-day notice of withdrawals, and once again this step had relieved it of pressure. As in the past, depositors were reassured to know that nobody else could deplete the bank's cash reserves. They were content to wait and see how the country would rescue itself.

⁕

A struggle between silver and gold might disrupt the nation. The President of the United States might be wondering how his handling of the crisis would affect the political future of his party. Some great financial institutions might be collapsing. None of these sources of turbulence could interfere with Stanford White's dedication to the completion of the bank's new building. He concentrated on it as he concentrated on every project he undertook, ignoring everything that threatened to distract him.

While construction was in progress, The Bowery once more used the vaults and premises of its first friend, the Butchers and Drovers Bank; and no one worked more earnestly with Stanford White or with sculptor Frederick MacMonnies, whose heroic figures overhang the bank's entrance, than did President Edward Wood. Yet Wood missed what might have been the most gratifying day of his life. Four months before the building was opened for business he became ill. Within a few days he was dead.

If his shadow lay across the formal dedication of the bank, everyone understood. The entire board of trustees, the bank's officers, and city officials attended the ceremonies. The new president, John Pomeroy Townsend, gray-haired, gray-moustached, stood in the entrance and made a dignified speech in which he lauded his predecessor, Edward Wood, as the father of this impressive structure. Then he invited the visitors to join him in an inspection tour of the premises.

President Townsend's personal pride was unmistakable. For 34 years he had served this institution as a trustee and more recently as a vice president. He could not help recalling, as he led his guests around the great hall, that *The New York Times* had described the bank as "without question the strongest financial institution of the sort in America, if not in the world."

Another newspaper wrote of the building's architecture: "The Bowery Savings Bank is a palace that is good to come to and sit in and feast one's eyes upon, with its marble pillars, its dome, its gilt, and its splendor. It is like some old cathedral, and the entrance through dim, pillared aisles —which is called 'The Chapel'—bears out the resemblance."

That day the place was filled with the spirit of Edward Wood. And though he had missed this occasion, he had lived long enough to enjoy another kind of satisfaction. He had seen the success of The Bowery draw other savings institutions to the street. The Dry Dock had established a branch at the corner of Third Street. The Metropolitan Savings Bank had opened its office a few blocks to the north, near Cooper Square. The Citizens had come to the corner of Canal Street. And there were commercial banks, too, that gathered around, principally the Manufacturers' Trust and the First National Bank.

"Though criminals had their lairs all around the Bowery," wrote historian Alvin F. Harlow, "there were no 'stick-ups' in any Bowery banking rooms, no blowing of vault doors, no tunneling into vaults from below by burglars, as was frequently done elsewhere. Money with the scent of liquor on it, mothball-scented money from clothing dealers, it all came trustfully to the Bowery banks. Even a communist taking part in a riot at the City Hall, shouting 'We want bread! We want work!' was found to have exhibited his faith in capitalism by depositing $2,622 in The Bowery Savings Bank."

Why were Bowery banks never robbed? A newspaper writer ascribed the fact to the "community pride" of local burglars. They would never molest "their own" institutions. That community pride extended to something else, too. Most women were regarded as fair game; but let a man dare to annoy a local Salvation Army lass, and he would be beaten almost to death.

So, in 1894, the bank celebrated the opening of its new building—and one other memorable event. After long months of indecision, after appraising every model on the market, The Bowery Savings Bank purchased its first typewriter.

Having bought it, the officers now discovered that only women had been trained to operate such machines. That posed a direct challenge to tradition; no female had ever before worked in the bank.

There is no record of how the trustees reacted to the necessity of hiring a woman. But it was obvious that the typewriter, having been paid for, had to be put to use, and so in this historic year, 1894, The Bowery employed its first female. She came to work as President Townsend's secretary.

The impressive new building helped to attract so many depositors that toward the end of 1895 the bank had more than 111,000 accounts and assets in excess of $60 million. An enterprise of such magnitude demanded long hours of labor from its employees. It was the policy of The Bowery to compensate people for their dinner expenses on evenings when they worked late. Recognizing the pressures of rising prices, the board of trustees met on September 9, 1895 and unanimously approved a resolution:

> That in consequence of the increased cost
> of nearly all articles of food—since
> the existing rate of 35 cents a head paid
> by this Bank for dinners for its employees
> was fixed over 15 years ago—the rate
> be increased to 40 cents per head.

The issue of silver still divided the United States, and one wonders how the industrialists who comprised the bank's board of trustees reacted to the strife of the day. At the Republican Convention of 1896 the wealthy Mark Hanna was appealing strongly to other men of means to support his candidate, William McKinley. Hanna, in the words of Henry Bamford Parkes, was a man "who, like Alexander Hamilton, believed in leadership by an elite group of wealthy men and in close union between government and big business. The platform he advocated called for the maintenance of the gold standard and promised opposition to the free coinage of silver."

Many a trustee must have nodded approval of such a program. But what were they to do about the 36-year-old young whippersnapper the Democrats had nominated as their candidate for the Presidency of the United States? Until recently he had been an almost unknown Nebraska congressman. Now people everywhere were quoting the rousing speeches of young William Jennings Bryan.

He had managed to identify gold with the "plutocrats who control it." Silver became the political adversary of gold, the standard around which non-plutocrats could rally.

"A growing number of Americans," said a Washington newspaper, "are becoming convinced that the economic system is fundamentally unsound and that the Federal Government should assume responsibility for the general welfare instead of leaving economic processes to work themselves out. For the time being, the forces of popular discontent are concentrated behind the demand for free and unlimited coinage of silver. In spite of its obvious inadequacy as a program of total reform, it has become the main rallying point for all who want a change in the existing system."

Bryan had brought the Democratic Convention to its

feet, cheering, with his defense of silver and of the rights of "little people"—the very kind who were Bowery depositors.

"There are two ideas of government," Bryan had declared. "There are those who believe that if you just legislate to make the well-to-do prosperous, their prosperity will leak through on those below. The Democratic idea has been that if you legislate to make the *masses* prosperous, their prosperity will find its way up and through every class that rests upon it. . . . We will answer their [the Republicans'] demand for a gold standard by saying to them: You shall not press down upon the brow of labor this crown of thorns, you shall not crucify mankind upon a cross of gold."

William Jennings Bryan or William McKinley?

Since in their private businesses the trustees were, for the most part, wealthy men, they were perhaps in sympathy with the Mark Hanna philosophy of leadership by the rich. Yet they could see the less affluent people—those who were making the bank a great institution—carrying "Vote for Bryan" placards up and down the Bowery. If any trustee felt a moral conflict of interest, he never manifested it at board meetings. Silver or gold, McKinley or Bryan—the bank continued to be interested mainly in safeguarding the savings of "little people"; and though its trustees might in principle be opposed to silver currency, their first obligation was to provide depositors with the dividends on which they depended. Whatever direction politics might take, the prosperity of the bank had to be maintained.

9

ONLY EXPERTS NEED APPLY

Professor Solomon Fabricant of New York University, who had been teaching economics for almost half a century, made this observation:

The very purpose of long-range saving in America has changed. It used to be that a family based nearly all its hopes for old-age security on the amount of cash it could amass in savings accounts. Today most people in the labor force can look forward to two other sources of income in their years of retirement. One is Social Security, which will send them monthly checks.

The second is the benefits to be derived from a pension plan. Considering the way the cost of living has been increasing, however, these two sources rarely meet the needs of the average family.

Fabricant's point is underscored by the findings of the Social Security Administration. Its surveys indicate that "35 percent of married couples over the age of 65 receive less total income than is needed to rise above the poverty level; likewise, 77 percent of unmarried people over the age of 65 do not have income sufficient to maintain even a modest level of living."

Fabricant continued:

> People now save largely to *augment* what they expect from Social Security and pensions. And to be comfortable in their later years, to augment their basic retirement income with substantial sums of savings, means they must save over many years.
>
> What you call a Savings Payout Account [The Bowery's name for a system it originated] enables depositors to arrange to receive monthly checks, drawn from their savings, over a ten- or fifteen- or even twenty-year period after retirement. I imagine thousands of families are finding this the wisest way of providing for the future. But in order to do so intelligently, in order to take the hazards of inflation into account, they require the expert guidance and counsel of competent officers in their banks.

Thus Fabricant fixed attention on a few of the modern obligations a banker has as compared with his problems of the past: the ability to offer sage advice on almost every monetary question; and the fiduciary responsibility of understanding how every family can be steered through the maze of complications and uncertainties in today's financial world.

The very language of banking has changed. No nineteenth-century economist ever heard terms like "floating rate notes" or "payment orders" or "Eurodollars," or even queries about Savings Bank Life Insurance. And how could anyone have discussed the advisability of an individual's buying tax-exempt municipal bonds in an age when there was no personal income tax?

It is precisely because the demands on bankers' knowledge have mounted in so many ways that a number of universities now offer comprehensive courses in banking. It has become a career which insists on specialized expertise—without which no modern bank can survive.

"The point is," said Earl B. Schwulst, "that the savings bank is no longer the bank exclusively for the simple, unsophisticated 'little guy' with a few dollars to save each week or month out of his pay check. It is a big financial institution progressively becoming an investment trust for the investment of non-commercial deposits of any size."

This evolution has never been interrupted. It is continuing more energetically than ever. As Morris D. Crawford, Jr. told the Senate Banking Committee: "We believe that mutual savings banks must develop into full-service family banks capable of providing all the financial services required by families over their economic life cycle."

The evidence of how broad a banker's interests must be in this generation lies in the questions he is asked by depositors. At The Bowery the officers meet daily for lunch. One has only to join them to discover, through their discussions, the wide variety of their functions. As a matter of curiosity I inquired about the subjects they had been called upon to deal with in a single week. Among them were:

☐ State and federal legislative developments.
☐ The effect of new electronic devices, especially as they relate to the use of computers for the instant transfer of funds to every part of the nation.
☐ Consumer loans and the use of credit cards.

83

- ☐ The expansion of branch offices.
- ☐ AMMINET—the Automated Mortgage Market Information Network, which quotes instantaneous information on the secondary mortgage market.
- ☐ Insurance programs.
- ☐ A new type of investment certificate—the aforementioned "floating rate notes."

And, of course, there were the perennial concerns of the supervisor of school accounts, maintained to encourage thrift among children; of specialists in home improvement loans, in education loans, in the Keogh retirement program for self-employed people; and the problems of overseeing the cash inflow and outflow amounting to hundreds of millions of dollars a year.

I mention these merely to suggest the vast gulf that lies between the interests of the original officers of the bank and the interests of those who have followed. The Bowery's first presidents were not bankers. Chosen from among the founding trustees, they were successful merchants who may have demonstrated business acumen in their own enterprises but had assumed their tasks at The Bowery with scant experience in banking per se.

As the institution grew in size, in importance, in the variety of its services, its leaders had to have knowledge commensurate with expanding needs. President John Pomeroy Townsend was an early example of the new type of executive. His financial background was impressive. A trustee since 1864, he had served as president of New York's Maritime Exchange, as treasurer of the New York Produce Exchange, and as president of the Knickerbocker Trust Company. He had traveled extensively in Europe, studying economic conditions, and he had written for such scholarly publications as the *Cyclopaedia of Political History and Political Economy of the United States.*

This, then, was a new type of Bowery president, a man

thoroughly conversant with the banking and economic problems of the day. He *had* to be outstanding to be confirmed by a board of trustees that included some of New York's most distinguished citizens—men like Hugh D. Auchincloss, George F. Baker, Charles Scribner, and James Stillman.

ᘒᔛᕀ

Weldon Welfling, chairman of the Department of Banking and Finance at Case Western Reserve University, has recorded this significant bit of history:

> Between 1865 and 1900 approximately 2,000 commercial banks, about four-fifths of them state banks, suspended operations. These frequent failures of commercial banks helped to maintain the position of savings banks as intermediaries. This factor operated, of course, most strongly where savings banks were already well established.

It certainly must have been a factor in the progress of The Bowery Savings Bank, since its growth continued in good years and bad. A curious aspect of this growth occurred in 1899. For sixteen years the dividends it paid had been an unchanging 4 percent. Then the rate was reduced to 3½ percent. Did this cause depositors to desert the institution, to carry their funds away in search of higher earnings? Not at all. During the next two years, until the 4 percent rate was restored, the number of depositors climbed from 121,006 to 123,564; at the same time the bank's assets rose from $70,865,758 to $76,044,031.

How explain such an anomaly? Was it because all banks were reducing their rates?

"No. There are a number of other reasons," said a Bowery officer. "First, there is the combination of loyalty to an institution and of simple human inertia. A person who feels his savings are secure in one bank isn't going to run off to another in order to get an extra ½ percent on a fairly small amount—and remember that most deposits at the time *were* modest. To a man with $500 in his account, the difference of ½ percent is only $2.50 a year. For $2.50 it hardly pays to go through all the trouble of changing banks. Incidentally, it is important to realize that the temporary reduction in rates was not the result of poor earnings. On the contrary, it was a step toward lifting the bank's net worth to a more secure level. There have been other times when we have had to reduce our dividend rates to safeguard the basic strength of the institution's net worth, and I believe that the more sophisticated depositors of a mutual savings bank understand and approve of such precautions. It is *their* interests we are protecting."

In newspapers of the period one finds no mention of The Bowery's rate change. In fact, during those latter years of the 1890s the activities of the bank received less than their customary notice in the press. Too many exciting national and civic events were demanding newspaper space.

For one, in 1898 the United States went to war. To be sure, it was a brief conflict limited to Cuba and the Philippines. Nevertheless, it was a war. From the sinking of the *Maine* to the Rough Riders' charge up San Juan Hill and in succeeding days, war stories preempted all other matters.

On the local scene, more than thirty years of resolute campaigning on the part of Brooklyn's Andrew H. Green resulted in 1898 in the joining of the five boroughs to form Greater New York, a metropolis with over 3 million inhabitants. Confronted by an event of such magnitude, reporters could hardly be expected to concern themselves too seriously with what was happening at The Bowery Savings Bank.

And a subway was being built. Though no newspapers emphasized the effect this might have on thrift institutions, it caused a great deal of excitement in The Bowery's mortgage department. A subway, by connecting outlying districts as far as 145th Street with the heart of the city, promised to increase real estate values near every station. Builders were buying land, projecting the construction of new homes. That would mean an upsurge in mortgage applications.

Nor was that all. Theodore Roosevelt was being elected governor of New York; Admiral Dewey was being hailed as a wartime hero in mammoth civic parades; the world's tallest skyscraper, the 26-story Park Row Building, just completed, was bringing gasps from all sightseers. Uptown, a group called the Floradora Sextette was winning endless columns of newspaper applause in the theatrical pages, outdoing even the notices given to the Metropolitan Opera's newest diva, Mme. Ernestine Schumann-Heink.

Still, the aftermath of the Spanish-American War was producing most of the headlines, even in the business sections. Among them was the question of purchasing the Philippines. President McKinley, addressing a convention of Methodist ministers, made one of the most extraordinary speeches ever delivered by an American Chief Executive. He told his audience that after praying for divine guidance, he had received what he firmly believed to be a message from God. In this communication, he asserted, he had been told that it was the solemn duty of the United States to acquire the Philippines in order "to educate the Filipinos, and uplift and civilize and Christianize them." He said little about a subject that other members of his Administration were discussing—the hope that the Philippines could become an American base for the expansion of trade and influence in the Far East. At any rate, the Philippines were soon bought for $20 million. (And it was there that a future president of The Bowery was to serve as Superintendent of Banks.)

With so many things happening in a historic year, it was understandable that the bank received less than its own usual share of publicity. Nevertheless, *The Times* did report the death of President John Pomery Townsend and the accession to the presidency of John D. Hicks. Also, the business pages briefly noted that President Hicks was creating a new executive position at The Bowery—the office of comptroller, to which he appointed Henry A. Schenck. As President Hicks said, an institution with $70 million in assets ought to have an officer in charge of its financial affairs.

One of the reasons for Schenck's appointment was that John Hicks had little time to concern himself with everyday disbursements for operational expenses. He was confronted by a serious decline of land values in several areas where the bank held mortgages, and in the final year of his administration he was obliged to give most of his time to mortgage readjustments. This he succeeded in doing before his retirement as president, when he yielded the post to William H. S. Wood.

Almost at once, the new president demonstrated vigorous ideas of his own. He felt that the bank had not been sufficiently energetic in seeking new depositors among the 3 million New Yorkers. To remedy this neglect, he instituted the first major advertising campaign in The Bowery's history, setting precedents which several other banks quickly adopted. Perhaps President Wood was driven to the recruitment of new accounts by an unexpected bill for $67,865.39 that came from the state government. The legislature had just passed a franchise tax on savings banks!

It was the first time the bank had been taxed for anything at all except the real estate it owned on the Bowery.

Yet Mr. Wood must have known that any new tax, once imposed, is likely to grow bigger with every passing year. His anticipation of such demands may have been one of the reasons he felt the institution ought to have more depositors and more money.

In January of 1904, he told a meeting of trustees: "Special efforts have been made to induce certain classes to save, especially actors and actresses, the Soldiers of the United States Army, and the Sailors of the Navy. We have sent out 14,000 copies of an illustrated booklet. We have also instituted a system whereby depositors can bank by mail, and the method is described in the 27,000 copies of another brochure we have distributed. In addition to all this we have issued to the laboring classes, through their employers, about three quarters of a million pay envelopes, each bearing advice as to the weekly saving of some portion of their earnings."

By 1906 his campaign for accounts had won more than 11,000 new depositors; and President Wood was able to notify his trustees, with a great deal of pride, that deposits *now exceeded $100 million.*

"It is the first time," he declared, "that any institution of savings has been the custodian of so huge a sum."

There could hardly have been a more spectacular way to enter the twentieth century—or to face the troubles, the anxieties, the wars, and the upheavals the century was to produce. To meet the challenge of the future, the nation's mutual savings banks now had to raise their sights to wholly new frontiers.

10

A CENTURY OF NEW CHALLENGES

It has often been said that no epoch in human history has wrought more technological changes than has our twentieth century. When philosophers remind us of the wonders of past ages—every invention from the wheel to telegraphy, from the steam engine to electric light—we counter with talk of aviation, television, space exploration, and scores of other innovations that have enriched our era.

Yet those who speak for the past and those who speak for the present can agree on this: The advent of any new technological process (especially one as revolutionary as the computer) involves changes in everything from machinery to law, from labor agreements to college courses. Banking has not been excluded from this pressure for change. The methods it employs today, even the regulations under which it operates, were in many instances undreamed of in the 1880s. For that reason and for purposes of comparison with later years, it is significant to appraise the status of America's savings banks at the birth of the present century.

In 1900 there were 626 such institutions throughout the country. By contrast, there were 12,427 commercial banks in the United States. Most of these, especially those in Eastern urban centers, had long considered savings accounts too petty to be of interest. But eyeing the combined assets of thrift institutions—$2.9 billion—some commercial banks began to change their attitudes.

In 1903 two of them queried the Comptroller of the Currency about the legal aspects of creating subsidiaries to deal in savings and trust functions. The Comptroller answered: "You are respectfully informed that there does not appear to be anything in the National Banking Act which authorizes or prohibits the operation of a savings department in a national bank."

Thus reassured, a number of commercial banks began to open savings departments. Within fifteen years they had over $3 billion in savings deposits.

This did not mean that mutual savings banks saw their own resources depleted by $3 billion. Their assets also rose. What they suffered was a diminution in their *share* of total deposits. By 1918 their share had dropped from 88 percent to 73 percent of the total savings in deposit institutions.

For now savings banks were competing for funds not only with commercial banks. The people of the United

States were putting more and more of their money into other ways of providing for the future—savings and loan associations, corporate securities, life insurance.

The Bowery itself, curiously enough, seemed only mildly affected by such trends. The frugal workers of lower New York continued to bring their extra dollars to the tellers' cages. They persuaded friends and relatives to join them. On the first day of the twentieth century, when the bank was 67 years old, it could count these resources:

Cash	$ 3,917,972
Government bonds	10,489,000
Other Bonds	33,935,500
Mortgages	23,094,053
Other assets	1,450,000

Five years later, on January 1, 1905, these assets of $72,886,525 had increased to $94,566,944.

Naturally such growth pleased the trustees. At one of their meetings they offered warm praise to President Wood for the quality of his leadership. He in turn was as gracious and self-effacing as any member of the board.

"I cannot help thinking," he replied, "that our position is largely due not only to the active efforts of the bank but to the high and well-known standing of the trustees and their indefatigable efforts to build up a tower of strength for the savings of the laboring classes. I consider such a record as we have made as one of which every trustee may feel justly proud. It is a remarkable testimony to the wisdom and conservative care with which they have for so many years administered the affairs of the institution."

While the president and the board exchanged congratulations and words of praise, neither mentioned one of the primary explanations of The Bowery's growth; immigration. More aliens than ever before were arriving in the

United States, most of them entering through the port of New York. There were years when over 800,000 came. Though many of them traveled on to settle in other parts of America, thousands remained in the city—and eventually many of them became depositors.

Also, the widespread advertising campaign President Wood had launched was having its impact. And then there was a brochure, first published in 1903, that went to areas far outside the city and described the expansion of a service that had previously been local. It announced:

> The Bowery Savings Bank, in order to widen the field of its useful activity, has inaugurated a system of "Banking By Mail" through which it extends to the dweller in northern Maine, southern Texas, or in the remotest sections of the world, the same protection that it does to the citizens of New York City or nearby towns.
>
> Every corner letter-box or smallest cross-roads country post office has thus become a convenient receiving teller, from which Uncle Sam's registered mail, acting as a trustworthy messenger, guarantees the safe delivery of funds and the return of a formal receipt from the Bank.

Since most states had no savings banks at all, the brochure drew a very gratifying response. The same leaflet, however, made a point which must fill every modern taxpaying American with nostalgia:

> One of the chief advantages of keeping one's money on deposit in a savings bank is that all funds thus are held free from taxation. The interest paid is therefore all profit and may be counted upon as a definite fixed income.

In any case, "Banking by Mail" proved successful, as did the advertising campaign, and internal affairs at The Bowery were going well. But there was an external trouble to meet—a trouble that threatened the entire economy—and in the face of this, the bank was helpless.

The United States experienced another of its periodic financial debacles.

This time, in 1907, the causes were diverse and cumulative. They stemmed for the most part from excessive, ill-advised speculation in which many commercial banks had indulged. Having in prosperous years accumulated more funds than they could invest prudently, they became reckless. Secretary of the Treasury Leslie M. Shaw was moved to say: "We who pray should ask God to save us from increased prosperity; we have all we can stand!"

(The clergy too were concerned—but each in his own way. One Sunday morning at Trinity Church, at the foot of Wall Street, the sermon dealt with "Bless the Lord for All Our Riches." That same day the sermon subject at St. Patrick's Cathedral was "The Root of All Evil.")

Prosperity notwithstanding, blow after blow now began to fall upon the American people, leaving them first appalled, then bitterly disillusioned. The shocks began to come when investigations disclosed incredible mismanagement and extravagance in the highly respected insurance industry. If you could not trust insurance companies, all under strict government scrutiny, whom *could* you trust? Next, the American maritime industry was shaken when the great Morse shipping combine failed. Soon thereafter, a chain of banks controlled by Morse and Heintze collapsed.

No one more clearly recognized the underlying reasons for all this than did Thomas Woodrow Wilson, then president of Princeton University. When he was invited to speak at a convention of the American Bankers Association, he stunned his audience with the candor of his accusations.

"The banks of this country are remote from the people," he charged, "and the people regard them as not belonging to them but as belonging to some power hostile to them. . . . Even the colossal enterprises of our time do not supply you with enough safe investments for the money that comes in to you; and banks here, there, and everywhere are tempted, as a consequence, to place money in speculative enterprises, and even themselves to promote questionable ventures in finance at a fearful and wholly unjustifiable risk in order to get the usury they wish from their resources."

Reading this in their morning papers, The Bowery's officers and trustees had the satisfaction of seeing that Wilson had urged commercial banks to do what local thrift institutions were doing.

"There would be plenty of investments," Wilson said, "if you carried your money to the people of the country at large and had agents in hundreds of villages who knew the men in their neighborhoods who could be trusted with loans and who would make profitable use of them. Your money, moreover, would quicken and fertilize the country."

But Woodrow Wilson's advice came too late. Throughout the land companies and banks were already failing, largely through mismanagement. When the president of the Knickerbocker Trust Company committed suicide rather than face charges of corruption, it proved to be the final blow. Fearing all banks were corrupt, people again rushed to withdraw their funds. They came in such frenzied numbers that, to save banking reserves from utter depletion, the federal government made a serious decision. Notices of it went to every part of the country, and of course The Bowery was included. On its doors hurriedly prepared placards went up to announce:

By government order all banks are forbidden to exchange hard currency for checks.

By its very harshness, the injunction against cashing checks exacerbated the situation. Now people were angry. They *demanded* currency. They needed it. If they had to travel, railroads required cash. If they went into restaurants, they were expected to pay in cash. And New York in particular offered all sorts of attractions for which one had to pay in currency: Were you planning to hear Enrico Caruso at the Metropolitan? Were you going to see Ethel Barrymore in Charles Frohman's production of *Captain Jinks?* Or George M. Cohan at the Palace? You *had* to have money.

Under this pressure, the federal government rushed $30 million in assistance to banks in New York and other cities. It was not enough. The ruin of many banks still seemed imminent as their funds flowed out.

At the height of this tension, Edward Harriman and John D. Rockefeller went one night to the home of the country's most influential banker, J. Pierpont Morgan. They urged him once more to help rescue the American economy. The elderly Morgan rose out of a sickbed, sweating and shivering, to go to his telephone.

(Some reporters later insisted that President Theodore Roosevelt himself asked Morgan to intervene, but one can doubt this. In his trust-busting activities Roosevelt had denounced many financiers, from whose number Morgan had not been excluded. "These men," the President later wrote, "demanded for themselves an immunity from governmental control which, if granted, would be as wicked and foolish as immunity to the barons of the twelfth century." So it may be assumed that whatever Morgan did that night was done for the broad welfare of the nation, not necessarily to please the administration in Washington.)

Throughout the night, J. Pierpont Morgan conferred with other financial leaders. Two days later *The New York World* reported that "national catastrophe had been avoided largely through the efforts of Mr. Morgan. In a series of all-night meetings in his library the 70-year-old

banker, dizzy with a cold, marshaled cash resources of
$25 million to save the banks threatened with runs."

During the crisis The Bowery, like every financial
institution, lost a number of worried depositors. But at
the same time, people who withdrew their money from
commercial banks brought it *to* The Bowery. In consequence of such public confidence, the bank had little
net loss in deposits and it gained enormously in prestige.

This prompted *The New York Tribune* to soar into
hyperbole. "No conceivable circumstance," it declared,
"no extremity of banking or financial disaster, could bankrupt the great Bowery Savings Bank."

It is doubtful whether any responsible economist would
accept so exaggerated a statement. But thousands of "little
people" read it. Thousands of "little people" gave it
thought. When next they had money to deposit, they
brought it to The Bowery.

⟨≈⟩

In the midst of the tensions and uncertainties of 1907,
The Bowery Savings Bank sustained an unexpected blow.
This came with the death of its president, William H. S.
Wood.

Wood's four-year administration had brought almost
10,000 new accounts to the bank, as well as the esteem
of the financial community. At a special board meeting,
his memory was honored by eulogistic comments from
every one of the 43 trustees.

They sat in the paneled boardroom which Stanford
White had tried to make the most beautiful in America.
They occupied two long rows of chairs which faced
a desk on a raised platform where the presiding officer
sat. The effect was rather like that of students in a class-

98

room facing their teacher. From the president's point of view, it must at times have seemed more like an accused man confronting a jury.

(In recent years the unwieldy size of the board has gradually been reduced. Today, with Ellis T. Gravette, Jr. as chairman, it consists of 16 trustees who gather around a long conference table.)

At the 1907 board meeting following the death of William Wood, respect for his judgment continued as did respect for his wishes. The trustees chose as their next president the man Wood himself had picked to be the bank's comptroller—Henry A. Schenck.

Before long, Schenck had the agreeable task of supervising the celebration of the bank's 75th anniversary. Presumably the staff was impressed by the speech he made, by the display of bunting over the entrance, by the formally clad presence of all trustees, by all such conventional trappings of an anniversary. But what must have delighted them most was the bonus of half a month's salary that went to every employee.

This was almost the last easy function that fell to the lot of Henry Schenck. In 1914, after the passage of the Federal Reserve Act, he had to warn his board that it must henceforth be prepared for more aggressive competition from commercial banks. The Act specifically recognized, as one analyst expressed it, "the growing practice of accepting time deposits and paying interest thereon by national commercial banks." It also permitted national banks "to make mortgage loans on improved farmland."

Clearly The Bowery, like all thrift institutions, would have to find ways of coping with this competition. Yet the problem was destined to be of minor importance during the next few years. For those years were to span one of the most trying periods in American and world history,

99

the years of World War I. The bank's age-old preoccupation with the welfare of "little people" would temporarily have to be put aside. Its first obligation would be to support the wartime needs of the United States.

One might have argued, of course, that the interests of "little people" dedicated to political freedom and of a United States dedicated to political freedom were really synonymous. Neither could survive without the other.

11

THE BANKS
GO TO WAR

Poets have long reminded us that no man is an island
unto himself, and they might have said the same
about banks. What affects the financial health of any
community instantly affects the repositories of its
funds. As one banker said to me, "We are not only
the mirrors of our times; we are its victims or its
beneficiaries, depending on circumstances."

Certainly this was true when the Allied nations
of Europe clashed with the forces of Germany and its
allies in 1914. In one way or another the banks of

America were instantly embroiled in Europe's war. Their involvement began immediately after the declaration of hostilities when an absurd rumor spread across the United States. It hinted that the federal government intended to confiscate all funds in American banks.

Who launched the rumor or why was never ascertained. But that, plus a brief closing of stock exchanges to forestall riotous trading, was enough to send frightened people running to their banks. They were convinced that something of a secret nature was wrong with the country's economy, something Washington was afraid to explain. The general attitude seemed to be "I want my money before the government takes it!"

Every financial institution was beset with long lines. At The Bowery, on the first morning of the rush, a single paying teller passed out $200,000 in cash during the two opening hours.

It was soon apparent that the cash reserves of all thrift institutions might quickly be dissipated. So the State Superintendent of Banks resorted to protective action. He took the same stern measures The Bowery itself had taken on previous occasions. He issued orders that every savings bank must insist on sixty days' notice of withdrawal. The only exceptions would be $50 disbursements in cases of demonstrable need.

Of course, the rumor of government confiscation faded as swiftly as it had spread, and depositors relaxed again. Some of them even looked sheepish as they brought their money back to the banks. President Schenck, walking among them on the banking floor of The Bowery, diplomatically greeted them as old friends. His confidence appeared never to have been ruffled.

Yet he must have wondered, as did everybody else, how the European conflict would affect America. Would it end the $2.5 billion in annual European trade, thus causing an American recession?

He need not have worried. The overseas war proved to be a bonanza for American business—and, as a corollary, a bonanza for American banks. With this country serving as the arsenal of the Allied forces, the nation's exports to Great Britain and France—principally in food, munitions, and supplies—rose in 1916 to nearly $5.5 billion. That was more than twice the amount reached in any peacetime year. According to the annual review of one business periodical, "Almost every branch of the American economy was in a state of feverish prosperity. Both profits and wages reached unprecedented heights."

And as people earned higher wages they increased their deposits in savings banks. By the end of 1916, The Bowery had record assets of over $119 million.

But the voracious, insatiable needs of warring nations continued to demand more and more goods from the United States. Factories worked double and triple shifts. Where there were shortages of men, women were recruited for heavy labor they had never done before. Every payday saw long lines of depositors bringing their earnings to tellers' windows.

Maybe a few of the peace-loving Quakers on The Bowery's board had private misgivings about prosperity linked to wartime killings. If so, they were helpless to do anything about it. No earthly power could stop what was happening. No earthly power even tried to stop it.

(One local event of the times, though unrelated to the war, is worth noting. New York's mayor, John Purroy Mitchel, decided to reorganize the city's operations. He placed responsibility for the project in the hands of the city's chamberlain, Henry Bruère. After two years in the job, streamlining many departments, Bruère streamlined his own by recommending the abolition of his office. He declared the chamberlain's functions, costing the city $12,000 a year in salary, could be performed by the comptroller. It was an unprecedented action that won wide public notice. It marked him as a man of unusual integrity and eventually helped lead him to the presidency of The Bowery Savings Bank.)

In the two years that the United States remained nominally neutral while shipping material to the Allies, President Woodrow Wilson repeatedly said, "England is fighting our fight." Meanwhile, German propaganda was spending $35 million a year to make Americans think otherwise. But the Germans vitiated the effects of their propaganda by resorting to sabotage and the destruction of American ships. When these acts reached a climax in the sinking of the *Lusitania*, Americans could no longer contain their fury. They went to war.

Even then, there were those who shouted that this country had been dragged into the combat not by events but "by bankers and munitions manufacturers." Bankers? The trustees of The Bowery must have been astounded to hear themselves denounced as warmongers.

They had little time to protest. There was a new job to do. The government needed immediate funds—$31 billion, according to the original budget. It called upon the banks to help raise the money, and what happened at The Bowery was typical of what was happening at other thrift institutions:

Posters urged depositors to use their savings to buy Liberty Bonds. Newspaper advertisements repeated the message, as did leaflets. Tellers were instructed to advise customers that they could make passbook loans for the purchase of bonds. On the banking floor, counters were set up where non-depositors could become bond buyers. Whenever a Treasury spokesman wanted to make a speech to crowds in the Bowery, he was welcomed to use the steps of the bank's entrance as a rostrum. All this continued through the issuance of four Liberty Loans and a final Victory Loan.

The Bowery itself set an example for its depositors.

Whereas it had owned practically no government bonds at the outbreak of hostilities, by the end of the war its holdings amounted to $9,880,600.

There is an aged Bowery denizen with whom I have occasionally discussed the Bowery of those times. "I was a kid then," he once told me, "maybe thirteen or fourteen. Shining shoes for a living. A nickel a shine, sometimes three cents. Used to work outside the Bowery Savings Bank on account that's where you could get customers with money as they went in or out. Anyhow, in war times the boys coming in from training at Yaphank would march off to their ships along Broadway. Even from here you could sometimes hear the bands playing. It would be *Over There* or *The Stars and Stripes Forever*, but mostly you'd hear *Over There*. People would run out of the bank to get over to Broadway to wave good-bye to the boys. Then they'd come back to finish their business in the bank, and sometimes you could tell they'd been crying— especially the women. And that song, *Over There*, you'd hear it all day long and all night long in the saloons. And after a while you'd hear other tunes like *Oh, How I Hate to Get Up in the Morning* and *K-K-K-Katy* and *Pack Up Your Troubles in an Old Kit Bag and Smile, Smile, Smile*. Those days we had songs a person could remember and *sing*. They were great days, all right, great days—till the bodies began to come back."

After the war, when there was no further need to invest in war bonds, people again put their money into savings accounts. Deposits in all thrift institutions began to swell. At The Bowery, assets climbed from $119 million in 1918 to $170 million in 1920.

And then, in 1920, the country's hundreds of savings institutions realized that, despite their size and common interests, they had never had a unified voice in the shaping of national policy. The American Bankers Association, powerful as it might be, was oriented primarily to the interests of commercial banks. State organizations of savings banks had their own special aims and problems. And so the National Association of Mutual Savings Banks was founded. Its purpose was "to assist the savings banks of the nation in their efforts to promote thrift, to represent the savings bank industry on all national issues, to further the interests of depositors in the promotion of sound banking procedures and in the extension of the mutual savings bank system to areas not yet served."

(That last phrase, "the extension of the mutual savings bank system to areas not yet served," is worth noting and remembering. It was to cause years of controversy. But the controversy did not reveal itself in the early 1920s.)

At that time, surveys made by the newly formed National Association indicated that thrift institutions were sharing in the country's general prosperity. With factories converting from the manufacture of war equipment to the starved needs of a peacetime economy, jobs were still plentiful and wages remained high.

Was this destined to be permanent prosperity? Many commentators were far from sanguine. They saw that people were producing and buying what had been denied them during the war. What would happen when their needs were satisfied?

"I don't think anybody at the bank was particularly worried about the future at that time," said a veteran officer who has long ago retired. "After all, deposits were coming in, and the mortgage business was booming. The construction of homes had been all but abandoned during the war years, and now builders—with eager customers waiting—were making up for lost time."

The Bowery's mortgage loans skyrocketed to over $100 million in 1920, and other savings banks were experiencing the same kind of demand. Viewing all these evidences of prosperity, President Schenck felt justified in approaching his board with an ambitious new project. He said, "I want to establish an uptown Bowery branch."

"Illegal," promptly replied the lawyer representing Cadwalader, Wickersham, and Taft. "You know the state legislature does not permit mutual savings banks to open branches—unless they can produce some incontestable reason. And I doubt that we have such a reason. We're doing very well where we are."

All of this was true. Schenck knew the objections of the state legislature were founded on the indisputable fact that all funds in a mutual savings bank are held for the exclusive benefit of its depositors. To open a branch could require a heavy investment in real estate, construction, equipment, and salaries. Years might pass before such a branch became self-sustaining. Money thus committed, the legislature maintained, meant that earnings on that sum must temporarily be forgone; the funds might be more fairly appropriated to increase the bank's net worth and the dividends to its depositors.

Schenck conceded the validity of such arguments. But he refused to believe that a branch of The Bowery must become a long-time drain on the bank's resources. "Thousands of our depositors have moved uptown," he reasoned. "The convenience of having a branch near their homes would bring them to the bank more frequently. And the population is now so heavy in the uptown area that we would attract thousands of new depositors. I am convinced that an uptown branch must be a profitable venture and a great service to the community in which it will be located."

Granting this was so, one trustee asked, how did he hope to persuade the legislature and the Banking Department to change their policies?

"That will not be necessary," President Schenck assured the board. "There is another way."

The method he outlined was remarkable in its simplicity. Not far from The Bowery, on Pearl Street, stood the comparatively small Universal Savings Bank. To acquire it by merger or purchase would yield two benefits. First, it would immediately bring added assets and depositors to The Bowery. Second, it would provide a legal advantage: *There was no legislative prohibition to moving the site of a bank.* Therefore the Universal, once it became part of The Bowery, could be moved to an uptown location, there to be reopened as the bank's uptown branch.

All very well, said the trustee; indeed, very clever. But would the Universal Savings Bank approve of such a merger?

President Schenck assured his questioner that exploratory talks with the officers of the Universal indicated their deep interest.

A thoughtful board decided it must have time to consider so revolutionary a proposal. The members departed to think. It was significant that nobody suggested moving the original bank uptown. That building was sacrosanct. The Bowery Savings Bank *belonged* on the Bowery. Besides, it was unthinkable that so beautiful a home should be abandoned.

On October 5, 1920 the trustees reconvened. If they were solemn, it was because they realized they were about to usher their 86-year-old institution into a new era. They passed a resolution stating that "The officers of the Bank be and are hereby authorized to effect a merger with the Universal Savings Bank, New York City, and to purchase a suitable site for the location of an uptown branch." In seventeen days the merger was completed.

A committee of trustees was promptly named to find a location for The Bowery Savings Bank's first uptown branch, and the new era was born.

12

THE SECOND CATHEDRAL

The primary qualification for membership on a Building Committee ought to be vision—the ability to see values beyond any immediate cost. This qualification was certainly possessed by the five trustees who set out to find a second home for their institution. They were all successful and highly respected citizens: George McNeir, William A. Nash, Thomas B. Kent, Arthur L. Lesher, and William M. Spackman.

The location they eventually chose was the corner

of Park Avenue and 42nd Street in the very heart of the city, opposite the newly built Grand Central Railroad Station—only to be denied this site by the Superintendent of Banks. He regarded it as too expensive a bit of real estate for a savings bank.

Nevertheless, this was an excellent neighborhood for a bank. Some 60,000 people passed here every day on their way to the railroad terminal. So the committee moved its recommendation to the middle of the 42nd Street block, which would be somewhat less expensive than the corner. To this selection, surprisingly enough, the Superintendent gave his consent. Negotiations began at once. Within three months after the merger with the Universal Savings Bank, President Schenck signed an agreement to purchase the buildings at 110 to 116 East 42nd Street for the sum of $1.4 million.

The architects retained to design the new branch, York and Sawyer, must have felt an obligation to equal the magnificence of the Stanford White creation on the Bowery. What they put on the drawing boards for the trustees' approval was a kind of Romanesque cathedral estimated to cost $4.5 million. Today, people walking into its great hall gaze up at the ceiling, five floors above them, and it is understandable if they whisper, "They don't build them like this any more." They are right. The spacious 42nd Street office, a city landmark, has been called the most beautiful bank in America. Its marble was imported from abroad. Its celebrated bronze doors were created by artists of the first rank.

In authorizing all this, Schenck must have foreseen that nothing like it would ever again be constructed in the United States. The functional age was already dawning. Architects no longer looked toward Rome or Greece. So The Bowery's president stinted on nothing and helped produce a masterpiece.

And yet, like Edward Wood—who had presided over the building of the first "cathedral" in the Bowery—Schenck never knew the joy of seeing the completion of his work. Four months before the uptown building was completed, Henry Schenck died.

He would have been proud of the glamor that surrounded the new bank's formal opening on June 25, 1923. Even the transfer of funds from the Bowery to 42nd Street—$202 million in cash, negotiable securities, mortgages, and other assets—was spectacular. *The New York Times* said:

> Fourteen armored motor cars, with portholes bristling with sub-machine guns, followed each other through the streets of crowded Manhattan. Besides machine guns, the guards, drivers, and other members of the trucks' crews were provided with side arms. More than 100 police were required to clear the route for the armored cars. . . . A motorcycle policeman preceded each car, and all along the route were posted detectives, plainclothes men, and uniformed policemen.

One need hardly add that no bandit was bold enough to attack the cortege.

As soon as the great bronze doors of the 42nd Street office were opened, crowds beyond anyone's prediction jammed into the enormous banking room. Many of the visitors were simply curious spectators, but not all. By three o'clock 2,712 people had opened new accounts, depositing a total of $439,590. Each of them received a diploma-like certificate designating him a first-day depositor. With these newcomers added to those that were transferred from the Universal Savings Bank, the uptown office started operations with 5,600 accounts.

Had Henry Schenck been alive he could have told his board, "You see, an uptown office *can* be profitable. This promises to be the most profitable step we have ever taken."

❧

In March of 1922, William E. Knox succeeded Henry Schenck in the presidency. Dignified and gregarious, respected by his associates, he had been The Bowery's comptroller since 1908, a trustee since 1918, and a vice president since 1920.

He was unquestionably an able and experienced executive. As the bank's representative at many civic gatherings, he proved also to be an excellent speaker—articulate, knowledgeable, distinguished in appearance. At that time The Bowery, like many other mutual savings banks, was a member of the American Bankers Association. Within a few years Knox was elected to its presidency, the first savings banker so honored. Thereafter his ability as a speaker was widely utilized. He appeared for the American Bankers Association at meetings and conventions throughout the country—causing several Bowery trustees to shake disapproving heads. He seemed to be giving the Association more time than he gave the bank.

How much The Bowery meant to its depositors was something Knox learned in a strange way.

A. P. Giannini's Bank of Italy, later to become the mammoth Bank of America, was expanding from California across the nation. In 1925 Giannini sent representatives to New York. Their mission was to find banks which could be purchased and added to the Giannini empire, thus giving it New York outlets. The emissaries found two such institutions.

One was the East River National Bank. The other was called the Bowery National Bank. Both were relatively small commercial enterprises. They had no connection with either the East River Savings Bank or The Bowery Savings Bank.

As soon as newspapers reported these contemplated acquisitions, alarmed depositors hurried to The Bowery. They insisted on seeing President Knox; no lesser authority would do. And they had anxious questions. Was their bank being sold? Was its character about to change? Would it henceforth have absentee management in California? The fact that many of these people had never heard of a Bowery *National* Bank explained their apprehension.

President Knox reassured everyone. The Bowery Savings Bank was not for sale to Giannini or anyone else. It would remain what it had always been. Yet the very anxiety he had to allay was a tribute to the intensely personal regard depositors had for "their" bank.

Considering all that Knox accomplished during his five years in office, one would wish it were possible to regard his tenure as an unqualified success. Unfortunately, it was not that.

"But don't underestimate the man," said Howard Hastings, one of his associates. "He made mistakes, yes. But also he made many outstanding contributions to The Bowery. Chief among them, you might say, was the matter of growth."

This was undeniable. During his presidency the bank expanded from 156,763 depositors to 212,221; from assets of over $183 million to well above $302 million. Such growth made Knox see that the 42nd Street building, big as it was, must before long be inadequate in size. With wise foresight he persuaded his trustees to purchase the adjoining property on 42nd Street, numbers 118 and 120, for which they paid $707,600. Here construction soon began on a sorely needed annex.

When I asked one of Knox's former vice presidents to list other achievements of his administration, the record was imposing indeed. "He installed the first mechanical posting system to replace the laborious, manual methods of the past," the man said. "He arranged for group insurance to cover the lives of all employees. He founded any number of employee clubs and activities to strengthen a feeling of personal participation in the affairs of the bank. He started publication of *The Chest,* the in-house periodical that disseminates bank news to the staff. I should say as important as anything else was the skill with which he integrated the operations of the two branches, ultimately making the uptown office The Bowery's real headquarters."

What, then, went wrong with his administration?

First, there was William Knox's misplaced faith in human honesty. This involved two young men he and his wife regarded as their protégés. Knox's personal interest in them was well known, and before long they held fairly responsible bank positions. The Bowery had inaugurated a policy of accepting school accounts—that is, the small savings of children—the purpose being to inculcate early habits of thrift. Bowery representatives even went to schools to lecture on the wisdom of saving. Knox's protégés were assigned to keeping the children's accounts. They discovered that the easy manipulation of school records made it possible for them to pocket money. By the time an audit disclosed their embezzlements, they had robbed the bank of more than $40,000.

Both men and an accomplice were seized; much of the stolen money was recovered. But the blow to Knox's faith was staggering. He seem to feel betrayed. That was the first of the emotional traumas he suffered.

The second was the result of an indefensible error in his own judgment. Without the knowledge of the trustees, he took part of the bank's considerable law business away from the firm of Cadwalader, Wickersham, and Taft. He transferred it to a small law partnership of which his brother Herbert Knox was a member.

One can understand the shock and outrage of the trustees when they heard this. Cadwalader, Wickersham, and Taft had represented The Bowery for half a century. Their services had been exemplary. There was absolutely no reason to make a change—except the enrichment of Knox's brother.

The board summoned the president to a special meeting. It was in no mood to be polite. After voting angrily and unanimously to restore full legal responsibilities to Cadwalader, Wickersham, and Taft, it censured Knox on additional grounds. Suppressed resentments exploded. The trustees openly accused the president of neglecting the affairs of The Bowery while traveling about the country to make speeches for the American Bankers Association. They charged that in self-aggrandizement he had all but turned his back on the bank.

In almost a hundred years, no president of The Bowery Savings Bank had ever had to confront such denunciations. Having no defense, Knox sat silent. When the ordeal ended and he finally rose, he was white of face and unsteady as he walked out of the room. One of his associates was beside him, and as they started across the banking floor the president muttered something about not feeling well. "I'm going up to rest," he said.

On an upper floor he had established a small apartment where he could spend the night when he worked late. Now he went to this retreat to recover from the acrimony of the board meeting.

A few minutes later Walter E. Frew, president of the Corn Exchange Bank, telephoned to ask if Mr. Knox was free for lunch. Perhaps Mr. Frew, a Bowery trustee who had witnessed the attacks on the president's pride, hoped in some way to comfort Knox.

Percy G. Delameter, the bank's secretary, took the call. Since there was no telephone connection in the upstairs apartment, he sent an attendant, Falton Hall, to summon the president. Hall found Knox seated in a deep chair, staring out of a window. Knox said, "Tell Mr. Frew I'll call back in a few minutes."

But twenty minutes later he had not yet come down. Did he suspect Frew had been chosen to demand his resignation? No one could say. But since the president was keeping Frew waiting, Secretary Delameter himself went up to the apartment. He knocked several times. There was no answer. Finally he opened the door—and stood unmoving.

William Knox was slumped forward in his chair, a revolver on the floor, a bullet hole in his chest.

∽

How do you explain such a tragedy to the public? How do you persuade depositors and others to understand that the suicide of the bank's president is no reflection on the bank's solvency? Soon the police and the press would be swarming into the doors. Decisions had to be made. Answers had to be prepared for the searching questions of reporters. Yet no one had any answers.

Vice President Victor A. Lersner delegated the task of meeting the press to a veteran in the bank's service, Howard S. Hastings. Long after his retirement, Hastings vividly remembered the confrontation with newsmen.

"Every paper in New York rushed reporters and photographers to the bank," he said. "I took them all to the office that had been Knox's. The place was jammed.

Everybody was throwing questions at me. Finally I got them to be quiet. I told them Mr. Knox's death had nothing to do with the solidity of the bank. It was due wholly to a nervous breakdown. I talked about the young protégés who had let him down. I said nothing about the tumultuous scene in the boardroom. I knew there would be headlines. William Knox had been an important, respected, and well-known figure. I could only hope no paper would suggest there had been discrepancies in the bank's accounts."

While Hastings talked to newsmen, the police and the Medical Examiner were in the third-floor apartment. They were still there when Knox's wife and two children arrived, so stupefied and unbelieving that—as Hastings put it—"There just wasn't anything you could say to them."

Of course, every trustee who happened to be in the city—which is to say, every trustee who had attended the morning meeting—was notified by telephone. They rushed back to the bank in private cars, in cabs, on foot. The first two to hurry into the building were Stephen Baker, president of the Bank of the Manhattan Company, and Lewis L. Clarke, chairman of the American Exchange Irving Trust Company. They were followed by Jesse Isidor Straus, president of R. H. Macy & Company. Then came Milton W. Harrison, president of the National Association of Owners of Railroad and Public Utility Securities; he had invited a number of guests to attend a dinner that very evening in honor of William Knox. It was to be held at the Union League Club. In his shocked excitement Mr. Harrison forgot, until almost the last moment, to cancel the arrangements.

By 4:15 that afternoon all the trustees had returned, some coming from Westchester and Long Island. After a tense conference, they sent a brief statement to the press again asserting that the affairs of the bank were in good order; that they had recently been audited by Peat, Marwick, Mitchell and Company, one of the city's leading accounting firms. Now the question was: How would the press handle the story?

Next morning the front-page headline of *The New York Times* announced:

W. E. KNOX, HEAD OF BOWERY SAVINGS, ENDS LIFE IN BANK

Nervous Breakdown Given as Cause of Suicide In 42nd St. Office

Official Affairs In Order

13

THE BRUÈRE YEARS BEGIN

Never in The Bowery's history had there been a more solemn board meeting than the one which occurred a few days after Knox's death. With Vice President Victor A. Lersner acting as chairman, the trustees' first duty was to elect a new president.

The immediate choice was obvious. Lersner was elevated to the executive position. But he was 62 years old. Recognizing that 65 had long been the traditional age of retirement from the bank, the trustees realized his term of office would be limited.

It therefore seemed wise to begin a search for a younger man who would be ready to replace Lersner within two or three years. To be ideally suited for the position, he would not only have to be a man of financial ability with inherent qualities of leadership; he would also have to be one whose distinction in the community would make him an outstanding representative of The Bowery Savings Bank.

Such a man would not be easy to find. Yet, surprisingly, the search ended very quickly when the trustees held an unofficial session at the Metropolitan Club—a meeting at which Lersner was not present. Why a secret session without the president? Though it was never explained in any records, it reflected the board's desire to be tactful. Lersner had been in the presidency so short a time that it might have embarrassed him to have a successor named so soon.

At any rate, a number of trustees had agreed on a candidate they now suggested to their colleagues. This was the man who had once recommended the abolition of his own $12,000-a-year job as City Chamberlain of New York. From that position he had gone first to become an executive of the American Metals Corporation, then on to head the Group Insurance Department of the Metropolitan Life Insurance Company. Though his experience did not lie in banking, he had displayed remarkable business acumen and integrity in every task he had undertaken. Mayor John Purroy Mitchel had appointed him to serve on various municipal commissions, and he had acquitted himself remarkably well in every assignment. At various times newspapers had described him as "an authority on municipal planning, finance, and social science," with an educational background that included a degree from Chicago University and studies in law at Harvard and New York Universities. Invariably these stories emphasized the fact that he had been an adviser to Presidents Theodore Roosevelt, Taft, and Wilson as well as a financial consultant for the Mexican government and a personal friend of Franklin Delano Roosevelt. One could scarcely hope to find a person with a better record.

His name was Henry Jaromir Bruère.

The trustees elected him to the position of First Vice President with the understanding that this would afford him the opportunity to familiarize himself with the operations of The Bowery before he became its president. But through oversight—possibly because every trustee felt one of his colleagues would do it—the board neglected to apprise President Lersner of what it had done.

On a morning soon thereafter, Lersner looked up from his desk at a tall, affable, extremely handsome man who smiled, offered his hand, and said, "Good to know you, Mr. Lersner. I'm Henry Bruère."

Though no one else was present except the secretary who had ushered the new vice president into the office, one can well imagine what happened. Lersner, quite puzzled, must have been jolted to open-mouthed amazement when Bruère identified himself as the bank's newly appointed vice president.

To the eternal credit of Victor Lersner, it must be recorded that, after swallowing hard, he took the announcement with grace and dignity. Nothing in the minutes of ensuing board meetings suggested that President Lersner ever upbraided or even chided the trustees for the manner in which he had been forced to meet his successor.

"Lersner was a quiet, self-contained man," one of his associates told me. "In all the years I knew him he never displayed a temper, never showed his innermost feelings. Yet in some ways he was eccentric. For instance, it was his habit to change his suits two or three times a day, and it seemed to me that after the arrival of Henry Bruère Mr. Lersner devoted more time to his appearance than ever before. He seemed to realize that the trustees wanted Bruère to gain experience as quickly as possible, and so he allowed Bruère to take over many executive functions. He himself spent hours every day alone in his office. What he did there, I never knew."

He must have done some writing, however, for contributions of his appeared in the *Bulletin* of the Savings Banks Association of New York. One of these revealed his idealistic attitude toward his work and toward his bank. He wrote:

> There is a certain sense of calmness and security in the very atmosphere of a mutual savings bank. There is a feeling that the methods as well as the objects of the institution must be such as would be approved by the whole body of people whose interests are involved.

Howard Hastings, who knew Lersner well, said, "He was a gentle man, not at all the aggressive type. I think that, deep down, he was relieved and glad to have Henry Bruère take many executive duties off his hands."

Within three years, on January 11, 1931, Henry Bruère was officially elected president. The minutes of that same board meeting state:

"Mr. Baker having taken the Chair, the nomination of Mr. Victor A. Lersner for Chairman of the Board was received, and one ballot having been cast by the Secretary, Mr. Lersner was declared unanimously elected Chairman of the Board."

⚬᷉⚬

It must not be assumed that Bruère's three years of apprenticeship—if a vice presidency can be so described—

were a quiet period devoted to learning a craft while marking time. Far from it. Robert W. Sparks, who had worked with Bruère at the Metropolitan Life Insurance Company and who had joined him at the bank as "a kind of personal aide," said of him; "He learned by doing things. He had a lot of ideas and he put them to work as fast as he could, sometimes over tough opposition from other senior staff members."

Could such opposition, I asked, have been attributable to professional jealousy? After all, Bruère had been placed in a position senior to that of all veteran bank officers except the president.

"There may have been an element of jealousy and resentment at the outset," Sparks conceded. "That would have been natural. But it all vanished within a year or two as the others came to like him and to respect his achievements. As for Bruère himself, I don't think he worried too much about jealousy. He had too many other things to think about."

That was understandable. Henry Bruère came to The Bowery during a period of national excitement which, by 1929, was to result in the most calamitous stock market crash the United States had ever experienced. Apparently no one, not even President Herbert Hoover, could change the downward course of the nation's fortunes.

What, for instance, could anyone do about the private debts that were piling up in the country? When the postwar demand for goods had been satisfied and consumption began to drop off, manufacturers—rather than reducing prices—offered credit for the purchase of everything they produced. Between 1923 and 1929, installment buying in America amounted to $5 billion a year. Borrowing for everything from small business to farming became an accepted way of life. By 1929 the total of America's private debts amounted to $200 billion. As one analyst described the situation, "Everybody seemed to be in debt to somebody else. This made the whole economy vulnerable, since whenever any group became unable to meet its obligations, the whole structure would start collapsing like a house of cards."

Yet even the most generous offers of credit could not persuade consumers to absorb everything American manufacturers were producing. So the manufacturers turned to foreign markets—actually extending credit to foreign customers for such purchases. This too was a precarious practice which depended wholly on foreign solvency.

It was especially misguided as it applied to a few Latin American countries whose governments were too frequently being overthrown by new dictatorships. Two billion dollars were taken from United States investors for reinvestment in Latin America. As historian Henry Parkes observed, "The dictators got the money, the Wall Street bankers got their commissions, and gullible American investors took the loss. Eventually all but two of the Latin American countries stopped payment on their foreign debts, and two-thirds of these loans have remained permanently in default."

Opposing such reckless manipulation of the people's money, thrift institutions were pleading with wage earners to put their funds into savings accounts. The Bowery was running daily newspaper advertisements directed at every sector of the working classes. One advertisement said:

38,000 SALESMEN SAVE AT THE BOWERY

Another:

45,000 MECHANICS SAVE AT THE BOWERY

A third:

66,000 HOUSEWIVES SAVE AT THE BOWERY

So the advertisements ran, touching scores of vocations. Other thrift institutions were using their own forms of appeal. And before long The Bowery, the Union Dime, and the Emigrant savings banks joined to place cooperative messages in newspapers and on billboards, all urging people to save instead of gamble.

They were too late with their exhortations. The stock market madness had already spread across America. Everybody was buying. Everybody was talking about this stock and that. *Not* to be in the market stamped one as an idiot. The Federal Reserve Board could have limited wild speculation by limiting brokers' loans. But this was vehemently opposed by commercial bankers, and nothing came of it.

Thrift-minded men like Lersner and Bruère could only shake their heads when "little people" drew their lifetime savings out of The Bowery to buy risky stocks. The very purpose of the stock market seemed forgotten. It was intended to provide a sound means of investing in reputable American industry. But in the madness of the late 1920s, it became simply an instrument for buying paper.

"People bought stocks," said a veteran Wall Street observer, "not because they wanted good investments—many, in truth, were buying the stocks of companies they had never even heard of. They bought paper on flimsy tips in the hopes that they could quickly sell at a profit to someone else. If they lacked cash, they bought on margin. And stock prices went on rising without any real relation to the companies' capacity for earning dividends."

Bankers in thrift institutions might warn depositors of the perils ahead. But why should a person listen to a banker who was paying him a measly 4 percent in dividends while everybody else was earning a fortune in Wall Street?

As always, the biggest and most experienced investors were the first to start selling. On October 19, 1929 they seized the opportunity to get peak prices. A few others quickly followed. And as the news spread that "the big men" were dumping their holdings, the avalanche started. Suddenly everybody wanted to sell. Everybody *had* to sell. And the market crashed into the utter chaos of October 29th.

That day, with 16,500,000 shares thrown on the market at collapsing prices, some $30 billion of paper wealth was destroyed, much of it never to reappear.

Nor was this the only American trouble. As people lost their money, sales of manufactured goods declined, and companies had to lay off employees. Unemployment became so rampant that between 1929 and 1932 the national income plunged from $82 billion down to $40 billion. And, as always, the greatest sufferers were the "little people" who lost their jobs. Those lucky enough to have savings had to draw on them. As for others, "They sold apples on the streets."

It was against this background of national economic and social turmoil that Henry Bruère began in 1931 his twenty-one years as head of The Bowery Savings Bank.

ॐ

According to Robert Sparks, Bruère was keenly sensitive to the ills of the country. He discussed them in a deeply troubled mood. Yet he did not allow them to interfere with the innovative services he gave to the bank.

"Even in the three years before he was elected president," Sparks said, "he brought changes into being which have become permanent features of The Bowery's operations." Sparks counted the changes off on his fingers:

☐ The establishment of an efficient annual budget for
   all departments, something the bank had never before
   had.

- The clear division of responsibilities between the treasurer and the comptroller, resulting in increased accounting-control of operations.
- The creation of Christmas Club accounts, then an original concept for savings banks.
- The inauguration of a Safe Deposit Box Department. At a cost of $175,000, this opened with almost 3,000 boxes priced from $5 to $55 annually and provided space for 20,000 additional boxes.
- Perhaps most important of all was the establishment of a funded and insured pension plan for employees—something until then unknown in mutual savings banks. Now that the Bowery plan has been in effect some 45 years, scores of retired employees are enjoying its benefits.
- The adoption of "teller checks." These permitted tellers to issue checks for withdrawals without the delays of waiting for a bank officer to approve and sign such checks.

"The significant thing about all this," Sparks concluded, "was that it kept the bank on a progressive course at the very time when the American economy was close to disaster. It proved, I think, the essential strength and stability of savings banks at a period of our history when many commercial banks, savings and loan associations, and insurance companies were failing. Yet in spite of all the withdrawals of funds The Bowery sustained, its assets rose from $318 million in 1928 to $444 million by 1931. There was no magic in this. Having been taught by bitter experience that gambling in stocks can bring 'little people' to ruin, these people—at any rate, those among them who had jobs—were quietly bringing their funds to the safety of thrift institutions."

14

DAWN OF
THE NEW DEAL

Bruère and those who have succeeded him as chief executive of The Bowery Savings Bank had to deal with governmental activities of a kind that had never confronted their predecessors. The same can be said, of course, of the modern heads of every other mutual savings bank in the country. How would any of their nineteenth-century counterparts have coped with the problems of the 1970s? Would they even have considered such problems possible?

As an example: In August 1974 the United States

League of Savings and Loan Associations announced that in the preceding month, July, the savings and loan institutions had suffered an outflow of funds that exceeded $582 million. Much of this was money that went into high-yielding investments offered by commercial banks. But at the same time, incredibly, the biggest competitor for the public's savings was the government of the United States. It was offering U.S. Treasury notes in low denominations that paid interest of more than 9 percent, while the savings banks were being limited to paying 5¼ percent on their regular accounts.

Why this deliberate federal bid for the savings in thrift institutions? Did the government really need the money? Or was it an attempt to reduce inflation by taking buying power—dollars—out of the public's hands? Whatever the answer, it was the kind of situation which had never challenged savings bankers of past generations.

Another illustration: Today, in estimating a family's ability to meet mortgage payments, banks are required by law to combine the earnings of husband and wife—even if she is eight months pregnant and likely any day to stop working. "She may even decide never to work again," one mortgage officer said. "That may permanently cut the family income in half. Still, legislation forces us to include her present earnings in our calculations as if they were to continue forever. Personally, I'd rather grant a mortgage loan to a spinster or a bachelor who has to rely on one source of earnings."

At the beginning of Henry Bruère's administration in 1931, such complexities of government activity could not be foreseen. Bruère had other problems.

For almost a century the mutual savings banks of the country, most of them located in the Northeastern states, had been a group apart. They had never enjoyed the wide variety of investment privileges accorded to commercial banks. Yet paradoxically, the very strictures placed on

their finances, removing them from indulging in speculative ventures, had made them an island of security in a
sea of banking turbulence.

Could they forever retain this character? The economic
pressures were too great to permit it. As a major source of
mortgage loans, they were confronted by the constantly
increasing need for American homes. That meant they
had to find more and more funds to satisfy the mortgage
demands made on them; and more funds could best be
acquired through growth.

That was why, at the very outset of Bruère's presidency,
some of his associates came into his office to urge the
opening of another Bowery branch. There was an excellent location, they told him, available at the corner of
Fifth Avenue and 34th Street, a corner passed every day
by tens of thousands of people.

Bruère hesitated even to consider such an undertaking.
"He seemed to have the idea," one of his assistants recalled, "that henceforth every Bowery building must be
as magnificent as the first two. This would involve the
expenditure of millions of dollars. He doubted that either
the trustees or the Superintendent of Banks would consent to such a project.

"But those of us who were pressing for a new branch
argued that it was not at all necessary to build another
cathedral. It was not even necessary to buy or lease an
entire building. All we needed was a street floor and a
basement for vaults. The records of the branch could be
kept at the main office. The quarters at 34th Street and
Fifth Avenue, we had ascertained, could be leased for
$30,000 the first year. The rental cost would increase to
a maximum of $50,000 over a fourteen-year lease."

But, Bruère wanted to know—and this was characteristic of his aesthetic sensitivity—would such a branch reflect the dignified image of The Bowery Savings Bank?

"We assured him that, though contemporary and functional in design, it would be impressive and beautiful in its own way. In the end we won his hesitant consent to talk to the board and, if they approved, to apply to the Superintendent of Banks for the required permission."

The trustees offered no objections; and when Superintendent Joseph A. Broderick held hearings on the application, he must have been surprised to find representatives of two other savings banks, the Emigrant and the Union Dime, present to testify in favor of the Bowery's plan. Presumably they wanted to liberalize the *principle* of branch banking, since it would enable them too to expand.

It did not take long for Superintendent Broderick to grant the permission the Bowery sought. Leases were signed, and the speed with which work on the new branch progressed can be judged from an entry in the minutes of the board of trustees' meeting of September 14, 1931. The president reported "that interior alterations were rapidly taking place and that on or about October 15 the branch would be opened with an equipment of six tellers' units capable of handling from 60,000 to 80,000 accounts."

Exactly four weeks later as planned, on October 15th, the Fifth Avenue branch opened its door to the public. In that single first day, 1,012 people deposited a total of $233,287. Within ten months this new branch was so busy that the next-door premises on Fifth Avenue had to be leased for purposes of expansion. The day of branch banking—without cathedrals—had begun for The Bowery.

❦

Though the year 1931 was difficult, even disastrous for some commercial banks, The Bowery had the single biggest windfall of deposits in its entire history. This was not because of its persuasive advertising techniques or because of brilliant management procedures. It happened because of the failure of the Bank of the United States.

(This was not the same Bank of the United States which had caused so much trouble for President Andrew Jackson. The 20-year charter of the original institution had long ago expired. This modern bank, though operating under the same name, had created problems of its own through years of high-handed practices that were suddenly revealed.)

Forewarned first by rumors of corruption and a deteriorated financial condition, then by newspaper stories of mismanagement, depositors hastened to withdraw their funds from the Bank of the United States. And what could they do with cash? The safest depository, as many decades had shown, lay in the savings banks. So people hurried to the thrift institutions. Many of these had astonishing increases in deposits, but none received as much as did The Bowery—a total of $75 million that came directly from the Bank of the United States.

"The Bowery was crowded with lines of people trying to deposit money," a veteran teller remembered. "Special desks had to be set up to accommodate them. We had never seen anything like it. You could call it a run on the bank in reverse. The money came in so fast that we had no room for it in our cash drawers. We filled wastepaper baskets with the bills and sent them down to the vaults as fast as men could carry them. They brought back the empty baskets, and we filled them again and again."

Bruère tried to discourage these deposits. Once he actually walked along the lines at tellers' windows and tried to persuade depositors to take their funds elsewhere.

But the reputation of The Bowery defeated him. An elderly, indignant woman waved a finger under his nose. "Young man," she demanded, "who are *you* to tell me not to deposit my money in The Bowery? I know this bank! Be good enough to mind your own business!"

Bruère, turning away in embarrassment, went back to his office. And money continued to pour into the tellers' cages.

Adding this tidal wave of funds to the regular inflow of deposits resulted, in 1931, in a total of some $85 million in new money. It was gratifying but by no means an undiluted blessing.

For the bank would have to pay *dividends* on that $85 million. The money would have to be invested as quickly as possible in order to have it yield immediate income. If sound investments could be expected to earn an average of 6 percent, then *every day the $85 million lay idle it was losing over $13,972 in potential earnings. In addition, it was costing $9,315 a day in 4 percent dividends to depositors.*

Faced with this situation, the bank needed time to make adjustments to such on overwhelming influx of funds. It certainly could not afford, at least for a while, to accept more big deposits. Therefore, on April 1, Bruère announced that until further notice new deposits would be limited to a maximum of $2,500. Three weeks later the limit was reduced to $1,000.

Meanwhile, in what was regarded as a protective measure, The Bowery began to grant mortgage money as fast as it could find borrowers. In its haste, as might have been anticipated, it made a number of unfortunate, ill-considered loans. These went to such applicants as golf clubs, theaters, and hotels—some of which were falling on evil days—and to some high-priced private residences. In short, money went into the kind of investments which in calmer, more prudent days the Bowery trustees would never have sanctioned.

The dangers attending a sudden, large inflow of funds were of course clear to the state's Banking Department. Superintendent Joseph A. Broderick knew that since 1918 The Bowery Savings Bank, like many others, had been paying dividends of 4 percent on deposits. He also recognized the perils of paying such dividends when they were not in satisfactory ratio to earnings. So, on December 14, 1931, the Superintendent wrote to The Bowery a letter marked "Strictly Confidential." In it he said:

> In the best interests of your institution and of general banking conditions throughout the entire State, we earnestly urge you, if you have not already done so, to reduce your dividend to be paid for the current quarter to a rate not to exceed 3½ percent per annum.

Naturally the bank complied. (Nobody could foresee that in the depression years ahead the dividend rate would continue to decline, going down to 3 percent, to 2½ percent, and finally reaching the nadir of 1 to 1½ percent fifteen years later during World War II.) In 1931, however, the great influx of funds was regarded as a temporary problem, not a catastrophe. It was seen as a tribute to the confidence enjoyed by The Bowery Savings Bank, not as a long-range threat to its net worth.

In fact, Henry Bruère was extremely proud of his 1931 record, the first year of his presidency. In his annual report, made on January 11, 1932, he told the board of trustees:

"Figures available to date show that for the year 1931, deposits in all the 146 savings banks of the state increased 10 percent. For 1931, deposits in The Bowery Savings Bank increased 21.23 percent. The bank's total deposits on December 31, 1931 were $485,249,000. This figure does not tell the complete story of the recent elevation of the bank to the outstanding position of the largest institution of popular savings in the world."

He explained the change in the dividend rate by saying: "This reduction was deemed prudent because of the lowered yield on new investments and because the rapid growth of the bank made it desirable to accelerate additions to the surplus account." And he reported with understandable pride: "In 1931 the total dividend paid was $17,036,351.07, a sum greater than the deposits in each of 72 of the 146 mutual savings banks in the state."

It was a glowing report, the more remarkable because it was made just a year and two months before the precarious affairs of American banks caused President Franklin Delano Roosevelt to declare the historic Bank Holiday. Yet, in spite of his pride in achievement, Bruère foresaw trouble. He concluded his first report with prophetic words based largely on what had happened at the Bank of the United States:

"We have seen in this year great public suffering because provision was not made in good times for bad times. We have seen millions of dollars of savings lost through inexpert and fraudulent management of banks, operated irresponsibly and inexpertly and without a sense of the high trusteeship involved in the custody of other people's money. The savings banks of New York have a different record to point to. Their aim is the aim of disinterested service, their method is the method of responsible trusteeship."

Unfortunately, not all mutual savings banks could live up to that ideal. Henry Bruère had scarcely made his report when his tribute to "responsible trusteeship" received a severe jolt.

❧

The Commonwealth Savings Bank of New York was in trouble. Burdened with bad mortgage investments and management problems, it was in imminent danger of failure. In an effort to save it, Deputy Superintendent of Banks J. T. Heenahan sent an urgent letter to other thrift institutions. He wrote:

When a savings bank is in danger of being closed, the whole structure of savings banks within that community, if not in the whole State of New York, is clearly jeopardized. If institutions in the community were to suffer runs under present circumstances, there is no institution in the State of New York which could pay its depositors in full. The real estate situation in New York City in particular is in such a condition of jeopardy, and the security market is in such a state of complete demoralization, that any explosion which could result in a concerted run upon savings banks would be the most trying calamity to which New York City could possibly be subjected.

He might have said the same thing of any city, of any state in which savings banks existed. There was no doubt that the shaky condition of the Commonwealth Savings Bank imperiled the welfare of all thrift institutions by undermining public confidence in them.

On the receipt of Heenahan's letter, the heads of 23 New York savings banks met in emergency session. They elected William L. DeBost, president of the Union Dime Savings Bank, to be chairman of the group. These 23 men, of whom Henry Bruère was one, quickly displayed a sense of cooperative responsibility and interdependence. They voted to rescue the Commonwealth Savings Bank with an advance of $900,000 from their own reserves. Since this sum was to be apportioned according to the size of the participating institutions, The Bowery assumed the largest single share of the obligation—$200,000.

As soon as Superintendent of Banks Joseph Broderick heard of the decision, he wrote to William DeBost:

> I was more than gratified to learn of the constructive and cooperative manner in which certain savings banks in your group have determined to handle the problem confronting us with respect to the Commonwealth Savings Bank. . . .
> I feel that you and your associates should be highly commended for this satisfactory solution to a very difficult problem.

It was not the only time when savings banks came to one another's rescue. In January of 1933 the Union Savings Bank of Mamaroneck found itself in desperate need of financial help. This time The Bowery itself assumed the responsibility. It lent the Mamaroneck institution $450,000, taking as collateral $850,000 in 5 percent mortgages. The debt, incidentally, was soon repaid.

And yet when it was suggested by a state legislator that the government establish a permanent Reserve Savings Bank for the State of New York, one whose reserves could help any thrift institution in emergencies, Henry Bruère opposed the idea. His opposition drew a series of editorial attacks from *The New York World-Telegram*. He was called obstructive and short-sighted—a blast of unfavorable publicity that stung the president.

He reacted by inviting the editors of the newspaper to lunch. They came. They found several trustees as well as Mr. Bruère at the table, and he used the opportunity to explain his objections to the contemplated Reserve Savings Bank.

First, he said, as a general principle he was against undue government interference with business. Second, there had been talk of a *self-regulating* Savings Bank Trust Company which the savings banks would themselves organize as a source of emergency funding. This would be owned and operated by member banks. It would not be a government agency, though it would be strengthened by credit commitments from the Reconstruction Finance Corporation and the Federal Reserve Bank of New York. This independent organization Bruère fully intended to support.

Either his arguments or his eloquence swayed the editors. Thereafter the attacks in *The New York World-Telegram* ceased.

⟨⁓⟩

Two American Presidents, Herbert Hoover and Franklin Delano Roosevelt, had to cope not only with a national economic depression that saw 20 percent of America's workforce unemployed in 1932, but also with a banking debacle which seemed incredible; almost 5,000 banks and building and loan associations had failed. Most were helpless victims of the general economic condition. Others revealed cases of mismanagement as flagrant as those of the Bank of the United States; a few were worse.

One of the things which most deeply troubled President Hoover was the inability of citizens in many states to obtain mortgage loans. The commercial banks in those states were concentrating on the quick profits to be earned from short-term industrial loans; a rapid turnover of funds was more attractive than being locked into long-term mortgage investments. As Earl B. Schwulst said, "Many home mortgages were being foreclosed and many more were in default. Mortgage money was extremely scarce, and many communities were completely without mortgage lending facilities. Construction of homes and other types of construction were at a standstill, and construction workers by the thousands were out of jobs."

To deal with this worsening situation, President Hoover called a White House Conference on Home Ownership in his final year in office. Out of it grew the establishment of the Federal Home Loan Bank System, whose principal function was "to supply its member institutions with credit to smooth their operations and enhance their service to the public." In this way it would "meet more fully the home-financing needs in many communities which would otherwise face serious obstacles in their development."

Surely this purpose was reasonable and commendable. Why, then, was it vigorously opposed by the American Bankers Association, by the insurance industry, and even by thrift institutions?

The answer lay in its stipulations: "The Board [of the Federal Home Loan Bank System] examines and audits each of the banks at least annually. The Board establishes the rules and policies under which the banks may make advances and accept member deposits. The Board establishes minimum liquidity requirements of member institutions within the ranges prescribed by law."

There were additional requisites for membership— many of them; but those quoted explain the primary objections of its opponents. Indignant Bowery trustees declared: "The System will impose strict federal regulations and federal interference on the banks!" This they refused to endorse. Other savings bankers shared their objections.

So, in spite of the Federal Home Loan Bank System's laudable motivations, it was at the outset virtually ignored. It brought little immediate improvement to the ills of the nation. On the contrary, matters continued to deteriorate. Banks were still being mismanaged and failing as President Hoover neared the end of his administration. In Michigan, after a big Detroit bank had collapsed, the governor declared a moratorium on banking operations. He closed all the state's banks on February 7, 1933.

Things were little better in New York State. On Friday, March 3rd—the day before the inauguration of Franklin Delano Roosevelt—Henry Bruère called a special meeting of his board of trustees. According to the minutes:

> He believed that a state of emergency existed in the banking situation, and especially as relating to savings banks, since the publication of the Michigan moratorium and since the many other happenings in the banking world. In the case of The Bowery Savings Bank, since February 7th (the date of the Michigan moratorium) the amount of $14,616,-000 had been withdrawn, $11,000,000 of that sum in the first four days of the current week. Similar proportionate withdrawals had been made from banks in Manhattan, and in Brooklyn, and in outlying districts.

Things were indeed bad. Whether this situation had been brought about by commercial banks or by savings banks did not concern the average citizen. For him, banks were banks. As he heard of more and more failures among them—in Detroit, Cleveland, New Orleans—he distrusted all banks. He wanted his money. He stood at tellers' windows and demanded it.

Seeing what was happening, Herbert Lehman, governor of New York, took the only measure he could have taken to protect the banks of his state from utter ruination. On the morning of March 4th, Inauguration Day, The Bowery Savings Bank received the following telegram:

YOU ARE HEREBY ADVISED THAT
GOVERNOR LEHMAN HAS DECLARED
A BANKING HOLIDAY EFFECTIVE TODAY
MARCH 4 AND MONDAY MARCH 6 DURING
WHICH ALL BANKING INSTITUTIONS
WILL BE CLOSED.

> J. A. BRODERICK
> *SUPERINTENDENT OF BANKS*

In Washington, almost as soon as Franklin D. Roosevelt sat down at his White House desk, he signed an order making the Bank Holiday nationwide. He explained his act in blunt words: "Some of our bankers have shown themselves either incompetent or dishonest in their handling of peoples' funds."

This was, of course, not true in the vast majority of our banks, but it was true in enough of them to shock the people for a time into a sense of insecurity and to put them in a frame of mind where they did not differentiate, but seemed to assume that the acts of a comparative few had tainted them all. It was the government's job to straighten out this situation and do it as quickly as possible.

The Bank Holiday was the only way of stopping the devastating drain on bank funds.

15

A HOLIDAY ENDS

Though the Bank Holiday did not rescue the nation from its depression, it did provide a respite during which the people of the United States could recover from terror and mass hysteria. It also permitted the fundamental good humor of Americans in time to reassert itself. People began singing *Brother, Can You Spare a Dime?* as if it were funny. Cartoonists were portraying millionaries and office boys strolling arm in arm, both grinning, neither with a cent in his turned-out pockets. In some ways the Bank Holiday seemed to become a great social leveler.

The Roosevelt Administration's faith in savings banks was demonstrated when these institutions were allowed to reopen within a single week—an order that did not include commercial banks. At the same time, the thrift institutions were shielded from runs. by a government edict that restricted withdrawals of savings to $25 a week. Within a short time the sum was increased to $250 (though this varied in different states). No crowds appeared to claim such allowances. The fact that the government regarded the savings institutions as sound was reassurance enough for most depositors.

Still, people were loath to *deposit* money. The knowledge that they could not draw more than $250 in any week discouraged them. Bruère was constrained to report that all savings banks were experiencing the ill effects of this limitation. "Persons desiring to open substantial new accounts," he said, "hesitate to do so. There is a marked decline in the funds coming into savings banks."

Other things, too, were going wrong for thrift institutions. With the entire economy in a state of depression, with wages reduced and little work available, mortgage holders could not pay their interest. Many real estate owners were also in default of taxes. More than ever the banks were finding themselves compelled, in desperation, to make foreclosures on properties they had no desire to own.

"And we shall be called upon to foreclose a substantial *additional* number of mortgages," Bruère warned in a monthly report. "Therefore we have organized a special staff to cope with the problem of managing and supervising the management of property."

During the next few years this special staff did everything in its power to deal with a plethora of foreclosures. The flood could not be stopped. By 1935 the bank held 431 parcels of foreclosed real estate whose value amounted to

$30 million. Earl Schwulst, in a review of those trying times when everything possible was done to *avoid* foreclosures, wrote: "Advances were made to owners by the Bank so that they might clear up delinquent taxes. To prevent owners from walking away from their properties, the Bank was reducing the interest rates on mortgages to 2 percent and even less. In some cases the Bank required no down payment at all on the sale of foreclosed real estate. It would even advance additional funds to the 'purchaser' for needed repairs or improvements. Of course, these were really not sales, and repossessions were the order of the day."

As one example of what was happening, the bank had to foreclose a piece of property on which it had lent $21,000 in 1901, when it had been valued at $42,000. Now it was vainly offering it to any taker for $4,500!

In the midst of these 1933 hardships, President Roosevelt asked his old friend, Henry Bruère, to come to Washington as a White House economic adviser. The trustees at once granted Bruère a leave of absence. For the next few months he spent most of his time in the nation's capital, where he witnessed at first hand the enactment of a number of New Deal undertakings.

One of them grew out of Roosevelt's concern for people whose money was unobtainable because their banks had closed, some of them never to reopen. Could the American public be protected against the recurrence of such a situation?

The answer lay, it was apparent, in some form of insurance to guarantee the safety of bank deposits. It would have to be dual-purpose insurance: to safeguard the interests of depositors on the one hand, and on the other to shelter the banks against future ruinous runs.

The idea was not uniquely Washington's. In New York State the thrift institutions, with the same thought, were still discussing the kind of self-insuring organization Henry Bruère and many of his contemporaries favored. This would be a fund supported by contributions from its member banks. It would hold in trust moneys that could be used to assist any member institution in distress.

The federal government, however, felt there was a need to protect depositors as distinct from the banks themselves, and that such protection should be nationwide. Therefore, in December of 1933, the Roosevelt Administration established the first Federal Deposit Insurance Corporation. I say the first because this one was generally regarded as a temporary measure to meet emergency needs. Known from its inception as FDIC, it originally planned to insure bank deposits up to a ceiling of $2,500. (Through the years this has gradually been increased to the present $100,000. A 1974 survey revealed that FDIC then insured 13,451 banks, covering 97.6 percent of all the nation's deposits.)

One would have thought—in view of FDIC's current wide acceptance—that The Bowery would have welcomed it from the start. Surely it was an instrument calculated to serve the "little man" as he had never been served before.

But it represented the Roosevelt New Deal philosophy, and to many people that philosophy was anathema.

"I for one want none of this FDIC," said George McNeir, an unshakable Republican conservative on The Bowery's board of trustees. "If it's New Deal, that damns it as far as I'm concerned."

He was not alone in this attitude. Board colleagues like Stephen Baker, Ward Melville, and Lincoln Cromwell staunchly supported him. For that matter, Bruère himself, though in many respects in favor of Roosevelt principles, was far from enthusiastic about federal intrusion into the banking business. Nevertheless, he saw its present necessity for reasons he patiently explained to the trustees:

Throughout the country, he said, there were any number of commercial banks that even now, nine months after the Bank Holiday, had not been permitted to reopen. Locked up, they were blocking economic recovery in their communities. They were prolonging distrust of bankers. They were doing nothing to shake off the nation's depression. The doors of these banks could be opened again only if the FDIC, as a nationally accepted entity, came into being to protect depositors. It was the only way to restore confidence in such institutions.

So Bruère recommended that The Bowery join the FDIC *temporarily* on the understanding that the bank could at any time withdraw. In that way it would set an example for other savings banks, and perhaps their support would give the American economy a sorely needed stimulus.

Bruère could see the board was not convinced. McNeir, Baker, and several other trustees were scowling and shaking their heads. It was a frustrating show of stubbornness. But the president continued to argue—and in the midst of his peroration he was handed a telegram. It came from Donald K. David, a trustee who had been unable to attend the meeting. Bruère scanned it quickly, then read it aloud:

> Even though there are no business reasons and perhaps certain severe disadvantages to entering FDIC plan, it seems to me clear that our institution, prominent as it is and located in New York City, cannot at this time stand out against movement to restore confidence, nor should savings banks generally be placed in position of less confidence than other banks. Have talked problem with men who have studied plan in detail and they concur in my conclusions.

The telegram from one of the board's most respected conservative members finally helped to sway the trustees, though they still remained distrustful of the New Deal. Reluctantly and grudgingly as it was given, Bruère none-

147

theless won the approval he sought for temporary membership in the FDIC.

Only then did he read aloud another communication he had received that day. This one was addressed to the entire board of trustees:

December 11, 1933

Gentlemen:

May I tell you, both personally and officially, how very greatly I appreciate the action of your Board in allowing me to have Mr. Henry Bruère in Washington this autumn. In addition to my old friendship for him and belief in him, he has rendered a very distinct service to the Government.

I told Mr. Bruère before he left that he has been so helpful to me that he might just as well break the news to his Board of Trustees that I fully expect to ask the Board to lend him to me again some day.

Also, I told him I hoped he would keep in close touch with the general savings bank situation and feel free to talk with me about it any time.

Very sincerely yours,
Franklin Delano Roosevelt

❧

As Bruère had predicted, when it was announced that The Bowery Savings Bank intended to affiliate itself with the FDIC, albeit on a temporary basis, other savings banks quickly followed.

For the most part they conceded that the concept of insuring deposits was a good one. They still felt, however, as did Bruère, that such insurance for depositors should be administered by the thrift institutions themselves, not by the federal government. Federal interference remained the bugaboo it had always been.

With this in mind, New York State's savings bankers met once more. They deliberated long and carefully. They sought the counsel of the Banking Department. And finally they established what they called the Mutual Savings Bank Fund. It was to be financed by annual assessments on its member banks. Its affairs would be handled by the recently created Savings Banks Trust Company. When a member bank found itself in distress, it could call on the new organization for assistance, whether in the form of a loan or a contribution to its net worth. Thus the Fund could enhance the liquidity and the strength of members that were in need.

"With this commitment of one for all and all for one," a veteran of those days recalled, "the future of the savings banks appeared to be secure. Everybody had so much faith in the arrangement that all except two of New York's mutual savings banks promptly withdrew from the Federal Deposit Insurance Corporation."

The two institutions that decided to remain in the federal agency were the Emigrant Savings Bank and the Franklin Savings Bank. The Bowery, to the relief of its anti-New Deal trustees, joined the rest of its sister banks in resigning from the Washington-controlled FDIC. It had been part of the federal agency for about five months. Now it became the largest contributor to the Mutual Savings Bank Fund.

It must not be supposed that this organization provided an instant panacea for all the difficulties that were besetting savings banks. They were still sharing the country's depression. They still had to adjust to the struggles of American business. The Bowery, apart from having to reduce its dividend rate to 3 percent to protect its own net worth, asked its staff to accept a sacrifice in pay. All salaries above $200 a month were cut by varying percentages, the highest executive compensations being slashed by a full 10 percent. Not a single employee resigned. Times being what they were, perhaps there was no place else to go.

☙

America's savings and loan industry owes an incalculable debt to a man named Horace Russell. He served as general counsel to the Federal Home Loan Bank Board. This Board had been set up to direct and supervise the Federal Home Loan Bank System, which had been created during the Hoover Administration. Though the organization was intended, as one of its purposes, to help mortgagors cope with the prospect of thousands of foreclosures during the depression, it had not fulfilled such expectations. Neither had it provided new mortgage funds in areas where there were no savings banks or other institutions ready to finance home construction.

President Hoover had so many depression woes on his mind that he did little to invigorate the Federal Home Loan Bank System. Having launched it, he probably assumed it would run itself. According to historian William Manchester, the President's plethora of pressing problems compelled him to employ five secretaries where previous Presidents had managed with only one. In any event, the Federal Home Loan Bank System was not revolutionizing the mortgage industry.

This was the situation when Franklin D. Roosevelt came to the White House. From the start he chafed under the System's lack of progress. Within a month after his inauguration he asked William Stevenson, chairman of the Federal Home Loan Bank Board, to find new ways of dealing with the mortgage problem. At the same time, he requested Congress to enact legislation which would bring financial relief to home owners who were in actual or imminent default on mortgage payments.

Chairman Stevenson in turn directed Horace Russell, his general counsel, to provide a blueprint for the required legislation. And Russell drew up what was called the Home Owners Loan Corporation Act. Its primary purpose, reflecting President Roosevelt's desire, was to help those home owners who were in trouble with their mortgages; this would be done by refinancing to avoid foreclosures.

But Russell went further than that. He conceived a plan that embraced what was to become Section 5 of the Act; this provided for a new kind of financing organization, the federal savings and loan association. "I had become convinced," he wrote in his memoirs, "that the mutual savings banks were the best examples of thrift institutions ever developed anywhere." But the savings banks were chartered by their individual states, and Russell was interested in creating a nationwide, federally chartered network of institutions. Several people who talked with him believe he approached leading savings bankers to spearhead and become the driving force behind such a network, only to find them unwilling to change their state-chartered status for an unpredictable future under federal regulation. This unwillingness, however, was not the explanation he gave for his decision not to involve the savings banks. What he wrote was:

> I was satisfied that we could not get Congress to authorize a system of Federal mutual savings banks. Opposition of bankers was too likely to develop. At the same time, I saw no reason why we could not authorize Federal Savings and Loan Associations and [thus] provide the simplest possible form of a mutual savings institution—and use the same primarily for sound and economic home finance.

So it was that in his Section 5 he provided for the establishment of a federal savings and loan industry.

Roosevelt recommended it to Congress. It was enacted. And on June 13, 1933 the President signed the bill.

But this did not result in an immediate American utopia. Russell's plan to revitalize the mortgage and construction industries was sluggish in its spread. Very few federal savings and loan associations were organized immediately after the enactment of the legislation. No doubt the reasons were partly political. Too many people with money still distrusted the inspirations of the New Deal.

The President, in his determination to restore prosperity to the nation, may have been impatient with such laggardness. By October, only four months after he had signed the bill creating the Home Owners Loan Corporation (which provided for federal savings and loan associations), Roosevelt decided on new action. Something had to be done to make the Act evoke a more satisfactory response. Mortgage money was not being made available as rapidly as he had hoped, particularly in areas that lacked home financing institutions. He needed experienced help.

To his knowledge, the most successful and experienced mortgage lenders were the country's savings bankers. So he turned once more to his friend Henry Bruère, and asked him to bring a delegation of leading savings bankers to a White House conference. Among the people who answered the summons were Philip Benson of New York, Stacy Lloyd of Pennsylvania, Wilson King of Rhode Island, and Myron Convers and A. George Gilman of Massachussetts. Gilman later wrote:

> I attended the meeting of savings bank men who were invited to The White House, where the President stated his intent to create a National Thrift Institution. He appointed Mr. Henry Bruère as liaison between the mutual savings banks and Government representatives. Mr. Horace Russell (who was also present) was assigned the task of preparing legislation with the objective in mind of creating a new National Thrift System.

Though the savings bankers listened with the respect due the President of the United States, they were not prepared to make instant decisions on behalf of their entire industry. They wanted time to think and discuss what was in effect a plan to spread their own type of operation across the land. So they went home to consider the idea, and Gilman reported:

> Henry Bruère invited some fifteen savings bank officers to attend a meeting in New York City at the Commodore Hotel. At this meeting Mr. Horace Russell stated this new thrift system was to be created.
> *He offered to the mutual savings banks an opportunity to become the foundation of the system.* [Italics mine.] He stated that all savings banks, cooperative banks, and building and loan associations would become members.
> This system was to be named the National Mutual Savings Bank System. Horace Russell went to great lengths to explain to the mutual savings banks that it would be a chance for them to head up this movement. . . . It is definite that the mutual savings banks were offered a chance, as Russell said, to be the "big factor" in this Federal system.

And what happened? Among those at the Hotel Commodore meeting were Philip Benson, president of the Dime Savings Bank of Brooklyn, and Henry Kinsey, president of the Williamsburgh Savings Bank. Both were adamant in their objections to the possibility of federal "domination." Granting that Roosevelt might not attempt to rule the savings banks, who could be sure of what Roosevelt's successors might do? Bruère, though less vigorous in his opposition to the plan, nevertheless shared many of his colleagues' fears. The upshot was that the group rejected the opportunity to become federally chartered.

Years later, in 1962, A. D. Theobald, president of the First Federal Savings and Loan Association of Peoria, Illinois, bluntly told members gathered at a convention of the National Association of Mutual Savings Banks that they had missed their big chance. Had they grasped the opportunity when it was offered to them by President Roosevelt, they could have created a coast-to-coast system of savings banks that would have obviated the need for a federal savings and loan industry. They could have been the leaders in a venture that might have revolutionized the mortgage business, or at least have directed it into new channels, to the great benefit of the American public.

In fact, the U.S. Savings and Loan League submitted a statement to Congress in 1963 in which the League said: "It is now acknowledged by savings bank leaders themselves that the Federal Savings and Loan System quite possibly could have been a Federal Savings Bank System if the savings bank leaders had acted and thought differently in 1932 and 1933."

In retrospect it is all the more ironic because the savings banks are today crusading for the very thing Bruère and his associates tossed aside. In May of 1974, Chairman Morris D. Crawford, Jr. of The Bowery, speaking on behalf of the National Association of Mutual Savings Banks, pleaded the case for federal charters before the Senate Banking Committee. He was accompanied by Grover W. Ensley, executive vice president of the Association, and by P. James Riordan, its general counsel.

Crawford championed the cause as he had been espousing it for years. He was convinced that "mutual savings banks must develop into full-service family banks capable of providing all the financial services required by families." And he added:

The realization of this goal requires three steps:
(1) A federal savings bank charter alternative, so that the progressive influence of the dual state-federal system of chartering and supervision long available to all other deposit-type institutions will be extended to mutual savings banks.

(2) The ability to provide the full range of financial services to consumers, including consumer loans, checking accounts, [and] credit card and other third-party payment services, including extension to thrift institutions of full partnership in the development of electronic funds-transfer services.

(3) The ability to invest in a wide range of federal, state, and local government and corporate securities, as well as in mortgages.

All these benefits the mutual savings bank industry might have had forty years before Crawford urged their adoption. They would have been granted during the Roosevelt Administration if the leading savings bankers of the day had not discarded the opportunity offered to them. Bruère, Kinsey, Benson, and their associates were great and distinguished bankers. They brought many innovations to their industry. But like so many other outstanding leaders of the American economy, they made their share of well-intentioned mistakes.

❧

It was evident that if Franklin Roosevelt abhorred any particular philosophy, it was one of *laissez-faire*. His reliance on hard, swift action—often of an unexpected and innovative nature—may have dismayed as many people as it inspired; but undeniably it set a stalled economy into motion. William Manchester said of him, "He ran his administration as a one-man show, and loved to exercise authority." But the authority he exercised was beneficial to so many "little people" that of the 8,000 letters he received every day, more than 7,000 were notes of thanks for the manner in which he had alleviated distress.

The banks of the nation posed a problem of their own. Months after the Bank Holiday, several thousand financial institutions were still shut down, unable to serve their communities. In an effort to rescue them, Roosevelt created an agency called the Deposit Liquidation Board, under the aegis of the Reconstruction Finance Corporation. Once more he summoned Henry Bruère, as a representative of New York's banks, to serve as a consultant.

Accepting the appointment, Bruère began a series of trips to Washington to confer with Reconstruction Finance Corporation officials. It was there he met Earl Bryan Schwulst.

To understand the developing relationship between these two men, one must first understand a quandary that faced the president of The Bowery Savings Bank.

One of the responsibilities of a chief executive is at some appropriate time to provide for his succession. As Bruère appraised his top-ranking associates at the bank, a dismaying fact became evident. Capable as these men might be, most of them were of his own age, some even older. That meant many would retire at about the same time he himself reached retirement age. Among the younger men he had not yet discerned any who had the wide experience in banking and the recognized stature in public affairs which, as he viewed the post, were requisite for the leadership of The Bowery.

The standards Bruère set for the post—at least in his own mind—were formidable. Writing in The Bowery's magazine, *The Chest*, he once asked: "What sort of man should be the leader of an institution such as this?" Then he listed a full page of qualifications. Among them were:

> He should be a person whom other business and community organizations wish to have in their councils. He should be actively interested in the welfare of the city and in the people his institution is intended to serve.
>
> The well-rounded executive should be without malice, indirection, guile, and free from envy and arrogance.

He must be inventive and progressive-minded.

He should be a good executive giving opportunity to others to manage their part of the enterprise, setting up standards of performance and inspiring others to achieve them. He must have three-dimensional loyalty: To his Board, to his colleagues, to his subordinates.

He should deserve the respect of the community. He should enjoy the friendship of the best men in his profession.

There were at least a dozen other stipulations, ranging from "good health" to being "economical of time, talk, and confabulations." One would have thought it impossible to find so many virtues in any individual. Yet those were the qualities Bruère sought in his quest for The Bowery's next president.

In Washington, in the offices of the Reconstruction Finance Corporation, Jesse Jones had placed responsibility for managing the staff of the Deposit Liquidation Board in the hands of Earl B. Schwulst. Jones had sound reasons for his choice. Ever since leaving Harvard, where he had been graduated *summa cum laude* in economics, Schwulst had devoted himself to banks and banking. His earliest training had come at J. P. Morgan and Company. Thereafter he had served for several years as the manager of the Credit and Loan Department of the Federal Reserve Bank of Dallas. In the course of these Texas years he wrote a book, *The Extension of Bank Credit*, which attracted considerable attention. It led eventually to his being appointed financial adviser to the Republic of Ecuador, where his responsibility was to set up a central banking system. And this in turn brought about an appointment as financial adviser to Henry L. Stimson, who was then governor-general of the Philippines.

In the islands, Schwulst's first task was to reorganize the system of bank supervision; it was in sad disarray. When this was accomplished and when other duties were fulfilled, he was appointed to serve as the islands' Superintendent of Banks, a tremendously important job for a man still in his early thirties. It compelled him to change all his plans; he had to relinquish the offer of an assistant professorship at Harvard. What he had originally thought would be a brief assignment in the Philippines turned into a stay of four-and-a-half years, for the financial problems he faced were enormous. But in the end, he led several of the islands' financial institutions out of serious difficulties into positions of stability. And the experience, as he later said, was priceless.

When at last he left the Philippines, Schwulst joined Jesse Jones in the Washington offices of the Reconstruction Finance Corporation. Starting as a special assistant to its board of directors, he soon received a number of specific assignments. These included positions as director of the Commodity Credit Corporation, director and president of the RFC Mortgage Company, and staff supervisor of the Deposit Liquidation Board.

It was in this capacity that he worked with The Bowery's president. The two men saw much of each other. Schwulst, some fifteen years Bruère's junior, certainly had more knowledge about banking than almost any young man The Bowery's head had ever encountered.

Their duty was to assist in determining which of the country's 5,000 closed banks could be reopened, and how much money would have to be advanced by the Reconstruction Finance Corporation to make such openings possible. Problems like that gave both men unique opportunities to appraise the workings of each other's minds. Though they did not always agree in their conclusions, they quickly developed respect for each other's opinions.

One afternoon, after more than a year of this association, Bruère invited Schwulst to see him at his quarters in the Washington Hotel. The call came at a time when

Schwulst had been working six and sometimes seven days a week, and often nights as well. He was exhausted. He and his wife were about to drive off for a weekend of rest in Virginia. When he tried to explain this to Bruère, the banker said, "I won't detain you more than a few minutes."

Once the two had sat down in the hotel room, Bruère seemed to forget the promise. He relaxed in a deep chair, crossed his legs comfortably, and spoke about countless trivial matters. Since his personal interests included literature, painting, and music, he was never at a loss for conversational material. Schwulst began to fidget. His wife would be waiting downstairs in the car and they had a long drive ahead. He was about to rise when Bruère sudenly said:

"Earl, how would you like to join me at The Bowery Savings Bank—as a vice president?"

Caught by surprise, Schwulst had no immediate reply. Besides, Secretary of State Cordell Hull, with the consent of Jesse Jones, had just asked him to go to Cuba as an advisor to the provisional government which had recently thrown out the dictator Machado. This assignment could well consume two or three months.

"You don't have to give me an answer now," Bruère said. "Think about it. Talk it over with your family and call me when you get back from Cuba."

"Have you spoken to Jones about this?" Schwulst asked.

"I haven't talked to anyone. Nor will I before I get your decision. At this point I just want you to know that I would be delighted to have you at The Bowery Savings Bank." Having said that, Bruère rose, smiling, and offered his hand. "Have a good weekend and a good trip to Cuba. If you're interested when you get back, phone me."

Two months later, on his return from Cuba and after long consultations with his family, Schwulst telephoned Bruère. He did not tell him that, as a courtesy and a duty, he had talked with Jones about the Bruère offer. Nor did he say that Jones had tried to dissuade him from going to New York—that Jones had offered him the presidency of a large Minneapolis bank. He said simply, "Henry, I'm interested."

This occurred shortly after the bank had observed its 100th anniversary. Schwulst was being asked to become part of a venerable institution whose assets now exceeded half a billion dollars. He was not *promised* its presidency. Bruère did not commit himself to that extent. But Bruère already knew, as he said in later years, where he hoped to see his new recruit eventually established. At the outset he was to be First Vice President. It was the same title under which Henry Bruère himself had entered the bank's service nearly a decade earlier.

16

THE WORST OF ALL TIMES?

Earl Schwulst could not have chosen a more challenging time to join a mutual savings bank—if one can define challenging as simply terrible. This was the peak period in which mortgage loans hastily made in days of plenty had to be foreclosed. Among other properties that fell into The Bowery's collection of unwanted real estate were several hotels. When you inherit hotels—concerned with guests and restaurants and bars—you inherit problems no bank is equipped to handle.

As an illustration, a young married woman was using the Hotel Montclair as a trysting place with various gentlemen. Her husband wanted evidence for a divorce. He hired a photographer to snap the kind of pictures he needed. The photographer, an expert in such matters, managed to get a key to the lady's room. He surprised her in bed with one of her many friends, and he succeeded in obtaining an excellent photograph.

The unusual feature of this situation was that the lady in question was the daughter of a respected and socially prominent Bowery trustee.

Summoned by telephone, Robert Sparks, then a vice president of the bank, rushed to the hotel. How could he prevent the newspapers from reporting an event which would reflect sordidly not only on the trustee but on a hitherto impeccable thrift institution which had no desire to be identified as the owner of an establishment in which such affairs could take place?

Sparks never explained what he did, except to say he invited the press into a private room directly behind the hotel's bar and had a heart-to-heart talk with reporters. The gentlemen of the press understood. Perhaps some of them went away thinking, "There but for the grace of God——" At any rate, the newspapers accorded the story what Sparks later termed "pianissimo treatment." A great deal of embarrassment was avoided.

Another memorable result of foreclosures involved the Williamsburgh Savings Bank of Brooklyn. It found itself the proprietor of a crumbling, empty, boarded-up building at 93 MacDougal Street. Nobody would buy such a wreck. The bank decided to have it demolished. The empty lot could then be devoted to a more modern structure.

The contractor hired for the demolition made a slight error in the instructions he gave his wrecking crew. He wrote the address as 93 McDonough Street. The men went there, found the building occupied, and were ordered to leave by the shouts of angry tenants. They saw, however, that the three-floor building next door, number 89, was empty and sagging in a sad state of disrepair. It was clear that their boss had made a mistake in address. So they went to work on number 89, ripped out plumbing and gas fixtures, and started to tear down the walls.

This foreclosed building was owned by The Bowery Savings Bank. When word reached the bank of what was happening, its men raced to the site and stopped the proceedings, but by this time they were the proprietors of a wreck.

In retrospect, such occurrences have their touch of humor. But there was nothing funny about them when they happened. They were symbolic of the disastrous wave of foreclosures that affected every thrift institution in America. Bank Examiner G. M. Aldrich found, in the case of The Bowery, that fully 44 percent of its mortgages were in default. At the same time, the funds it had committed to railroad bonds were in a state of collapse, with some 10 percent of them—representing investments of over $94 million—also in default.

Possibly this accumulation of blows explains why Henry Bruère sustained the first of his heart attacks. This one kept him out of the bank only a few weeks, but it made him realize that he ought to delegate more of his duties and worries to associates; and one associate he had in mind was Earl B. Schwulst.

Schwulst's appointment had, of course, to be ratified by the board of trustees. He came to New York to meet a few of them, all men of distinction like Frank L. Polk, former Undersecretary of State; Arthur A. Ballantine, one of the country's most eminent lawyers; Stephen Baker, president and chairman of the Bank of the Manhattan Company. And an obstacle instantly rose in the person of Trustee Baker.

A crusty, outspoken man who occupied an imposing

Wall Street office, Baker made no pretense of friendliness. Across his desk he glared at Schwulst.

"Young man," he said, "The Bowery Savings Bank is an old and respected institution. It is well run and directed and we don't want any young New Dealer coming up here from Washington to tell us how to run the bank. Is that clear?"

Schwulst promptly bristled. "Mr. Baker," he retorted, "I'm not here to defend myself or the New Deal. Permit me to say that I did not ask for this job. I was invited to take it."

"I am aware of that. Nevertheless——"

"What's more, I went into the Reconstruction Finance Corporation in the Hoover Administration. I was hired by Charles Miller—a Republican, former head of the Utica Savings Bank—who at the time was president of the RFC. May I also say that I served four and a half years in the Cabinets of three Republican governor-generals of the Philippines, Henry L. Stimson, Dwight F. Davis, and Theodore Roosevelt, Jr. I've worked for and with Republicans before there was such a thing as a New Deal. If a cause is good, Mr. Baker, I am not interested in whether it is Republican or Democratic. And if this attitude disqualifies me for The Bowery, I'm sorry. Thank you for your candor." He rose to leave.

White-haired Stephen Baker stared. He was not accustomed to such rejoinders. Abruptly a smile erased his severity. He waved to the chair and said in a friendlier tone, "Sit down, sit down, Mr. Schwulst. I'd quite forgotten. You *did* serve in the Hoover Administration."

❦

Every period of depression seems, to those who experience it, to be the worst the country has ever known. Admittedly the ordeal of the 1930s was unique. It differed from all others in the circumstance that President Roosevelt took measures never before attempted in his struggle to restore equilibrium to the American economy.

Among those with whom he conferred during his early days in office was economist John Maynard Keynes, introduced to the White House by Felix Frankfurter. Later Roosevelt wrote Frankfurter that he and Keynes had enjoyed "a grand talk." But apparently the President was not immediately swayed by the Keynesian philosophy of deliberately expanding and contracting a nation's money supply to meet the exigencies of the moment. Keynes advocated "spending the country out of depression" and, conversely in times of inflation, reducing government expenditures so as to diminish the amount of currency in circulation.

Of course, eventually Roosevelt did lead the nation into vast spending programs to overcome depression. Future historians may debate the influence of Keynes, but, like commentators of the past, they will probably never agree on a conclusion.

Roosevelt's New Deal, arousing the resentment of conservative Bowery trustees as it antagonized many other financiers, was derided as a succession of "boondoggling" experiments. Many an economist charged that the President was leading the country straight to ruin. Business leaders groaned as they saw one new federal agency after another created to erode their freedom of action.

First came the National Recovery Administration, authorized under General Hugh S. Johnson "to draft for each industry a code of fair competition that would have the force of law." What made this intolerable to certain industrialists was that it favored higher wages and shorter working hours as well as "collective bargaining through representatives of labor's own choosing." As if this were not Bolshevistic enough, the Wagner Act of 1935 set up a National Labor Relations Board to assert the right of workers to join unions and bargain collectively. ("This President is crippling the country!" corporation heads cried.)

And the President had only started.

Agency after agency came into existence, some as controversial as the Tennessee Valley Authority, which would spend billions; others as unheard of as the Civilian Conservation Corps, set up to provide temporary jobs for young men between the ages of 18 and 25. Such innovations, according to the New Deal Congress, were essential, for more than 5 million persons were living on relief, and some 7 million were unemployed. When the WPA—the Works Progress Administration—was established to *make jobs* for these unemployed, the country's conservatives became hopeless. Their government had gone mad.

No doubt the critics had some justification for their bitterness. In seven New Deal years, the gross national debt of the United States rose from $22,539,000,000 to $44,458,000,000.

And thrift institutions had no way of escaping the nation's depression. Between 1935 and 1938 The Bowery's assets declined for the first time in its history; and yet it was doing better than most savings banks. To strengthen its net worth, it now cut its dividend rate to 2 percent.

If one wonders why depositors remained with the bank when their compensation was so low, there were two answers: First, on an idealistic level, their faith in the institution remained unshaken. Second, on a more pragmatic level, all other savings banks were being forced to cut their dividend rates. There was no other place to go.

Mutual savings banks like The Bowery were not the only ones concerned about the welfare of "little people." In California a man named Francis Everett Townsend had proposed a plan to have the federal government give $200 a month to every citizen past the age of 60. His idea attracted more derision than support. Political candidates who espoused the Townsend Plan were soundly defeated. (What would they have said about the payments later distributed under the name of Social Security?)

Another man whose ideas were scorned in the early 1930s was "that visionary, impractical, misguided Socialist, Norman Thomas," who campaigned repeatedly for the Presidency of the United States. Thomas was castigated by right-thinking critics because he championed such unconscionable ideas as unemployment insurance, minimum wage laws, slum clearance, low-cost housing, health insurance for the aged, public works, the abolition of child labor, civil liberties for all, a five-day week, old-age pensions, and similar "un-American" notions. As J. E. Edgerton, the president of the National Association of Manufacturers, told a Senate committee, *he* attended to all such matters, "social welfare stuff, in my church work."

One may doubt that some of the conservative trustees of The Bowery, devoted though they were to the needs of "little people," could have sanctioned such bizarre ideas as Thomas advanced. But then, they were just as deaf to the dictatorial pronouncements of Huey Long and to the Nazi-like broadcasts of Father Coughlin. Their conservatism kept the bank out of the storms of political strife.

This was the situation to which Earl Schwulst was introduced when he joined The Bowery Savings Bank in 1936. The quiet, dignified interior of the institution might have seemed as isolated from mundane problems as a secluded temple. That was an illusion. Almost the first problem Schwulst had to face was the deplorable condition of the bank's mortgage portfolio. Every savings bank in the state, perhaps in the nation, was still being undermined by losses inherent in foreclosures.

"State Examiner S. I. Chittenden," Schwulst recalls, "had just completed a study in which he placed the amount of The Bowery's foreclosed real estate at more than $46 million. There were still $262 million of mortgages on the books, and of these, 35 percent were in arrears."

Fortunately, The Bowery's assets now totaled more than half a billion dollars—$556,847,618, to be precise. This put the institution in a stronger position than many of its contemporaries. It prompted Examiner Chittenden to report "a satisfactory financial condition. This institution is apparently under very competent management."

Unfortunately, not everyone could agree with Mr. Chittenden. Not long thereafter, a small, quiet, scowling man walked into the offices of The Bowery Savings Bank. He produced credentials to identify himself as another bank examiner. His name was Lawrence Geser. And though nobody realized it then, his presence was a threat to everybody in the bank.

17
⌒~⌒
TROUBLE
NAMED GESER

With the arrival of the bank examiner, a normal
enough event, Henry Bruère ordered as always that
all records and facilities be placed at Mr. Geser's disposal. From that point on, the examiner's contacts
would be principally with officers in the comptroller's
department, with the mortgage and real estate staff,
and with any others he chose to interview.

Near the end of his examination, Lawrence Geser
asked to meet with the president himself. He wanted
to discuss his findings. The result was an immediate
clash of personalities.

One has to visualize Henry Bruère, tall, remarkably handsome (despite the baldness about which he was over-sensitive), a patrician and aristocratic figure, a man of broad cultural interests who was accustomed to the company of the nation's leaders in government, finance, and the arts; one of the chosen few in the Social Register. Lawrence Geser was the antithesis of all this—small, worried, with no claim to fame, more interested in statistics than in people.

Earl Schwulst, then a vice president of the bank, had this to say about Bruère and Geser: "Mr. Geser was a stiff and rather dour individual. He was thorough and competent, but no diplomat. President Bruère was often unpredictable, temperamental, and proud, but also no diplomat. He could be sharp, short. Neither man was blessed with a sense of humor. Bruère was the highest-paid savings bank officer in the state, with a salary of $60,000 a year (quite opulent in 1938). Geser could not have been making more than $7,000 or $8,000 a year. To Bruère, Geser was little more than a clerk who should be properly deferential to the leader of the country's savings bank industry and the head of its largest savings bank.

"Geser, however, was unimpressed. He bluntly implied (to those he talked with later) that Bruère was incompetent and had not been giving the bank the expert guidance that might have avoided, or at least ameliorated, the serious condition in which he, Geser, asserted he had found the institution."

In those troubled days, with every mutual savings bank in America plagued by foreclosures and repossessions, Geser would undoubtedly have found similar faults in any thrift institution he visited. They were all steeped in the woes of the depression. The Bowery, being bigger than the others, understandably had a greater number of problems. Geser chose to focus on them almost to the exclusion of the many benefits Bruère had brought to the bank.

As for The Bowery's president himself, after the irritation of their meeting had subsided, he gave Geser little thought. He had too many other things on his mind. His service on national, municipal, and banking committees demanded much of his attention. His talks with Franklin Delano Roosevelt made him worry more than did most men: In Europe Hitler was threatening the very foundations of Western civilization, and at home the American economy, while rushing help to the Allies, was trying to adjust itself to a worldwide upheaval.

Moreover, one small crisis after another arose to harass him at The Bowery Savings Bank. Some were so petty as to be ludicrous, yet they frayed his nerves. As a minor example, there was the case of the lady who came into the bank one afternoon to withdraw $7,000 she claimed to have on deposit. She had no passbook. She told the teller that she had long ago mailed the passbook to a brother in South Africa. The teller regretfully informed her that without the passbook he could not give her the money.

The lady, clad in white from head to foot, thereupon became explosively angry. She created a noisy scene that brought Bruère hurrying out of his office. When he identified himself and attempted to calm her while scores of depositors looked on, she declared that she would not leave the premises until she had her money.

"I'll stay right here day and night till you pay me!" she screamed. She sat down and refused to be budged. Reluctant to remove her forcibly, which could have resulted in wretched publicity, Bruère went back to his office and telephoned for advice to DeCourcey Fales, senior partner at Cadwalader, Wickersham, and Taft.

"Above all," Fales said, "don't call in the police. Don't

make a worse scene than you already have to contend with."

"But she threatens to stay all night," Bruère said.

"Let her do it. Meanwhile get some of your men to find out if she has any relatives. If so, notify them. She sounds irrational."

At the closing hour the lady was still sitting stubbornly in the banking room; so Bruère had a cot prepared for her in the ladies' lounge. He ordered security guards to watch the door overnight. When he returned in the morning, the lady was still there. So Bruère had a breakfast tray sent in to her.

An hour later he was told that a sister of the woman had been located in the Bronx. "The sister is on the way here," the man reported. "She says this woman has been under observation for mental disorders."

After the lady in white was led off by her sister the incident seemed ended—except for its unexpected dénoument: The brother in South Africa mailed in the missing passbook. Irrational or not, the lady had had a just claim on her savings, and the bank duly paid out the $7,000.

Bruère had scarcely put this contretemps out of his thoughts when another occurrence of a non-business nature jolted him. Again the reputation of the bank was in jeopardy. The manager of a hotel that The Bowery had acquired by foreclosure telephoned in distress with a bewildering story.

"Last night," he said, "a young woman ran out of her room, drunk and naked, and went shrieking up and down the corridor. She was infuriated with a man in her room. She woke everybody on the floor, and there was a wild scene. We finally managed to throw a blanket around her and get her quieted down in another room. Some reporters heard of all this, and they're standing around in the lobby, waiting to question her. The trouble is, Mr. Bruère, she says she's an employee of The Bowery Bank."

Bruère tried to divert his mind from the problems of mortgages and net worth and calls from Washington. "Who is she?" he asked. When he heard the girl's name, he groaned. Her flamboyant manner and her style of dress had caused quite a stir among the male employees of the bank; they had given her the name of Hot Pants.

"Get her through a back door and bring her here," Bruère directed. Then he called Vice President Robert Sparks. "Bob, you handle this," he said. "Get her off the bank's payroll. Do anything you like, but get rid of her."

Sparks got rid of "Hot Pants" by getting her the job of cigarette girl at another big city hotel not owned by The Bowery. A few months later, wearing an expensive mink coat, she returned to make a sizable deposit at The Bowery and to thank Sparks for the opportunity he had given her.

With such distractions as well as the demands of the bank and of his government commitments to absorb him, Henry Bruère had scant reason to think about Examiner Lawrence Geser. And Geser went doggedly, silently, about his job of ferreting into and reporting on The Bowery's finances and activities.

The result was a blistering examiner's report to the Superintendent of Banks.

Geser criticized the organization and management of the mortgage portfolio. He criticized accounting procedures, audit control, and various other facets of operations. He even criticized the expenditures for advertising. In fact, he found almost nothing he liked in the way The Bowery was being run.

William R. White, who was then Superintendent of Banks, must have been appalled by the report. His deputy, Edward Pierce, immediately sent copies to Henry

Bruère and to the trustees. He asked in effect, "What about all this?"

Bruère was stunned by what he read. It was unbelievable. The Geser report was couched in terms which seemed to hold the president of The Bowery personally accountable for incredible mismanagement. Like many a proud and able man, he was profoundly sensitive to criticism and easily hurt. As he studied every charge Geser had leveled against him, he must have wondered if he had indeed failed the bank.

When he faced the board at its next meeting, he was a shaken man. Looking from one solemn face to another around the oval table, he may well have feared that these men secretly agreed with Lawrence Geser's appraisal of his administration.

And so, after the Superintendent's letter and Geser's report had been duly read aloud for the record, Henry Bruère rose and, for the welfare of the bank, quietly offered his resignation.

☙

Of course, it was declined. Not only was it declined, but the secretary was instructed to omit all mention of a resignation from the minutes of the meeting.

Within a few days the Superintendent of Banks and his deputy, Edward Pierce, telephoned Schwulst to suggest a meeting to discuss the Geser report. The next afternoon they met at the Harvard Club.

"Since I was a comparatively new man in the bank's senior management," Schwulst recalls, "and because I had at one time been a banking superintendent myself, they thought I might have some objective suggestions to offer. I told them that Bruère had just given me supervisory responsibility for the real estate and mortgage depart-

174

ments and that steps were already under way to deal with the matters which had disturbed Mr. Geser. I said all his criticisms would receive immediate attention."

Schwulst outlined the plans he had for future operations, and the government officials thoughtfully nodded. Summarizing the meeting, he told me:

"Whether my assurances that reforms were under way and the examiner's recommendations would be carried out forestalled more drastic action by the supervisory authorities, I do not know."

The outcome was that the state Banking Department decided to see what future examinations would reveal. The same examiner, Lawrence Geser, was assigned to study the bank's operations in several succeeding years, 1941, 1946, and 1947.

To his credit as a fair-minded man, Geser's 1941 report spoke of The Bowery as a "model organization." He added, "Your examiner commends to the attention of the Trustees the members of the personnel who are responsible for the accomplishment of this great improvement and the continuance of good mortgage procedure." His subsequent reports were equally laudatory.

When he was replaced by a new examiner in 1949, this man, M. L. Masson, reported, "The Bank is in sound financial condition and is well managed."

Clearly—though Lawrence Geser may at the outset have been crotchety, overzealous, and irritated by Henry Bruère—he did The Bowery Savings Bank a very real service. He compelled it to pull itself out of the morass of unhappy situations into which it had been thrown by the national depression.

And Superintendent William White himself must have appreciated the soundness of the bank's condition; after he left the Banking Department, he accepted membership on The Bowery's board of trustees.

18

THE FDIC BECKONS AGAIN

These were days in the early 1940s when long lines of troops paraded down Fifth Avenue, bands blaring, flags waving; and the sounds carried the two short blocks to the bank on 42nd Street. For this was in the midst of World War II.

Again, as in World War I, The Bowery urged its depositors to buy War Savings Bonds. At its own windows it accounted for more than $65 million in bond sales. If this meant people were withdrawing funds—as they were—one could only say that nothing was as important as financing and winning the war. The outflow of funds continued at all thrift institutions. Yet the savings banks had to conserve earnings, to build up their reserves. This could be done only by reducing dividend rates. The Bowery's rates went down to 1½ percent.

One hundred and eleven of the bank's employees—over 20 percent of its personnel—joined the armed services. The older men, from Bruère and Schwulst down, worked on almost every war-related civilian committee that came into being, locally and nationally. And through it all The Bowery remained strong.

Indeed, a number of savings banks throughout the United States were in better condition after the war than they had been before its start. That was because the American people now had jobs and money. One must remember that World War II (ten times as costly as World War I) compelled the United States to expend some $300 billion, $49 billion of it in lend-lease to Great Britain and Russia. The presses had never been busier printing money. To build the biggest navy in American history, the biggest army, and the biggest air force, the country had to create the biggest labor force it had ever known. Sixty-four million men and women were employed.

A gauge of their prosperity was this: Only 4 million Americans had paid income taxes in 1939. The number rose to 30 million by 1943. No doubt some of this increase was attributable to the fact that on July 1, 1943 a 20 percent withholding tax went into effect on wages and salaries. But the real cause was that the national income streaked from $72 billion to $198 billion during the war years.

Though 12 million men had gone off to the armed forces, as well as thousands of women, those who remained at home performed wonders beyond belief. They increased the number of war vessels from 380 to 1,100; the number of planes from 2,100 to 96,356. They created wholly new industries that had never before been dreamed of—electronic enterprises like those essential to the manufacture of an atomic bomb; industries like synthetic rubber. They produced tanks and ammunition and gasoline and hand weapons not only for American troops but for the country's allies. And they sent an endless supply of food across the sea.

All this provided Americans with jobs and purchasing power at a time when normal peacetime goods were scarce. In a repetition of what had happened during World War I, the competition to buy goods sent prices soaring. Roosevelt refused to let this continue. To the anger of some, to the relief of others, he resorted to strict government controls. Another New Deal agency, the OPA—Office of Price Administration—found it necessary to freeze prices and wages.

But the freeze did not stop millions of people from earning good wages. And they were patriotically buying war bonds. For a while, the savings banks feared that the government's energetic efforts to induce people to buy such bonds would result in fewer savings deposits. The bankers held a worried meeting at which several of them urged that the government be asked to modify its advertising campaign for bond purchases. President Kinsey of the Williamsburgh Savings Bank rose to oppose this. He predicted that with inflation and restrictions on consumer spending caused by the scarcity of goods, the savings banks would soon have "money pouring out of their ears." As most banks were to discover, he was not wrong. Despite the millions of dollars people were investing in war bonds, they also saved. Between 1942 and 1947 The Bowery's deposits rose from $463 million to

$660 million, an increase of 45 percent. Other savings banks had the same experience in varying degrees.

"When scarcity combined with inflated prices lifts the cost of goods to levels people cannot afford," an editorial writer observed, "consumers simply stop buying. They put their money aside in either savings accounts or conservative investments until such time as prices again seem reasonable and goods are available."

Another commentator said, "Though Americans were generously pouring funds into war bonds, many of them remembered that after World War I hard times had struck the country. And so, with prudent foresight for whatever the future might bring, they put funds into savings accounts, too. Their deposits almost equaled their purchases of bonds. What they were doing was saving money in *two* ways—bonds and cash." The savings banks, of course, were involved in both types of transactions, and their personnel had never been busier.

Throughout all this, quixotic as it may sound, Henry Bruère found time to write lyrics for songs. He staged colorful pageants at the bank and proved himself not only a born impresario but a thwarted thespian who often sang his own songs. The kind of lyrics he wrote are well exemplified by a patriotic *Ode to The Bowery* he penned to the melody of *America the Beautiful*. The great hall of The Bowery resounded with the voices of hundreds of employees singing:

> *O beautiful for stately halls,*
> *For aspirations high,*
> *For rugged honor's legacy*
> *That no man can deny.*
> *O Bowery, O Bowery,*
> *Continue on thy way,*
> *Keep up the fight with all thy might*
> *To bring a better day!*

"The astonishing thing about this remarkable man," Schwulst said, "is that with his heart really elsewhere, he brought The Bowery Bank successfully through the most trying period of its history—through the Great Depression and through two wars, the Second World War and the Korean conflict. But he paid a heavy price for his exertions and achievements. He suffered two major heart attacks and a number of smaller ones during his tenure."

Between heart attacks he devoted himself to innovative programs for the bank. He led the institution into the Savings Bank Life Insurance System. (It has since become the leading life insurance bank in the state.) Perhaps his greatest challenge and opportunity, however, came when the government invited all savings banks to join the permanent Federal Deposit Insurance Corporation—on which, a few years earlier, Bruère had turned his back.

One of Bruère's assets—or failings—was that he could always see both sides of a possibility. That often left him in the middle, indecisive. He was in this mood the day he sat down to discuss the FDIC with Earl Schwulst.

"Earl," he asked, "what do you think?"

"I think," Schwulst said, "that we must join."

"Why?"

"Many reasons. The first is that the Mutual Savings Bank Fund, as now constituted, does not really protect depositors as they have been led to believe it does. Its assets are too meager. It may serve to protect depositors in a *small* bank or two. But how can it cover the hundreds of millions on deposit in a bank like The Bowery? Its assets amount to hardly 10 percent of our deposits. In a general crisis, the Fund would be helpless. We know that. But the public does not. The only way honestly to insure all savings deposits in the United States is to have the wealth of the United States behind the guarantee."

Bruère gave this long thought. Finally he said, "If we're

to convince our trustees that you're right, we ought to have a way of weighing all the advantages of the FDIC against its disadvantages. In other words, a pro and con document. Could you draw one up? You will be working with a committee of trustees made up of Ward Melville, Rolland Hamilton, and Frank Polk."

Schwulst at once agreed. The report he prepared was destined to become historic. It was later reprinted at the request of many other thrift institutions and was studied by the officers of hundreds of mutual savings banks.

Since its impact was so extensive and since its influence proved to be so strong, some of the major points of the document bear repetition. At the outset it said:

> The facts and considerations upon which the Committee's recommendations are based may be summarized as follows:
>
> (a) Many depositors of savings banks believe they are protected by Federal Deposit Insurance, because that is the only kind of deposit insurance they have been told about in the public press and otherwise. It would seem advisable to provide depositors with the type of protection they *believe* they have, particularly since it appears to be the best available kind of protection.
>
> (b) In the public mind, Federal Deposit Insurance is identified with the Federal Government, and therefore banks enjoying such insurance have the maximum protection against the loss of depositor-confidence so long as depositors have confidence in their Government. Behind Federal Deposit Insurance there is substantial Government financial backing in addition to moral backing.
>
> (c) Nearly 13,500 banks in the country are members of the FDIC. Only a few hundred banks (nearly all of them savings banks) are not members. In view of the prevailing uncertainties arising out of the War, it would seem to be advisable to have all the banks of the country bound together in a common plan for the provision of protection for their depositors.
>
> (d) The FDIC is overwhelmingly stronger [than the Mutual Savings Bank Fund] in relation to any emergency

situation that might confront The Bowery Savings Bank. The FDIC (on December 31, 1941) had approximately $473,000,000 in cash and government securities, a sum equal to more than 100 percent of the deposits in The Bowery Savings Bank on that date. By comparison the cash and governments in the Mutual Fund on that date amounted to only 10 percent of the deposits in The Bowery Savings Bank. . . .

It would appear to be the obligation of the Trustees of the Bank to provide its depositors with the best available type of deposit insurance. It is conceivable that under certain circumstances the Trustees might be criticized for *not* having provided it.

(e) Mortgage and real estate investments in New York City and Westchester have been severely hit by the depression, and it appears that they face additional problems as a result of new conditions created by the War. This is another reason why savings banks in this area should avail themselves of the general protection afforded by the FDIC.

(f) The annual assessment paid by this Bank into the Mutual Fund, of which it is at present a member, amounts to $450,000. This is at the annual rate of $\frac{1}{10}$ of one percent of deposits. The corresponding annual assessment paid to the FDIC amounts to $375,000 at the annual rate of $\frac{1}{12}$ of one percent. The saving to the Bank would therefore be $75,000 a year.

There followed in the report analysis after analysis, comparing the government's offer to that of the self-regulated Mutual Fund. For example, membership in the Mutual Fund exposed the bank to additional emergency assessments that could amount to $2.7 million. No such assessments were threatened by the FDIC.

In spite of all these contentions, there were surely some advantages the Mutual Fund retained—at least on paper—and the report gave these unbiased consideration. The Mutual Fund professed to insure *all* deposits, whereas FDIC, at the time, granted coverage only up to $5,000. That meant, as the Schwulst appraisal pointed out, that "Somewhere between $20 million and $25 million of deposits in The Bowery Savings Bank would not be covered by the FDIC."

Then, too, "Whereas a savings bank can withdraw from the Mutual Fund without difficulty or embarrassment," the report noted, "its entrance into the FDIC is a marriage from which there is likely to be no practical way of obtaining a divorce. . . . There is no reason to believe, however, that this alliance would be unduly burdensome (it has not proven to be so to other members of the FDIC). It would seem to be unwarranted to assume that the Corporation would single out a particular member for arbitrary or capricious treatment—particularly if the management of the bank is competent."

After weighing all such factors, the committee of trustees—Messrs. Melville, Hamilton, and Polk, together with Schwulst—reached this conclusion:

> The Committee has carefully considered the advantages and disadvantages of membership in the Federal Deposit Insurance Corporation and it has reached the general conclusion that the advantages outweigh the disadvantages. In the light of the many uncertainties which now prevail and which may prevail into the indefinite future, it appears advisable for the banking institutions of the country to be united in a strong, common bond of protection for their depositors. . . . It is clear to the satisfaction of the Committee that FDIC can provide for the depositors of a large bank, such as The Bowery Savings Bank, much more adequate protection against all hazards, both seen and unseen, than the Mutual Fund can provide.
>
> Federal Deposit Insurance, because it is well known to and trusted by the public, affords the most effective insurance against the loss of depositor-confidence, and this is the real hazard which deposit insurance should meet. *The Committee has therefore recommended that The Bowery Savings Bank apply for membership in the Federal Deposit Insurance Corporation and withdraw from the Mutual Fund.*

If I treat the FDIC issue in some detail, it is because FDIC has turned out to be one of the most important protective measures ever devised for the deposits of the American people. The knowledge that deposits are secure has forestalled runs on banks. There has not been a run like those of past years since the FDIC was instituted. (Insurance coverage on each individual account amounted to $20,000 in 1974, and legislation was later passed to increase the coverage to the present $100,000.)

This must be said for Henry Bruère: Once he was convinced by the committee's report that joining the FDIC was the right and intelligent thing to do, he campaigned for that step with courage and determination. He soon won the support of his own board—only to discover, in dismay, that almost every other mutual savings bank in the state refused to have any connection with FDIC!

All the more disturbing was the fact that Bruère had recently served as president of the Savings Bank Association of the State of New York. Now he found himself in disagreement with the majority of his fellow members.

To give formal consideration to an invitation to the New York City savings banks to become members of the FDIC, the Association called a special meeting—a step which Superintendent of Banks Elliot V. Bell had recommended. More than a hundred savings bankers and their lawyers gathered in the Sert Room of the Waldorf-Astoria Hotel. Before the meeting was formally called to order, those opposed to membership in the FDIC went among their colleagues, noisily urging a negative vote. At the same time Schwulst, with equal fervor, talked to all who would listen about the importance of *joining* the FDIC. One banker, Myron Short, then president of the state Savings Bank Association, bitterly accused him of being a crusader for a wrong cause.

"It was as excited and divided a crowd as you can imagine," Schwulst said. "At moments the clash seemed to leave Henry Bruère shaken, mopping his forehead. Yet he did not yield to pressures. He clung to what he believed was the proper course to take. Our own attorney, DeCourcey Fales of Cadwalader, Wickersham, and Taft, turned against us. As vociferous as everybody else, Fales insisted that The Bowery should go along with the opinion of the majority. Bruère refused. When Fales swung around to argue with me, I also refused. It must have amazed many a banker to see us clashing with our own counsel."

The battle of the Waldorf-Astoria did not go to The Bowery. That afternoon Bruère and Schwulst could not persuade all the others present to concur in the wisdom of membership in the FDIC. Most bankers continued to maintain that they feared the possibility of federal interference.

And so, after the Waldorf meeting, The Bowery Savings Bank, acting independently, sought membership in the Federal Deposit Insurance Corporation.

And the letters began to arrive. Edward A. Richards, president of the East New York Savings Bank, wrote:

> All of us, I am sure, regret very much that the largest savings bank in America and the one over which the former president of our Association presides, should have found it desirable to ask admission to the Federal Deposit Insurance Corporation.

Richards correctly described it as "a step which vitally affects every savings bank in America." Others seemed to wonder if there were hidden *personal* explanations for The Bowery's "radical" decision. John B. Corwin, president of the Newburgh Savings Bank, wrote:

I would greatly appreciate it if you would advise me in strict confidence either your personal reasons, or those advanced by your committee, for concluding that under present conditions Federal Deposit Insurance is more desirable than insurance by the Mutual Fund.

Of course, there were letters of support, too. Bruère and Schwulst *had* persuaded some bankers to share their convictions. It was Henry Bruère alone, however, who went to Washington to confer with Chairman Leo T. Crowley of the FDIC regarding the bank's admission to the Corporation.

Once that was consummated, it was inevitable that others should follow. The very fact that The Bowery could now advertise that its depositors' funds were insured by an agency of the government would have compelled others to join so they could make the same claim as a matter of competitive self-protection. But there was no need for them to make this decision; it was made by Superintendent of Banks Elliot Bell, who personally induced all New York State savings banks to join the FDIC.

"One of my happiest memories," one Bowery veteran told me, "is the knowledge that our bank was among the leaders of those that brought the savings bank industry into FDIC. It was, in my opinion, one of the most significant and important achievements of the whole Bruère administration. It strengthened the future security of every savings bank in America—and of every depositor on their books."

19
THE MORTGAGE
CONFERENCE

Good times or bad, America has always yearned for the relief of laughter. During the early 1930s you could be sure that every evening millions of people would turn from the problems of depression to listen gratefully to the broadcast problems of *Amos and Andy* or *The Goldbergs* or *Fibber McGee and Molly*. Later in the evening they would concentrate on the hilarities of Milton Berle, Jack Benny, or Fred Allen.

Henry Bruère was different from the masses only

in the *type* of entertainment he sought as escape from reality. "Bruère loved Wagnerian opera, especially *Parsifal*," Robert Sparks once reminisced. "When there was a matinee performance of *Parsifal* at the Metropolitan, he would hurry there to attend a single act, then rush back to his desk."

If his spirits needed this kind of revivification it was because, during his long term as president and chairman of the bank, he managed to become involved in more crises than had any of his predecessors.

For instance, he was one of 33 distinguished men—all executives of leading banks, trust companies, title companies, and insurance companies—who were stunned when their institutions and some of them as individuals (including Bruère) were threatened with criminal charges. Their cases actually went to a grand jury. Had they all been tried and convicted, and had the individuals been sent to jail, the United States would have been confronted with one of the most disruptive financial traumas in its history.

This terrifying situation resulted from a speech which Bruère delivered, innocently enough, as early as December 17, 1931 before the Savings Bank Association of New York. No one ever doubted that his intentions were wholly idealistic, aimed at serving the best interests of the American public as well as of American financial institutions. He proposed the establishment of "a mortgage institute" which, by the cooperative action of lending institutions, would establish the mortgage lending business in New York on a "scientific, coordinated, and thoroughly efficient basis."

"By doing this," he said, "we shall make a contribution of great value to the stabilization of America's economic order . . . and we shall more rapidly restore the country's general condition to one of stable prosperity."

Could anything be wrong about such a proposal? Could anyone criticize its statesmanlike objectives? Coming in the midst of the country's financial woes, it won the praise of all who heard it.

For more than a year the idea was discussed among bankers and others interested in mortgage lending. Finally, in December of 1932, Robert L. Hoguet, president of the Emigrant Savings Bank, invited a group of colleagues to a luncheon at which he suggested that Bruère's original proposal be implemented. What he hoped to found was "an informal conference body to discuss common problems, particularly those emergency problems precipitated by the depression."

By unanimous agreement of those at the luncheon, a special committee was appointed to form what was to be known as a "Mortgage Conference." Its purpose was indisputably laudable. As described by the special committee, the primary aim of the organization would be:

> To influence united and concurrent action on important problems of emergency affecting the present mortgage situation which are not being dealt with by other agencies; and to consider measures for the advancement of improved and more standardized practices for lending on bond and mortgage.
>
> Conditions demand that every practical and possible effort be made for the permanent preservation and protection of real estate values and of income. It would seem reasonable that many of the questions with which mortgage lending institutions are struggling today could be treated more comprehensively and effectively if they were studied by joint effort and dealt with by common agreement rather than by independent action.

With some of the city's most eminent bankers in attendance, and Henry Bruère serving as chairman, the motion to create the Mortgage Conference was unanimously adopted. Considering its lofty purpose, no one could have objected except, perhaps, a good lawyer. The gentlemen present forgot to consult a good lawyer.

They organized their association and soon had 37 member institutions. When the term of the first president, Philip Benson, expired, Orrin C. Lester, a vice president of The Bowery, became its head. Several financial writers asked him more clearly to define the purposes of the Mortgage Conference. Its Articles of Association described the organization as intended "to protect and further all interests in real property and in mortgage investments through cooperative action." Could Mr. Lester clarify the meaning of this?

Lester tried to satisfy the curiosity of the press with several releases. The first said:

> The Conference is intended to perform a service heretofore almost wholly neglected. It is designed primarily as a forum of mortgage lending institutions for discussion of their common problems of real estate financing and any collateral matters which affect the security of real estate investments and the stability of real estate values. . . . It is of the first importance that values shall be restored, rents stabilized, and the whole problem of recovery dealt with in a highly responsible way.

Another release asserted:

> Mr. Lester believes that the old system of everybody for himself and devil take the hindmost must yield to the more modern and intelligent procedure of cooperative thinking and common protection.

All this sounded high-minded and irreproachable. Nevertheless, the press still asked questions. How did the Conference propose to deal with its problems?

Lester replied in a third release:

The Mortgage Conference is not a code-making agency. It is essentially an organized effort to advance institutional cooperation and to eliminate unnecessary and unsound competition. [Mark that last phrase. It was to haunt many men.] It is designed progressively to bring institutions to better understand each other's conceptions and practices.

After that, the press seemed for a long time to lose interest in the undertaking. There were too many more urgent matters to occupy the attention of newspapers, aside from the extraordinary innovations of the New Deal. Overseas, one saw the alarming aggressions of Adolph Hitler in Germany and the threats of his posturing partner in Italy. In the end, there was the fury of the war itself, with American troops and munitions pouring across the Atlantic. All such events were far more important than the Mortgage Conference, and so it was allowed to follow its course, almost unnoticed, throughout the years of combat. In war as in peace, it continued to disseminate information to its members. It tried to maintain the ethical standards it had announced at the start.

For more than a dozen years, in fact, the Mortgage Conference was unmolested. It served its members as a collector and disseminator of information. It issued a periodic *Bulletin*. It recorded major applications for mortgages, those granted and those rejected. It revealed and berated practices that were unethical. In March of 1945— fully twelve years after its inception—the Conference entered into a "servicing agreement" with the Savings Banks Trust Company, which would thereafter maintain all its records.

It was at about this time that a builder, whose unsavory reputation had made it difficult for him to obtain loans, complained to the Department of Justice. He insisted he was a victim of discrimination.

Whoever the man was to whom the complaint came—

some minor official, possibly, with an idle afternoon at his disposal—he wearily read the Articles of Association that governed the activities of the Conference. But slowly his casual attitude gave way to the excitement of discovery. He became more intent. He read and studied. He sent for *Bulletins* issued by the Conference. Finally he hurried into the office of Lee Loevinger, head of the Anti-Trust Division of the Department of Justice.

"Mr. Loevinger," he said, "here's an organization that's in direct violation of the Sherman Anti-Trust Act."

⊙∽⊙

The case was quietly investigated by the Department of Justice. The staff of the Mortgage Conference probably thought this was a routine examination of records, for they raised no alarm. None of the implicated bankers had any warning that the case was being rushed to the Grand Jury for the Southern District of New York, where criminal indictments were sought. And the leaders of the "conspiracy" were named as Henry Bruère of The Bowery Savings Bank and Philip Benson, president of the Dime Savings Bank of Brooklyn.

"By the time the members of the Conference finally did learn of what was taking place," said Earl Schwulst, "the grand jury was on the point of handing down the indictments. Consternation seized Bruère and Benson. Both men were eminent community leaders. It was inconceivable in their minds and in the minds of all who knew them that they could have conspired to commit or did commit criminal acts, or that they could involve their prestigious institutions in such acts."

They were not alone in their amazement. Every institution in the Mortgage Conference, 37 in all, found

194

itself being charged with participation in a criminal conspiracy. Among the allegations made to the grand jury were assertions that there had been illegal collusion to:

1. Restrain competition
2. Fix interest rates on mortgages
3. Dictate amortization policies
4. Unite in appraising property values
5. Discriminate against racial groups
6. Dictate where new construction was to be permitted
7. Agree on fixing rents
8. Establish uniform practices in dealing with other groups
9. Compel nonmembers to follow Conference policies
10. Exchange confidential information
11. Coordinate mortgage commitments

Once the news of their danger spread, bewildered telephone calls flashed among bankers. What was to be done? Understandably, no one felt more shocked than Henry Bruère himself. It had been at his suggestion that the Mortgage Conference had been organized in the first place. Was his leadership now to confront 37 leading American financial institutions with the possibility of conviction on criminal charges and some of their officers with the possibility of jail sentences?

For advice, the harried Bowery president called in Sims McGrath, a senior partner of Cadwalader, Wickersham, and Taft. McGrath studied all the allegations, then shook his head. In his opinion, he said, "The bank would find it difficult to interpose a successful defense in a court trial." In brief, McGrath saw no way of circumventing the threat of grand jury action.

"That," said Schwulst, who was present at the meeting, "was the end of participation by the bank's general counsel in the Mortgage Conference matter. They formally withdrew, and Paul Windels, a member of The Bowery board, was named as substitute counsel with Oliver and Donnally, counsel for the State Association."

At this critical point, Schwulst suggested to Bruère: "Let me go to Washington to see what can be done." His experience in the capital, plus the fact that he knew many government officials who would be concerned, made it possible that he might find a way out of the situation. Bruère instantly agreed.

First Schwulst flew to Chicago to confer with Leo Crowley, the former FDIC chairman. Then he went to Washington to talk with Maple Harl, the current chairman; with Jake Vardaman of the Federal Reserve Board; and with John Snyder, Secretary of the Treasury. All were either old friends or former associates of his in the Reconstruction Finance Corporation. They urged him to discuss the problem directly with Attorney General Tom Clark. Since the Department of Justice had initiated this criminal action, only the Department of Justice could rescind it.

Schwulst had never before met the Attorney General. But he recalled that years before, in Texas, Tom Clark's father-in-law had run for governor, and his campaign had been managed by a close friend of the Schwulst family. Also, Clark's father-in-law had given Schwulst one of his first jobs. All this helped to create a more personal atmosphere.

"Attorney General Clark knew something about the case," Schwulst told me, "but he was not familiar with its details. I called his attention to the fact that Section 10 of the Banking Law of New York proscribes 'unsound and destructive competition.' The institutions that had formed the Conference, following the ordeal of the early days of the depression, were well aware of the law. They were not trying to suppress competition in any way. They were simply trying to correct practices which had resulted in losses of many millions of depositors' money. I suggested further that criminal indictments might seriously disturb the depositors of savings banks and might cause runs on these institutions. Such a result would clearly not be in the public interest, and some other solution ought to be found."

Thereupon Schwulst analyzed each of the many criminal allegations that were being presented to the grand jury. "It was true, of course," he had to concede, "that the members of the Mortage Conference had for years been exchanging information through their *Bulletin*. But there was neither a criminal act nor a criminal intent in this. It was no more unusual or reprehensible than the information exchanged by doctors in medical journals, or by the members of any trade association. Throughout the existence of the Conference there had not been a single act in restraint of trade, not a single instance of any attempt to fix prices or to destroy competition, though there might have been loose talk that gave a contrary impression."

Nevertheless, the Attorney General pointed out, the *potential* for such criminal procedures lay in the Mortgage Conference's Articles of Association. That was true, Schwulst granted. But the Conference members had never taken advantage of that potential. Surely they should not be held accountable for what they had never done.

At that, the Attorney General sank back in his chair, gazed at the ceiling, and did some silent thinking.

"Finally," Schwulst said, "Clark suggested that a civil rather than a criminal action might be the proper course for the government to take, and that a consent decree dissolving the Mortgage Conference might offer a fair and just way out. He further suggested that if the Superintendent of Banks would be willing to appear before the grand jury and state that in his judgment the defendants had had no criminal intent, and perhaps had had some justification for forming the Mortgage Conference, the grand jury might weigh that view very carefully and come up with a finding that would fully serve the public interest, eliminate the Mortgage Conference, and save the banks from the possibility of depositor-disturbance."

Schwulst could not have asked for a better solution. He hurried back to New York. There he, Henry Bruère, and Philip Benson held an immediate meeting with Superintendent of Banks Elliot Bell. The Superintendent appreciated, perhaps even dreaded, the consequences of criminal indictments. He agreed to help, and promptly appeared before the grand jury.

Since the prosecution, too, had been made aware of the Attorney General's recommendation, a civil action was quickly substituted for the criminal action, to the relief and delight of everybody involved (except those grand jurors who might have felt their time had been wasted in the original effort to obtain criminal indictments).

But the criminal trials were avoided. A consent decree dissolved the ill-fated Mortgage Conference. And 37 relieved bankers, insurance executives, and their associates could once more breathe easily and turn their attention back to the normal operations of their institutions.

20
ON RAISING
$100 MILLION

One of the most illuminating ways of studying a man's career is to talk with his wife. Her observations, especially if she can be objective as well as sympathetic, reveal many professional aspects which the man himself is apt to take for granted; or else he glosses over them as a matter of modesty.

The wife of one banking veteran told me, "I came to regard the bank as my husband's other wife. He gave it not only his days but endless evenings. The higher he rose in executive status, the more demanding the job became. He had to represent the bank on committees, in seminars, in appearances at government investigations. He was asked to write articles for banking journals. He was invited to speak before all kinds of groups, not only in financial circles but at colleges and even before women's clubs whose members were interested in the intricacies of the investment world. Then there were charity drives, municipal activities, real estate conferences. How I yearned for his vacations when I could claim him for myself!"

Though she spoke of her own husband, what she said is applicable to many bankers—all the more so if they happen to be associated with a large institution. The officers who served The Bowery during the years of World War II—especially Henry Bruère, Earl Schwulst, and Robert Sparks—offer dramatic confirmation of the lady's observations.

Bruère, apart from being president of the Savings Bank Association of the State of New York, was appointed by Mayor Fiorello LaGuardia to the city's Defense Council. Later he became one of the sponsors of a committee to preserve the Metropolitan Opera as a national civic enterprise. Almost simultaneously, he was elected a trustee of the New York Public Library and of the Henry Street Settlement. He was named to be the liaison between the U.S. Treasury and the nation's thrift institutions, with the responsibility of promoting the sale of defense bonds and stamps. He was appointed to the War Finance Committee, and in 1944 he was asked by the City Fusion Party to become a candidate for the office of Mayor of New York, an invitation he declined. All these are but a sampling of the activities that demanded his time outside the bank.

Similarly, Schwulst found himself engaged in countless enterprises. As executive vice president of The Bowery and a member of its board of trustees, he appeared before congressional committees to discuss a wide spectrum of financial problems. He urged the Federal Housing Administration to raise the limitation of its insured loans on individual apartment projects from $3 million to $6 million. He asked that the government (state and local as well as federal) subsidize the construction of low-rent housing projects, for which the need was desperate; as treasurer of the Regional Plan Association, he was deeply concerned about the building of residential and industrial communities. In 1946 he became vice president of the National Association of Mutual Savings Banks; in a year he became the Association's president. Eventually he served also as president of the state Savings Bank Association. Locally he was named to a number of national and municipal commissions. In time he became head of the Greater New York Fund, which raised money to help meet the needs of health and welfare agencies and voluntary hospitals in New York City.

As for Robert Sparks, in addition to serving on civic committees, he was given a leave of absence from the bank to become director of the Treasury's national defense savings staff, which had been organized to implement the sale of war bonds and stamps through savings banks. Even after his retirement from The Bowery, new duties came to Sparks. He was sent by the National Association of Mutual Savings Banks to head a bank in Alaska which required experienced guidance to lift it out of its troubles.

One could lengthen the public-service list with the experiences of other Bowery officials of that era—William Lumsden, Walter J. Tietjen, James and Robert Stenhouse, William H. Switzer, R. Benson Ray, Peter I. Menzies, and many more. Bankers in other cities had comparable public duties—and still do today. One of them told me, "The management of money sometimes seems to me to be the least time-consuming of my obligations."

During the war years all such obligations were multiplied by patriotic demands. In their efforts to stimulate the sale of war bonds, Bowery executives set up counters in the bank, selling savings stamps as well as bonds. They organized and managed a payroll deduction plan for funds that would go directly into bonds for defense needs. At the same time, aside from their services to the nation, they instituted new projects for the welfare of The Bowery's employees. Well-meant and praiseworthy as these were, not all proved successful.

One notable failure was the attempt of the officers to provide for their personnel, through the Aetna Life Insurance Company, a health insurance program. It was intended to cover all members of every employee's family. What eventually happened to it was wryly described in a report to the president: "Plan went bankrupt. Bowery employees produced too many babies."

❦

For more than a century, the mortgage business had been the chief concern of thrift institutions. It had been repeatedly undermined by circumstances the savings banks could not control—like the importance of channeling funds into the war effort rather than into the building of homes; or because competition for deposits by other institutions, including the government itself, had eroded the amount of cash that thrift institutions could lend; or because of losses incurred through a nationwide spate of foreclosures.

Then, abruptly, there was a new and tragic uncertainty to face.

At 5:47 P.M. on April 12, 1945, a shaken press secretary at the White House telephoned the Associated Press, the United Press, and the International News Service on a simultaneous conference call. "This is Steve Early," he said, and his voice broke. "I have a flash. The President died suddenly this afternoon at Warm Springs, Georgia."

It came as abruptly as that.

Throughout the world, newspapers recorded the events of that tragic day. The Washington press told of Harry Truman's rush from the office of Speaker Sam Rayburn, where he had been chatting when the news came. He went directly to the upper floor of the White House to comfort Eleanor Roosevelt. Was there anything he could do for her? Mrs. Roosevelt's historic answer was: "Harry, is there anything *we* can do for *you?* You are the one in trouble now."

No one could foresee how Harry Truman would handle the problems he was inheriting. At the height of the war, he was being catapulted into the responsibilities of Commander-in-Chief of all the Armed Forces. The country—indeed, the world—looked to him for leadership, for decisiveness. If bankers were among the many men who were apprehensive about the future, that was understandable. Bankers knew that Roosevelt had always demonstrated deep concern for the strength of the American banking system. It had to serve as the strongbox of all the Allies. Now the question was: What would Truman do? What sort of man was this untried President?

Within hours after he was sworn into office, his caliber as a human being was revealed to half a dozen people in the Office of War Information; revealed through circumstances I have never read in the writings of any historian.

At about 6:15 that evening, a secretary at the White House telephoned the OWI. The new President, the secretary said, was expected to address the nation at 8:00

P.M. The White House staff was steeped in such grief and distress that no one there could prepare a speech for Mr. Truman. Would the writers at the Office of War Information compose a brief address designed to reassure the country?

Elmer Davis, head of the agency, was in London. It fell to those on duty in Washington to write the speech. Because I was among them, I shared the general dismay. All of us had the same thought: At a moment of such profound emotional stress, how could the President of the United States utter words that had been prepared for him by others? If he could not speak out of his own heart, ought he not to remain silent?

The speech was duly written. Noble Cathcart, the OWI's liaison with the White House, put the three-page manuscript into a briefcase and left to take it to the President. The rest of us sat silent and depressed, waiting to hear the eight o'clock speech.

Within half an hour, Cathcart was back with his briefcase. "The President," he reported, "refused even to look at the speech. Apparently he was unaware that we had been asked to write it. He said that until he knew exactly what *he* wanted to say, he would make no address at all—and right now the only thing he wanted the country to know was that the war would be pursued with all the vigor of which we are capable."

It was as if a brilliant and glorious light had broken through darkness. We all rose, reassured and proud. We knew then that the United States had a President worthy of the office, a man who would not be pushed around.

But no one else had witnessed this disclosure of the Truman character, and businessmen continued to worry. Savings bankers in particular had cause to view the future with doubts. Throughout the years of depression, when people simply could not pay their bills, the number of foreclosures had been devastating. What would happen under this new President?

As early as 1941, The Bowery had originated a plan to ease the burden on hard-pressed mortgage holders. Its advantages were outlined to the board of trustees in these terms:

1. The mortgagor would receive the advantage of a revised interest rate, ¼ percent less than the original 4¼ percent rate.

2. The mortgagor would be required to make fewer interest payments on the principal. As an example, he would pay off a 25-year mortgage (which was typical of the thousands in effect) in 22 years; a 20-year mortgage in 17 years and 11 months.

3. The mortgagor's interest would cost less. On a 25-year mortgage, paid off in 22 years, he would save as much as $139.32 on each $1,000 of principal (or $2,786.40 on a $20,000 loan); on a 20-year loan, paid off in 17 years and 11 months, he would save as much as $101 interest on each $1,000 of principal.

This plan was only one of many expedients that The Bowery, as well as other banks, had adopted to meet the foreclosure crisis. And the granting of *new* mortgage loans remained difficult as long as the government continued to preempt, for wartime expenditures, much of the money that might have gone into the construction of new homes. (After the war, in 1947, Bruère delivered an analytical speech to a group of economists. In it he revealed the fact that some 63 percent of the assets of all savings banks were now lodged not in mortgages but in government bonds. "These," he said, "have replaced mortgages as our chief investment concern.")

Was this good? Bad? The only answer was that it had been essential.

Afterwards, with World War II relegated to history, Bruère hoped the thrift institutions could concentrate on their original mortgage purpose. To do that successfully, to meet current demands for loans, they needed more funds. And the president of the bank saw a way, with a single act, to add over $100 million in deposits to The Bowery's resources.

What he proposed was a merger with the North River Savings Bank.

This institution, founded in 1866, had an excellent location on 34th Street and Seventh Avenue—excellent because it was adjacent to the Pennsylvania Railroad Station. Considering the crowds that passed the North River Savings Bank every day, a merger would serve to give The Bowery its fourth office in a spot that could attract thousands of new accounts. It was convenient not only for commuters but for all those who worked in the surrounding garment industry.

Bruère and Schwulst, together with other officers of the bank, had already held a number of preliminary conversations with executives of the North River Savings Bank, especially with its president, Harris A. Dunn. They had also investigated the attitude of the state Banking Department toward such a merger. Everywhere they had encountered good will, approval, and a cooperative spirit. And all these factors swayed the board of trustees toward its own consent.

On a winter afternoon, Harris Dunn came to Bruère's office for a final discussion of terms. As they talked, The Bowery's president noticed that Dunn's eyes constantly rose to study Bruère's bald head. This became annoying. (Bruère was so sensitive about his baldness that once, when he posed for a studio photograph, he insisted on wearing a hat.) He was understandably irked when he saw Harris Dunn so fascinated by his shiny head.

At last the conference ended. The two men rose to shake hands. And again Dunn's glance rose. But this time, Bruère saw in surprise, it was not fixed on his bald head. It was focused on a painting that hung on the paneled wall just behind Bruère's seat.

"I've been admiring that picture," Dunn said. "It's beautiful."

It was indeed beautiful—a misty landscape painted by Claude Monet. Henry Bruère had brought it from his home to his office so that he might enjoy its presence throughout the day. The relief of knowing Dunn had been interested in the picture, not in the baldness, brought their meeting to a most cordial end.

When the merger between the two banks had been consummated, the arrangement not only added $109 million in deposits to The Bowery's assets; it brought in thousands of accounts and an experienced group of bank officers. Harris Dunn himself was made vice chairman of The Bowery. An impressive office was prepared for him, furnished as elegantly as those of Bruère and Schwulst. Along with Dunn came—among trustees and capable North River officers—John W. Larsen, destined one day to become The Bowery's president.

On the February morning when Dunn arrived to occupy his new office, he eased himself into his commodious leather desk chair, leaned back—and abruptly straightened to stare. There, on the wall opposite him, hung the Claude Monet painting he had admired. He was still blinking at it, unbelieving, when Henry Bruère entered, smiling at Dunn's astonishment.

"Couldn't think of a better way," the president said, "to welcome you to your new office."

That day, February 15, 1949, every newspaper in New York carried a full-page advertisement announcing:

> The Bowery Savings Bank and the North River Savings Bank were merged today. Total deposits of the greater Bowery Savings Bank are now more than $787,000,000. The new Bowery starts with more than 500,000 depositors.

The advertisement added, among other things:

> The purpose of the merger of these two old and well-known banks is to permit increased service to its present and prospective depositors. . . . Since the war [World War II] the two banks now consolidated have financed 29,351 homes of all types in the amount of $176,371,350. This total includes 26,191 homes financed by $162,940,218 in Federal Housing Administration-insured and Veterans' loans.
>
> The greater Bowery Savings Bank will strive to . . . aid the community ever to improve as a place in which to live, to work, and to raise useful, healthy, and happy families.

Soon thereafter, advertisements named some of the many distinguished people who were Bowery depositors. Their pictures, plus brief comments on the wisdom of saving, featured Eleanor Roosevelt, Dale Carnegie, Lowell Thomas, Kate Smith, Frances Perkins, John Golden, Grantland Rice, Nanette Fabray, Russel Crouse, Faith Baldwin, and many others of note. The intent, of course, was to make potential depositors feel, "That's good company to be in; perhaps I too should save at The Bowery." The campaign worked well.

Indeed, it worked so well and brought in so many new depositors that Henry Bruère was inspired to seek ways for even greater growth. Continued expansion, he now realized, would require the establishment of more and more branches. Yet this was the kind of program on which the Banking Department still looked with dubious eyes.

How, then, could the Department's attitude be liberalized? How could the savings banks achieve the same right to open new branches that the commercial banks already enjoyed? The first step toward such a consummation, Bruère must have decided, was to win the support of public opinion. In the speeches he made, he discussed the need for branching so frequently that *The New York Sun* finally sent a reporter to interview him on the subject. The following day *The Sun* published this story:

BRUÈRE VIEWS BRANCH OFFICES AS NEEDED BY SAVINGS BANKS

Bowery Bank Head Says Institutions Should Be Permitted to Expand Home Mortgage Lending

Savings banks, being past their period of readjustment to the depression of the 1930s, should now look forward to a period of expanding their services to depositors in a manner that will fully capitalize their "magnificent inheritance" of depositor confidence, Henry Bruère, President of The Bowery Savings Bank, said in an interview with a New York Sun reporter today.

"Despite all the shifts of population and the development of new areas of growth," he said, "the majority of depositors still make personal visits to their savings banks, and most of them do a lot of walking." That is why, he explained, savings banks want to open branches that will make banking more convenient for their depositors, present and prospective. . . .

"I have suggested to the Banking Department that they make a study with a view to determining where branches would be desirable and feasible," said Bruère. "These locations could then be assigned in some fair plan of the Department's devising. What we are interested in is a plan to make savings banks easily accessible to everybody."

His interviews, like his speeches on branching and his admonitions to legislators, brought no immediate results. But then, neither did the efforts of any other savings banker. They were joined in what seemed a hopeless crusade, and its repeated failures must have brought deep discouragement.

Nevertheless, Henry Bruère persisted in seeking growth through branching. That he so doggedly persevered in spite of repeated setbacks was in itself noteworthy, for he was by nature an impatient man. He had little tolerance for failure, either his own or that of anyone else. This impatience applied to petty, personal endeavors as well as to great industrial efforts. Robert Stenhouse, who was then treasurer of the bank, remembered an occasion when Bruère was given a set of golf clubs by a friend. He had never before played golf. It seemed to him that it must be easy to hit a ball in the desired direction. So he went out on a golf course in Toronto, played for the first time in his life, and discovered after four or five holes that he could *not* control the flight of a ball as he had planned to control it. His patience did not endure even to the sixth hole. Utterly disgusted, he turned and gave the clubs to his caddy. "They're yours," he said, and walked off the course.

As far as anyone knows, he never again played golf. He was too impatient to give time to perfecting his skill. That would require a persistence which Henry Bruère lacked.

Therefore it was all the more remarkable that he continued, on the bank's behalf, to ignore failure and go on pressing for new branches. He was still trying on July 1, 1949, when the bank entered a new era.

That was the date on which Henry Bruère was elevated to chairman and Earl Bryan Schwulst became the fifteenth president of The Bowery Savings Bank.

FIRST REPORT

OF THE

BOWERY SAVINGS' BANK,

IN THE CITY OF NEW-YORK.

TO THE HONORABLE THE LEGISLATURE OF THE STATE OF
NEW-YORK, AND THE HONORABLE THE MAYOR,
ALDERMEN, AND COMMONALTY OF THE
CITY OF NEW-YORK.

PURSUANT TO THE ACT OF INCORPORATION.

NEW-YORK.

PRINTED BY HAMMOND WALLIS.

1835.

PORT

GS' BANK,

-YORK,

EIGHT HUNDRED
R.

---

act, entitled "An act
Bank," the Trustees
now beg leave to present their First Report, as follows,

First.—That the Bank commenced its operations on
Monday the second day of June last, and has been opened on Mondays and Saturdays of each week, from five to
eight o'clock, P. M.

Second.—That the Trustees have received, from Ten
Hundred and Thirty-six depositors, from the second of
June to the twenty-ninth of December, inclusive, the sum
of seventy-two thousand, seven hundred and forty-two
dollars, in the following manner, viz.

Lamp-lighter,	1
Lamp-maker,	1
Locksmiths,	4
Looking-glass maker,	1
Looking-glass frame maker,	1
Livery-stable keeper,	1
Machinists,	6
Manufacturers,	6
Marble cutters,	4
Marble polishers,	3
Masons,	32
Merchants,	7
Milkman,	1
Milliners,	9
Musician,	1
Nurses,	3
Oystermen,	3
Packers,	2
Painters,	22
Paper-maker,	1
Paper-ruler,	1
Pedlars,	2
Pavior,	1
Piano-forte makers,	5
Pilot,	1
Philosophical instrument makers,	2
Plane-makers,	2
Plasterers,	11
Physicians,	8
Plumbers,	3
Pencil-case maker,	1
Pocket-book maker,	1
Police officers,	3
Porters,	4
Portrait-painter,	1
Printers,	18
Quill-dressers,	4
Rope-maker,	1
Sail-makers,	3
Saddlers,	3
Sash-maker,	1
Sawyer,	1

Hatters,	14
Hat-trimmers,	4
Hinge-maker,	1
Hostler,	1
Hucksters,	3
Jewellers,	11
Joiners,	6
Keepers of prison,	2
Laborers,	44

The Bowery's new home on its original site (c. 1855).

Dividend day at The Bowery Savings Bank. From a woodcut in *Harper's Weekly*, July 23, 1870.

The Bowery, "busiest street in New York" (c. 1903).

Courtesy of The Bowery Savings Bank Archives

Making the most of an advertising opportunity: In 1932 The Bowery was the first to apply advertising posters to outdoor scaffolding, which was erected in front of the 42nd Street office.

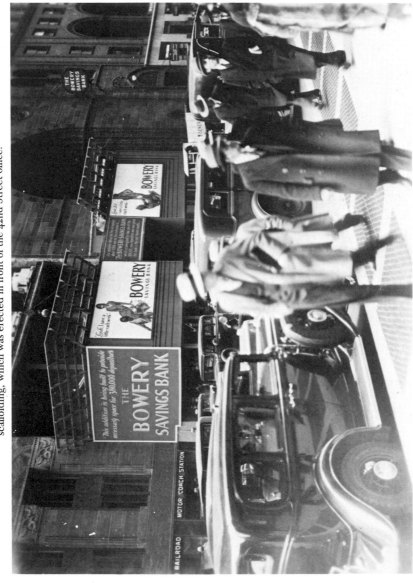

A Bowery ad in Times Square, 1938.

Courtesy of The Bowery Savings Bank Archives

An advertising poster inspired by the 1939 World's Fair.

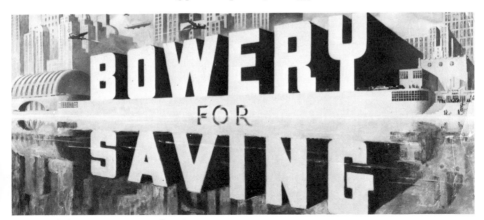

Courtesy of The Bowery Savings Bank Archives

The Bowery's first renewal project in Harlem—"stateliness instead of slums" (1953).

The magnificent bronze doors of the 42nd Street office, now used as interior wall decorations.

The inauguration of The Bowery Travel Service.

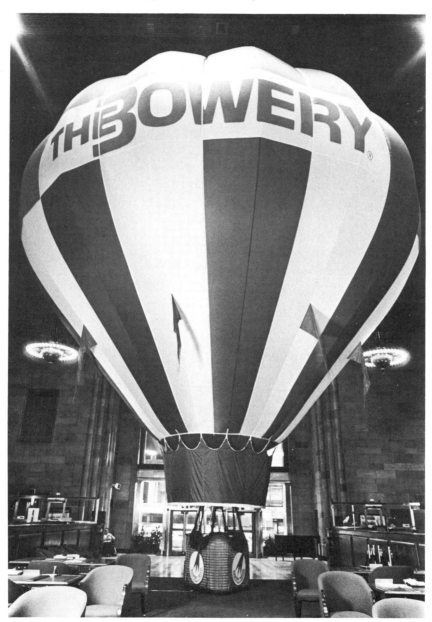

Carole Erger/Courtesy of The Bowery Savings Bank

The Bowery celebrates the Chinese New Year.

Carole Erger/Courtesy of The Bowery Savings Bank

The Bowery training quarters: a simulated bank.

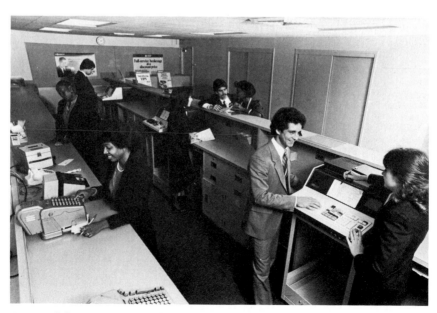

Courtesy of The Bowery Savings Bank

The Trustees of The Bowery Savings Bank, 1983. Seated left to right: James J. O'Leary, John W. Larsen, Morris D. Crawford, Jr., Ellis T. Gravette, Jr., Joseph P. McMurray, William H. Donaldson, and Walter N. Rothschild, Jr. Standing left to right: Christopher F. Edley, George S. Johnston, Stuart D. Root, Eugene H. Luntey, Ralph F. Leach, Jerald C. Newman, Walter B. Shaw, Richard R. Pivirotto, George Faunce III, and Edgar R. Fiedler.

Courtesy of The Bowery Savings Bank

The staff of 130 Bowery in 1894.

Courtesy of The Bowery Savings Bank Archives

The staff of 130 Bowery in the bank's landmark building, 1983.

Courtesy of The Bowery Savings Bank

From generation to generation: Morris D. Crawford, Jr. (left) to Ellis T. Gravette, Jr.

21

QUIET YEARS?

Earl Schwulst has referred to the years of his presidency and chairmanship as a relatively uneventful period in the bank's annals. "Those who preceded me had many serious problems to contend with," he said. "And those who succeeded me in the presidency, Rusty Crawford and John Larsen, certainly have had stormier and more complicated matters to face than I did." Records indicate, however, that he too faced his share of difficult challenges. He had actually had his baptism of fire, as he put it, during the Bruère administration.

"I recall a time in the late '30s or '40s," he once said, "when I was engaged in a dispute with DeCourcey Fales, who had left the firm of Cadwalader, Wickersham, and Taft to become head of the Bank for Savings. While he'd been The Bowery's counsel, he had rendered a legal opinion that the National Housing Act, under which the Federal Housing Administration was set up, was unconstitutional. That meant we should not have been buying, and should not buy in the future, home mortgages insured by the Federal Housing Administration. The opinion did not impress either Bruère or me, and we paid no attention to it. Soon thereafter, when Fales became head of the Bank for Savings, *he* immediately started buying FHA mortgages!

"One of his favorite territories was Long Island. We had not been making FHA-insured loans on Long Island. But we decided to enter that market. In order to get a footing there, we had to agree to take the mortgages on a somewhat lower yield basis than that on which Fales had been able to obtain them."

Though this was common enough competitive procedure, it infuriated DeCourcey Fales. He telephoned Schwulst and asked him to come to lunch at the New York Yacht Club. It was not a peaceful luncheon. The head of the Bank for Savings did not conceal his annoyance. He accused Schwulst of "breaking" the Long Island market and threatened to lodge a complaint against him with The Bowery's board of trustees.

"That made me angry, too," Schwulst said. "I told him bluntly to go ahead and do it."

Fales went directly to Henry Bruère. The president, always one who saw both sides of a controversy, began to wonder if the bank *was* doing the ethical thing. Somewhat uneasily, he asked Schwulst if he thought that "possibly we were a bit hasty in cutting the FHA mortgage rate." What arguments, he wanted to know, could they present to the trustees?

At that, Schwulst went back to his desk and wrote a forceful memorandum on the entire situation. He saw no reason to allow the head of the Bank for Savings to dictate Bowery policy. When Bruère read this, his hesitation vanished. "You are absolutely right," he said. And The Bowery continued its resolute and successful Long Island campaign.

Two principal factors were making Long Island a mortgage-hungry region. One was the construction of expressways leading from the city to Nassau and Suffolk counties, a project under the supervision of Robert Moses. These highways were invitations to suburban living. Thousands of families followed them to a new and refreshing way of life, and most of those families were eager to own their own homes. They created a building boom which depended on mortgage loans. Not to heed this opportunity would have been remiss on the part of the bank's management.

A second factor commanded attention on humanitarian as well as business grounds. This was the result of a calamity. In 1938 one of the worst storms in history, a hurricane accompanied by disastrous floods, struck Long Island. Sweeping in from the sea, roaring over sand dunes, it demolished hundreds of homes in waterfront communities. The Hamptons were among the worst hit, but other towns suffered almost as badly. When the storm at last abated, Long Island residents looked dazedly at the wreckage of their homes and at the prospect of rebuilding them. This too would require mortgage assistance.

Before long, Nassau and Suffolk counties were in the midst of a building boom. Apart from homes that had to be rebuilt, new communities were appearing where once Long Island had been an expanse of potato farms and duck farms. Builders poured into the region. Some of them like the Levitts constructed "developments" that were in themselves full-fledged towns with schools, churches, shopping centers, police and fire departments.

One of these was Levittown, and here The Bowery made a total of 7,736 home loans. For everybody concerned, it was a gratifying operation. By 1951 only 29 of these were in arrears. Illness accounted for 17 of the delinquencies; economic conditions for 5; absence on military duty for 4; marital difficulties for 2; and the last was attributable to the death of both husband and wife in a Pennsylvania Railroad wreck. For the most part, Levittown was populated by families who were moderately well-to-do and proud of their homes.

"I would say," a Bowery mortgage officer told me, "that our Levittown investments were among the most satisfactory we made in those days."

But this did not mean that times in general were good.

Seen in retrospect, the presidency of Earl Schwulst began at a time when the entire mutual savings bank industry of the United States faced the danger of being undermined. Its vulnerability lay in its tradition of specialization. It had been organized to serve the interests of "little people" who wanted to invest their savings in rigidly circumscribed ventures—ventures that were safe and sheltered depositors from the perils of rash speculation.

The more the commercial banks encroached on these historic provinces, the more the savings banks' share of the country's thrift deposits diminished. In 1945 the savings banks had 29.1 percent of the nation's savings. By 1965 this had dwindled to 17.9 percent. It was scarcely to be wondered at, then, that these thrift institutions sought more productive fields for their operations. They were fighting for their very future.

The Federal Reserve System was well aware of this.

One of its governors, John L. Robertson, acknowledged it when he spoke before the Illinois Bankers Association.

"It is insufficient," he said, "merely to grant mutual thrift institutions broader *lending* powers. Desirable as this may be, it would seem to leave us just about where we are now. . . . To meet the problem of these institutions, I suggest that we need a major change in our philosophy about them. We must not regard them as permanently tied to a specialized function, *but as potential candidates for full-service financial status.*"

In 1951, it must be remembered, few Americans outside of banking circles gave thought to such matters. Too many other things were monopolizing newspaper headlines. There was the Korean war, for one, and President Truman's unprecedented, almost unbelievable act of summarily relieving General Douglas MacArthur of his command. In Washington there were the infamous revelations of interstate crime uncovered by a senate investigating committee headed by Estes Kefauver. In New York, Julius and Ethel Rosenberg were being tried and sentenced to death on the charge of committing wartime espionage, while street crowds of their supporters and opponents almost came to blows.

Meanwhile a Japanese peace treaty was being signed in San Francisco, and in Europe six nations were organizing what was to become their Common Market. The world was indeed full of exciting events—especially in New York City, where the Yankees were beating the Giants in a hometown World Series encounter, and Joe DiMaggio was slamming balls into the wild blue yonder, the same Joe DiMaggio who years later became the television spokesman of The Bowery Savings Bank. With so many dramatic things happening, the banks could not remain a haven of tranquillity in a seething world.

One of the first crises President Schwulst had to meet,

215

in common with the officers of all thrift institutions, was the federal government's move to impose income taxes on savings banks. The thrift institutions were just beginning to recover from the trials of the depression years. "Like a groggy boxer," one commentator wrote, "getting up from his knees." At this point, heavy federal taxes would be a staggering blow.

A group of commercial bankers led by Arthur Roth, president of the Franklin National Bank, was *demanding* that Congress pass such legislation. Roth's attitude symbolized the ever increasing, ever toughening competition between commercial banks and savings banks.

Since Schwulst had become chairman of the Committee on Taxation of the National Association of Mutual Savings Banks, the Roth challenge became his personal responsibility. Working with officers of the Association and with his colleagues at The Bowery, he prepared for battle.

Edward K. Smith, Jr., who is now comptroller, says of those days: "Schwulst wanted to be armed with every available statistic. In our offices we worked day and night. Every evening my staff would assemble the day's findings, and I would rush them up to Earl's apartment. He would sit up late, basing his case on incontrovertible facts and figures. Those figures showed that many thrift institutions, especially the smaller ones, simply could not sustain the added burden of federal income taxes at that time. We were fighting for every mutual savings bank in the country."

There were moral, ethical, and philosophical issues at stake as well as financial considerations. What a mutual bank earned after providing for reserves, it passed on to its depositors in the form of dividends. On these dividends the depositors themselves paid income taxes. Was it equitable to place a double tax—the bank's as well as the depositors'—on the same earnings?

Moreover, thrift institutions had incurred so many mortgage losses during the depression that they were assuredly entitled to time to recover, time to write off an accumulation of bad debts.

Schwulst and his team of associates went to Washington to plead their case for the savings banks before the House Ways and Means Committee. They testified at hearing after hearing. The questions from congressmen were searching. The debates with Roth adherents were bitter. In the end, Congress attempted to mollify both sides: Though federal income taxes were imposed on mutual savings banks as of January 1, 1952, these institutions were granted the bad-debt deductions Schwulst sought. Such offsetting exemptions served to relieve most savings banks of federal tax liability. And that could be interpreted as a partial victory.

If the country at large gave the Schwulst hearings scant notice, it was because the far side of the Capitol was pre-empting attention. There Senator Joseph McCarthy was hounding Alger Hiss and other State Department officials. The senator's droning, endless, almost monotonous charges of Communist infiltration into the American government overshadowed all that was happening before the Ways and Means Committee.

Earl Schwulst's effectiveness, however, was eloquently summed up in a letter written to Chairman Henry Bruère by J. Wilbur Lewis, who was then president of the National Association of Mutual Savings Banks. Lewis wrote:

Dear Henry,

I would be remiss if I did not convey to you, and the other members of your Board of Trustees, the reaction of our membership to the decision of the House Ways and Means Committee relative to the continued Federal tax exemption of mutual savings banks.

Although the recent action of the Committee must be ac-

217

cepted without assurance for all time, our members are nevertheless greatly relieved and have been given renewed strength and courage. . . . To me the most singular reaction of our members, as well as of the savings bankers of all other states, was their clear recognition of the fact that the development and presentation of the savings bank case was from the start under the leadership of Earl Schwulst.

The gravity of the situation caused all of us to follow intently each step of the undertaking. There were times when we despaired of the outcome, but throughout the entire period Earl's confidence that our cause was just gave his associates and consultants the courage to follow his course of action. We shall never be able to express to him our appreciation for the time and effort he expended on behalf of our system.

Unfortunately, the clash before the House Ways and Means Committee did not subdue the determined animosity of Arthur Roth and of those who joined him in his crusade against the mutual savings banks. The crusade continued for years, stirring anger and even vituperation. It was Roth and his adherents who had tried to have the mutuals expelled from the American Bankers Association; and though the effort had failed, it had left so harsh a residue of ill will that many savings banks withdrew from the organization. "We could no longer feel," one of their officers said, "that the ABA represented our interests. So we made our own home in the National Association of Mutual Savings Banks."

One sidelight of these disputes merits being recorded. Throughout the tax discussions, Schwulst had been impressed by the arguments made on behalf of the American Bankers Association by a young economist named Elmer M. Harmon. "Despite all the efforts *we* had put into preparing a strong case," Schwulst said, "Harmon, it seemed to me, had outdone us in the breadth and depth of his presentation. Though he had figured powerfully in our inability to reach a reconciliation with the ABA, I had to respect his thoroughness and efficiency."

Back in his office in New York, The Bowery's head found himself thinking repeatedly of Harmon's work. A man of that ability, he felt, ought to be working *for* the bank, not against it.

Not long thereafter, there was a bankers' convention at White Sulphur Springs, West Virginia. Schwulst attended. When he came down to breakfast one morning, he saw Harmon eating with a friend at a nearby table. Making a quick decision, he went to the economist and said, "I'd appreciate a chance to talk with you when you're free. Could we meet later?"

Though he looked startled, Harmon agreed. A few hours later, in a private conference, Schwulst went directly to the point. "Within a few months," he said, "we will have an opening, due to retirement, in The Bowery's research department. I should be very glad to have you join us. Does this interest you?"

Harmon must have been amazed. No doubt he had anticipated a continuation of the tax debate. Now he had to realign his thoughts. Would a career in the American Bankers Association be as attractive as a career with the prestigious Bowery Savings Bank?

"I'd like time to think about it," he said.

"Naturally. Let me know at your convenience."

They shook hands, and Harmon left. Thereafter they met on several other occasions before the economist reached a decision. In the end he accepted the offer. He remained with The Bowery for years, until his retirement as a senior vice president.

As for the inter-bank dispute, The Bowery was not among those banks that immediately left the ABA. In recalling those days, Morris D. Crawford, Jr., The Bowery's former chairman, told me: "I could sense an increasing estrangement from the ABA. Nevertheless, whenever I discussed this with Earl Schwulst, he seemed to feel there was more to be gained than lost in remaining in the Association, and we continued our membership."

The forces opposed to thrift institutions were still relentless. They supported a bill, introduced in the New York State Legislature, which would have compelled savings banks either to convert to commercial banks or to liquidate. It accused thrift institutions of deceiving people. Superintendent of Banks George Mooney promptly helped crush this attempt. "It is presumptuous and arrogant," he declared.

"But the attacks against us continued in one way or another," Crawford said. "A time came in the early 1960s when, as president of the National Association of Mutual Savings Banks, I was an *ex officio* member of the ABA's Executive Council. One day I received the customary notice of a meeting. The notice made it clear that federal taxation of mutual savings banks would be discussed, but the usual agenda was not included. Thinking it was an accidental oversight, I telephoned the ABA offices to report the omission. An embarrassed staff member told me it had been decided that copies of the agenda would be sent only to commercial bankers. For me this was the ultimate affront. When I told Schwulst of this latest act, we agreed we could take no more. The Bowery Savings Bank resigned from the American Bankers Association."

Earl Schwulst's "quiet years" were largely concerned with the welfare of Bowery personnel. As far back as 1949, he called the trustees' attention to the difficulties of retired employees who were trying to match their pensions to rising living costs. The outcome was a resolution to increase pension payments by an amount equal to half the monthly payments of the Social Security Act.

Succeeding changes in the bank's pension system were even more innovative. Employees themselves were no longer required to contribute to the pension fund out of their salaries; The Bowery paid all such expenses—and even returned moneys previously paid by employees. Schwulst notified the entire staff that:

> The new plan will provide the same schedule of benefits as offered by the old plan, but will have several benefits for the employees which the old plan did not and could not provide. . . .
> Under the new plan the employee may, if he so elects five years or more before his normal retirement age, avail himself of what is called "a contingent annuitant option." This enables the employee, by accepting a lower amount of pension when he retires . . . to spread the pension over the life of his wife or some other designated dependent, thus making the pension, although in a reduced amount, cover two lives rather than one. . . .
> There will be no additional cost to the employees under this new plan. [The bank assumed all expenses, as part of the policy it soon adopted of paying all pension costs.]
> Let me assure you that the discontinuance of the old pension plan and the taking out of the new and more up-to-date plan are in the best interest of both the Bank and the employees.

The Bowery's pension system was particularly noteworthy because it was the first of its kind in savings banks. But the burdens of rising costs lay also on those who were still employed. When the trustees learned of some trying emergency needs that employees were encountering, they granted the bank the right "to *prepay* salaries or wages in amounts not exceeding $3,000 in the aggregate at any one time." And shortly thereafter, all personnel other than officers were aided in meeting higher living expenses by being granted a bonus "equal to 5 percent of the first $4,500 of salary."

However, such internal affairs, gratifying as they were to all concerned, could not detract the attention of the officers from challenges outside the bank—like the issue of expanding into Harlem. This began when The Bowery once again requested the right to open new branches. And again the request was denied. But this time the Superintendent of Banks made a counter-suggestion. It was unexpected and intriguing.

Lunching with Bruère and Schwulst, he spoke of the old Harlem Savings Bank, founded in 1863. He pointed out that for more than a quarter of a century not a single new savings bank had been opened in Harlem's black community. That left its residents at a serious disadvantage. They were limited in the sources to which they could go for mortgage loans. And no community in the city was in more desperate need of new housing.

If The Bowery would undertake to open a Harlem branch, the Superintendent said, he was certain permission would quickly be granted. A pressing need would thus be met.

Bruère's obvious question was: Why wasn't the Harlem Savings Bank itself, or some other bank in the community, being advised to open a new branch?

And the answer: That would not provide Harlem with a new alternative, a competing institution. What some banks might not be able to offer, The Bowery perhaps could. The presence of The Bowery would mean an infusion of newly available capital.

Before making any decision, Bruère and Schwulst sent investigating teams into the Harlem area. Their mission was to assess public opinion as well as to seek a suitable site. They made exhaustive surveys, all of which were favorable. And eventually they recommended a location at the corner of St. Nicholas Avenue and 145th Street, an important Harlem traffic and transportation center.

Not that their motives were wholly altrustic. "The Bowery was interested in a Harlem branch for several reasons," Schwulst admitted. "It had large mortgage investments in the area, it wanted to further the economic welfare of blacks and other minority groups, and it thought the public-service aspects of the action would be beneficial to the bank. Also, it was hoped that the action would stimulate other capital improvements in the area."

After the demolition of existing structures, which were antiquated, a new building would have to be erected on the site suggested by the investigators. But was it a sound idea to build only a bank on so costly a corner? Surely better use could be made of the land.

To evaluate the potentials of the undertaking, Henry Bruère invited a number of Harlem's leading citizens to lunch. Among them were civic leaders, clergymen, political figures, and businessmen. To his delight, he encountered general good will. It became clear that The Bowery Savings Bank would be a welcome newcomer to the Harlem scene. Moreover, the visitors offered some inspiring ideas.

And so, in 1953, The Bowery began the construction of a twelve-story apartment house on St. Nicholas Avenue—modern, attractive, geared to reasonable rents. Its street-level floor was designed to provide space not only for the bank itself but for a number of stores. Upon its completion, it was one of the most beautiful structures ever to rise in Harlem.

Because of the Banking Department's very restrictive policies in the matter of branching at that time (particularly where the country's largest savings bank was concerned), this was the only new branch the bank was able to launch during the seventeen years that Schwulst served as president and then as chairman. "From a purely economic point of view," he later said, "the project was only a moderate success, if that. In twenty years it accumulated 38,000 accounts and deposits of $65 million. Those are modest figures. But it has served a very useful purpose in demonstrating The Bowery's interest in promoting the welfare of minority groups and in helping them to take their proper place in the life of the city."

22

THE PERSONALITY
OF A BANK

The Schwulst administration began at a time when
the free world was rebelling more forcefully than
ever against the Hitler philosophy of Aryan suprem-
acy. In the United States the insistence on ethnic
equality was being heard from any number of powerful organizations: the National Association for the
Advancement of Colored People, the Anti-Defama-
tion League of B'nai Brith, the National Conference
of Christians and Jews, many more. All of them existed because prejudice, racial and religious, had not
yet been eliminated in America.

Since Earl Schwulst had been reared in Texas, some people may have wondered, when he joined the bank, what his Southern-trained attitudes might be toward blacks, toward Jews, toward other minorities. The answers came almost from the start.

A White Plains resident wrote a bitter complaint to F. D. Richart, then manager of the bank's real estate department. He and his wife had inspected a six-room apartment in a Bronxville building owned by The Bowery. Its superintendent had been most cordial and eager to rent—until he learned the couple's name was Cohen. Then he froze. He explained that it was the policy of the building's owners not to lease apartments to Jewish people. "If they did," the superintendent had added, "they feel all the other tenants would move out."

Mr. Cohen's letter emphasized his resentment because he, his wife, and many of their relatives were depositors in The Bowery. He intended to withdraw his funds from the bank at once.

Troubled and astonished, Richart took the letter to Schwulst. Schwulst promptly said, "Ask Mr. Cohen if it would be convenient for him to come in and see me." Within two days Mr. Cohen came. His disappointment in the bank was unmistakable as he sat down to talk.

"I cannot blame you for being resentful," the banker told him. "I feel as unhappy about this as you do. The facts are simple: We now own that building because we recently had to acquire it by foreclosure. When we did so, we had no idea that the previous owners had any anti-Jewish bias. Nobody mentioned it. Nobody here even thought to ask about such a thing. As for the superintendent you saw, he was accustomed to following the orders of the previous owners. As soon as we received your letter, we called him and instructed him that the former owners' policy was abhorrent to us; that it was to

226

be completely and immediately discarded. If you still want the apartment, Mr. Cohen, it's yours."

Mr. Cohen stared. "What if the other tenants do move out?" he asked.

"Let them. If they do, they are not the type of tenants this bank wants."

Mr. Cohen rose and held out his hand. "I'm relieved and pleased," he said. "We've already rented another apartment, so that we won't need yours. But at least we don't have to go look for another savings bank."

A second test of Earl Schwulst's "Southern training" developed in Pennsylvania's Levittown development. Not a single black family had bought a home there. When the first such family made an offer, counting on a Bowery mortgage, they found themselves unable to acquire any home insurance. The deal was about to collapse when word of the situation reached Schwulst.

Levitt developments involved thousands of Bowery mortgages. On a purely financial basis, it was far from politic to oppose the feelings of Levittown residents. But Schwulst was not thinking of financial advantage. He contacted the black family and assured them that *he* would arrange to have their home insured. "If you still want to buy the house," he said, "and take your chances with the community, we'll back you all the way."

The deal was consummated.

"As a Southerner," Earl Schwulst once told me, "I had plenty of opportunity in my boyhood to observe the effects of racial prejudice, and I never liked what I saw. My own grandfather, brought up in another age, all but disowned me at one time because of my friendship with a black fellow student at Harvard. But my grandfather eventually mellowed as all intelligent men and women have to mellow. As for a bank that accepts deposits from all people, it must *respect* all people. And that goes for those it hires as well as for those it serves."

(As a matter of record, over 33 percent of all present Bowery employees, men and women, are black. The other 67 percent include whites, Puerto Ricans, Chinese, representatives of practically every ethnic and national group one can find in New York. The board of trustees, likewise, has black as well as white membership, Catholics and Protestants and Jews and, for all I know, even atheists.)

In fact, it was Schwulst's personal opposition to racial discrimination which led him to accept the chairmanship of the Commission on Race and Housing. In this post he could further the interests of minority groups, both social and financial—sometimes against stubborn opposition from surprising sources.

In one such case, Schwulst's convictions brought him into conflict with a government agency. At a Waldorf-Astoria dinner, where he received an Urban League award for his support of civil rights, he shared the rostrum with Norman P. Mason, Federal Housing Commissioner. Facing an audience of some 300 civic leaders, Schwulst presented a program to eliminate discrimination in housing. One newspaper, *The Amsterdam News*, reported the event this way:

> Mr. Schwulst wasted no words. He came straight down the middle and charged the Government, through the FHA, with aiding and abetting discrimination in housing against minority groups by insuring mortgages for builders who bar minorities from the homes they build.
>
> "To deny a person the right to live where he chooses because of the color of his skin, or because of his religion, is both unjust and damaging to him," Mr. Schwulst said.

Reporting the response of Commissioner Mason, the newspaper added:

228

The net effect of what Mr. Mason answered was, "Those of you who know me know where I stand." He never got around to stating that the FHA, which had been indicted by Mr. Schwulst, would take positive action to end discrimination against minority groups.

In the long run, the urgings of Schwulst and many others did have their effect. American policy toward minority groups has steadily been moving closer to the Constitutional concept that "all men are born free and equal," and equally entitled to mortgages.

The criticism The Bowery's chairman aimed at the Federal Housing Administration during the Urban League meeting was neither the first nor the last time he commented on the agency's policies. In many cases he *defended* those policies. At one time in 1954 the FHA was accused in the press and before a congressional committee of making it possible for certain venal builders to reap enormous profits by "borrowing out"— borrowing from lenders the full cost of a housing project on the basis of unrealistic and excessive FHA appraisals.

Some publications castigated President Eisenhower for permitting such scandalous activities to occur. Other periodicals, like *House and Home* magazine, excused him on the grounds that he was not an expert in real estate appraisals or mortgages. "We cannot blame the President," the magazine said. "He has too many other responsibilities to study and understand the intricacies of government relationship with any one industry. . . . But why was there no one among the White House advisors with the knowledge and courage to tell him about the FHA scandals?"

The facts had to be publicized by people outside the White House. Among these, Schwulst was one of the most articulate, especially in a searching analysis he presented to his board. He made it clear that the fraudulent procedures of a few unscrupulous real estate operators should not lead to blanket condemnation of the whole FHA program. He granted that there were inequities in the agency's methods of appraisal and financing, but he showed how these could be eradicated; and the FHA acted on a number of the suggestions he and other savings bankers made.

House and Home magazine, long a bitter critic of the agency, was ultimately able to publish an editorial in which it said:

> Because we have never condoned what is wrong with FHA, we are proud to be the first to reaffirm that (1) FHA is the best thing that ever happened to the home-buying public. It has enabled millions of families to own far better homes than they could otherwise afford. (2) FHA is the Number 1 example of government and business partnership at no cost to the taxpayer.

"What Earl Schwulst and other critics proved," said one of his former associates, "is that honest criticism can be the best service one can render to a friend."

I record all this because when Schwulst was elected to serve as both president and chairman of the bank, he had said of himself: "I came from a thrifty family. And I grew up in the banking business under the tutelage of 'old school' conservative bankers. So it was natural that my administration at The Bowery would emphasize economy and try to avoid the flamboyant. I had not been exposed to, and had therefore escaped infection by, the more modern and more fashionable idea that the American family and its government need not live within their income."

Such an attitude was clearly well suited to the head of an institution which had for more than a hundred years encouraged thrift and prudence.

Through the years of his chairmanship, he carried his

ideas far outside the bank. Testifying before a congressional committee in support of "Truth in Lending" legislation, he once made a memorable statement against "the growing practice of merchants to encourage teenagers to open charge accounts and to buy on credit." He insisted that "teenagers should be taught to save rather than enticed into spending money which they do not have." The statement appeared in newspapers throughout the country and inspired eloquent editorials.

Schwulst, however, brought more than fundamental ideas of thrift to his administration.

"He brought us a more relaxed atmosphere," one officer said. "I would never have dreamed of walking into Henry Bruère's office without first telephoning to ask if he could see me. Yet I never hesitated to go in to talk to Earl Schwulst, because I always felt at ease and welcome.

"Of course," he added, "we knew we had an outstanding, experienced banker among us, and that meant a great deal. If we tried to explain a problem, he could grasp it before we had half-finished describing it. He would clarify it with a single bull's-eye phrase. If we made a mistake, we could count on a quiet, rational discussion of how the mistake could be corrected. Whereas in the case of Bruère, who was frequently short of temper and intolerant of mistakes, it was always a stomach-wrenching trial to face him with an admission of having made an error."

At the time Schwulst became chief executive of The Bowery, the nation was being tested not just by demands that ethnic and religious discrimination be abolished. Something else was occurring—something far less idealistic, far less inspiring; something that shocked and infuriated the country.

There was an increasing prevalence of bank robberies. One would have imagined that the practice had lately become fashionable in the underworld. The Bowery did not escape its share of such incidents. None were of major significance. None involved large sums of money. None were spectacular. On the contrary, a few had aspects of grim humor—for the bank, that is, not for the thieves.

There was the case of the man in the 42nd Street office who slipped a note to a teller, demanding all the money in her cash drawer. "Don't try to be smart," the note added. "I have a gun in my pocket. If you try anything, I'll shoot straight at your head." The teller, a woman with several years of experience, nodded and filled his bag with bills. The instant the thief started for the door, she cried out, "Stop that man!" The robber broke into a wild run for the 41st Street exit.

A security floorman near the door saw the robber coming. He did not attempt to tackle him, which might have impelled the thief to draw a gun. Instead he allowed the man to get into the revolving door—and as it turned he inserted his foot in it. The door stopped. The thief was trapped. He could not push the door back and he could not push it on toward the street. The delay allowed other security guards to converge on the exit while an alarm went out for police. The thief and his bag of money never reached the sidewalk.

Another robbery attempt occurred in the Harlem branch. There again a man passed a note to a woman teller, demanding all the money she could gather. She looked straight into his eyes and said quietly, "There are four people on line behind you. They'll become suspicious if they see me fill your bag. Step aside while I take care of them. Then I'll do as you ask."

Startled, perhaps bewildered by so unexpected a request, the thief automatically stepped aside. But the line behind him grew longer. He became impatient. Pressing his way back to the window, he whispered, "You do as I say *now!* Or I'll——"

She promptly interrupted in a loud, angry voice, "Listen, you miserable little crook! You get out of here or I'll scream! You're nothing but a——"

She had no need to finish. The terrified thief was already bolting for the door.

In talking of hold-up efforts, a Bowery security officer told me, "It is almost futile these days for criminals to take chances in banks. Sooner or later they'll be caught. A whole battery of electronic alarms and safety devices is aligned against them—hidden cameras to take their pictures, hidden signals to focus security guards' attention on them, automatic connections with nearby police stations. The trouble is, most would-be robbers don't realize what fools they are until they stare in amazement at the handcuffs on their wrists."

❧

It took the bank 116 years, from 1834 to 1950, to reach a level of one billion dollars in total assets. Once it had that initial billion, it needed only thirteen additional years to reach the $2 billion mark in 1963; only five years more to attain $3 billion in 1968. Certainly the most recent increase reflected the general economic boom of the 1960s. New industries were flourishing. Computers, for instance, were multiplying beyond the calculations anyone had ever made: In 1960 government observers had predicted that within a few years there might be as many as 15,000 computers in use throughout the United States, and by 1967 the actual figure exceeded 40,000. At the same time xerographic copying machines, in wild demand everywhere, were creating thousands of new jobs. Commercial and military aircraft were being ordered from American manufacturers by customers in every part of the world, and in Michigan the automobile industry was responding to almost insatiable consumer demand. The automotive aspect of prosperity caused observers like William Manchester to recall Will Rogers' prediction that "the country was going to the poorhouse in an automobile."

Since much of the nation's affluence flowed toward New York, the country's financial center, the city's banks, including The Bowery, shared a unique geographical and financial advantage.

It was not surprising that an institution with multi-billion-dollar assets should attract the attention—and arouse the acquisitive instincts—of commercial banks. On separate occasions Schwulst was approached by representatives of two such institutions. Both were among the largest in the country, and each broached the matter of a merger.

In the case of the first, Schwulst listened quietly to the proposal. Then he reminded his caller that what they were discussing was impossible since it was not authorized by law. The visitor granted this. But if The Bowery were interested, he said, a way could be found to amend the law.

Schwulst shook his head, a gesture which in a sense affected every savings bank in America. As he later explained, "I could not consider an action that would benefit only the stockholders of the commercial bank involved. There was no hint that anything would be paid for The Bowery's good will or for The Bowery's very substantial net worth. Therefore, under the circumstances, I saw no advantage whatever for The Bowery and its depositors. Besides, and of much greater importance, the precedent created by such a merger might well have spelled the doom of mutual savings banking in New York State, and possibly for the whole country. That alone was reason enough for rejecting the suggestion. I took the same position with the second bank, and that was the end of merger discussions."

Because Schwulst had served as president of both the National and the State Associations of Mutual Savings

Banks, his rejection of merger offers did indeed have broad significance. There was always the thought that as The Bowery went, so others would go. The responsibility of leadership lay heavily on the bank, and its chairman never forgot it.

Not that all mergers could be considered bad; certainly not those among mutual savings banks themselves. Indeed, at one time in 1964 The Bowery and the Manhattan Savings Bank actually agreed on a merger. In May their attorneys filed long briefs to obtain the approval of both the Federal Deposit Insurance Corporation and the State Superintendent of Banks. Their arguments appeared to be unassailable. It was the belief of both banks that the merger would result in broadened opportunities for service to the depositing public as well as some worthwhile economies in operation.

The Banking Department, however, had the opinion that the merger would reduce savings bank competition, particularly in the Grand Central area and on the Lower East Side of Manhattan (each bank already had offices in both areas). Therefore the Department withheld its approval, and the merger could not be consummated.

The Bowery's very bigness involved another kind of responsibility, this directly to its customers. It had to find some means of investing large sums in projects that would assure reasonable dividends to the depositors. Such a quest was not always easy. Nor was it easy to preserve a satisfactory ratio between the deposits and the net worth of the institution.

In 1951, when Schwulst began his administration, the relationship between earnings, deposits, and net-worth requirements was out of kilter. That was because 22½ percent of The Bowery's assets, about $235 million, was in low-yield government securities. When an investment of that magnitude brings only 2 percent in interest or thereabouts, it is hardly feasible for a bank to pay more to its depositors.

"This top-heavy investment in low-yielding government securities had to be reduced," Schwulst said. "At the same time, better-paying mortgage holdings had to be heavily increased."

Therefore The Bowery set out to diminish its portfolio of low-yield securities and at the same time to increase its mortgage investments of higher yield. It first began to sell off some of its bonds which brought the highest prices. But John Larsen, then a vice president, argued that it was wisest to sell off the lots that brought the least so that larger losses could be taken when the bank later became subject to federal income tax; losses could then be offset against otherwise taxable income.

He was right. His idea resulted in preserving deductions of over $800,000.

By December 31, 1966, the bank's low-yield government holdings had been pared down to 4½ percent of assets (reduced from 22½ percent). Higher-yielding mortgage loans were increased to 84 percent of assets (up from 64 percent).

In some endeavors, however, the Schwulst administration was less successful. For instance, it made futile protestations against the fact that savings banks—especially the biggest of them—were increasingly engaging in destructive competition and trying to undercut one another.

This was particularly noticeable in their lavish and often frenetic advertising. Full-page newspaper insertions proclaimed that this or that bank was offering the highest interest rates. The truth was, of course, that virtually all savings banks were paying the same rates. All of them had to observe a ceiling set by law or regulation. Any suggestion of "highest" dividends was at best a half-truth.

In private, many savings bankers objected to such dissimulation. One official said, "I wish we had the good sense to cooperate, to spread the message to the public of the value of *all* savings institutions. Instead we continue this dog-eat-dog habit of trying to make people believe they really get higher dividends in a particular bank." He shook his head. "All you have to do is read and compare the advertisements of a dozen banks on any single day, and the fallacy of the 'highest dividend' claim becomes evident."

The Bowery's staff condemned the practice. Yet its protestations did not change anything.

Neither could Schwulst, Crawford, Larsen, or anyone else at The Bowery end the wild giveaway policy—free gifts rewarding those who made new deposits. The Bowery's officers were not alone in their objections. The East New York Savings Bank bought a full-page advertisement in *The New York Times* to say:

> The question we ask is this: When will financial institutions come to their senses and stop trying to tempt more and more people into fund shifting for the sake of a $5 or $10 gift? When will they learn that free toasters could burn the whole mutual savings bank system?
> The time is long past when savings banks can continue to neglect their primary responsibility: protecting depositors' funds, managing them prudently and fostering the health and welfare of the community as a whole. After all, we are nonprofit institutions. Our founders never expected us to engage in reckless, destructive competition.

In reviewing some of the other competitive measures of the period, Earl Schwulst recalled that one institution, the East River Savings Bank, had sent out 200,000 letters offering one dollar in cash to anyone who opened an account with a minimum of $10. The Newton, Massachusetts, Savings Bank dispatched gift packages to the hospitalized mothers of newborn babies. In addition to the gifts came the offer to start an account for the baby with

$1. All the mother had to do was present the letter to a teller (and hopefully, of course, continue thereafter to make deposits for the child). Such efforts were simply variations of the basic giveaway practice.

Like his predecessors, Schwulst tried and failed to persuade the Banking Department to allow more liberalized branching privileges. Here he encountered, among other obstacles, a matter of semantics. What is a branch? When is an added office *not* a branch?

In 1957 Crawford, at Schwulst's request, had pointed out to the bank's attorneys that the bank's property, acquired with the merger of the North River Savings Bank, touched upon the Pennsylvania Railroad Station. He asked the law firm for a ruling on the legality of opening an annex on property leased from Penn Station but adjoining the bank's own land. The lawyers produced the opinion that such an office would be entirely legal since it would be a "contiguous lateral extension"—a phrase which only long legal training could evolve.

To build the annex, however, it would be necessary to cut a tunnel across 33rd Street, and this the bank proceeded to do. The operation was called to the attention of a bewildered Deputy Superintendent of the Banking Department. He immediately telephoned Crawford. "What the devil are you fellows doing on 33rd Street?" he demanded. "Where did you get the right to break up a street?"

Crawford explained, "We're tunneling in order to connect with an annex we plan to open in the station on leased property adjoining our own property. It's for the convenience of customers."

"Who gave you the authority to do all this?"

"It's perfectly legal," Crawford assured the official. "A matter of contiguous lateral extension."

"A matter of *what?*"

"Contiguous——lateral——extension."

There was a moment of silence as if the official needed time to recover from a blow. Then the voice on the telephone murmured a somewhat dazed, "Contiguous lat—— Well, I didn't know about that."

Crawford sent the Department a copy of the legal opinion, and he heard no more about the contemplated annex. In time, the tellers' windows opened in Penn Station.

A decade later, the Banking Department finally yielded a little to the requests of mutual savings banks. It ruled that a thrift institution could open a "public accommodation office." This was defined as an auxiliary office within 1,000 feet of an existing office. Under this authorization, The Bowery and the New York Bank for Savings were enabled to open offices within the Grand Central Railroad Station. (The rationale for such permission lies solely in public service: having windows for deposits and withdrawals made more conveniently available to people who pass close to a main branch.)

Chairman Crawford once observed, "When we opened these offices we congratulated ourselves on the fact that suburban dwellers could now make deposits or withdrawals on their way to and from their trains. It was a pleasant idea. But we overlooked the *wives* of these commuters. We soon learned that in general it was the wives who deposited the family's weekly savings, and the wives were still out there in the suburbs. *They* found it more convenient to deposit their funds locally. And so, though our public accommodation offices have certainly paid for themselves—including the $300,000 we spent in building an escalator from our subway office to the street level on 42nd Street—these satellites did not really attract all the suburban deposits we had hoped to get."

No one can guess right every time—something every bank official has learned from experience. "But," Earl

Schwulst once told me, "there was one area in which I could not *afford* to make a wrong guess. That, for the sake of the bank and its depositors, was in finding the right man to be my successor."

How, then, did he make a choice?

23

THE OBLIGATIONS
OF LEADERSHIP

"The matter of providing for an able successor commanded my attention almost from the day I became
chief executive," Schwulst has said. "As I looked at
my colleagues I realized—as had Bruère and others
in their time—that the senior officers were of approximately my own age or older. That meant they
would be retiring at about the same time I retired.
As for the younger echelon, while many of them
were unquestionably competent in what they were
doing, they were for the most part either too young

or too untried to have produced among them one sufficiently qualified to be considered as a possible successor."

Like Bruère, Schwulst had to face the fact that an exceptional type of person had to be chosen to head and represent the biggest savings bank in the country. It had to be a man whose personality, ideas, background, executive ability, and general intelligence matched the heavy obligations he would have to assume. It had to be a man who could cope with political, social, economic, and even legal issues. It was not an easy set of qualifications to find.

An executive search of that kind is not uniquely characteristic of The Bowery Savings Bank. It occurs in corporations and institutions of all types. When *Finance* magazine made its 1974 "Banker of the Year" award to Gaylord Freeman, chairman of First Chicago Corporation, it gave as one of the reasons: "An exemplary achievement was the manner in which he provided for management continuity following his own forthcoming retirement. Freeman personally recruited, selected and guided the executive team that has now been installed to succeed his administration."

Schwulst, after considering several outstanding choices, none of whom fully satisfied his requirements, discussed his problem with his friend John Redfield of Cadwalader, Wickersham, and Taft. Over a thoughtful luncheon, Redfield mentioned three of his younger partners. "Although able," Schwulst later conceded, "two of them did not strike me as having quite the personality for the position, and the third was unwilling to give up his law career. So Redfield suggested one of his still younger men whom he described as 'a rising star,' not yet a partner but certain to become one in the near future. This was Morris DeCamp Crawford, Jr. I asked Redfield to have Crawford come in to see me."

Within a couple of days Schwulst glanced up from his desk at a tall, lean man whose hair instantly explained why he was called "Rusty." As he rose to shake hands, the chairman recalled everything John Redfield had said about this young lawyer.

Graduating from Harvard University *magna cum laude,* and then from Harvard Law School, Crawford had gone to work for Cadwalader, Wickersham, and Taft. But World War II had interrupted his legal career. He enlisted as a private and attained the rank of major on the staff of General Douglas MacArthur. After the war, back in civilian status, he rejoined Cadwalader, Wickersham, and Taft. That had been some thirteen years ago. "He's not a banker," Redfield had conceded, "but I think he'll surprise you by the speed with which he learns."

When Schwulst and Crawford sat down to talk, the chairman could not help wondering if anyone with so bright a future in one of America's leading law firms would *want* to change careers. What the chairman could not guess was that Crawford had for some time felt restless as a sedentary lawyer. He often envied the businessmen he represented. They lived in a world of action, of enterprise, of excitement which seemed somehow more stirring than his own. Perhaps eight years of immersion in law books and briefs was enough. As for banking, in its broadest sense it dealt with the lifeblood of America, with financial participation in every imaginable industry, in the very lives of the people it served.

It was clear to both men as they talked that no firm commitment could be made by Schwulst as to what the future might yield. That depended on Crawford's ability. Moreover, he would have to meet with some of the trustees; the board would have the final voice in any selection the chairman might propose.

As it happened, Crawford impressed the trustees as

favorably as he had impressed Schwulst. On October 1, 1953 he was elected Vice President and Office Counsel.

❦

Several years before the U.S. government made it possible for self-employed people to provide a pension plan for themselves (through the Keogh Act), The Bowery recognized the need. To meet it, Earl Schwulst devised what he called the "Savings Pay-Out Plan." In some respects this was similar to an annuity. On retiring from his job a depositor could arrange to have his savings, plus all accumulated dividends, paid out to him in regular installments, generally monthly. These would continue until the account was exhausted. If at any time a depositor wished to withdraw his funds in a lump sum, or change any aspect of the plan, he could do so. Perhaps the most astonishing thing about so simple and practical an arrangement was that it had never before been adopted. Within a short time after it became one of The Bowery's services, it spread to other banks.

The ability to make such innovations comes with growth. One can hardly equate the services of a multi-billion-dollar institution, such as Schwulst headed in the 1950s and 1960s, with those of the small Bowery Savings Bank of a century earlier. During his administration, Schwulst spent days—nights, too, for that matter—poring over the problems and the responsibilities inherent in the custody of billions of dollars. More than half a million depositors depended on the bank's management to assure them of the safety of their funds, a fair return in dividends, and the constant availability of their money.

No previous system of handling so many accounts could really be called efficient. Indeed, every working day made it clear that new methods would have to be adopted to keep pace with the ever increasing complications of management. Fortunately, the world of electronics was constantly developing new equipment for dealing with the exigencies of business growth. Such equipment was expensive, however; so a special committee appointed by the board of trustees studied all available systems. Acting on the committee's recommendations, the Schwulst administration was one of the first among savings banks to install a wholly new concept for handling its accounting needs, the Univac "on-line" system. This called for an outlay of $2 million—a sum that would have appalled earlier regimes at the bank. But, as Schwulst said, "It handled virtually all the accounting and statistical work with a great saving in time and expense and a great improvement in speedy service to the public."

Still, such things were mechanical matters. Schwulst, always a believer in prudence, concerned himself more intensely with the tougher problems of banking: making certain that the institution would have not only a strong net worth but also—just as important a consideration—sufficient liquidity at all times to meet non-crisis demands for cash.

It was true that The Bowery was a member of the Savings Banks Trust Company. The Company could and did make emergency loans to a member bank that needed funds in a crisis. A small bank might feel secure with such backing; it would never require very large loans. But what about giant institutions like The Bowery, the Dime, the Dry Dock, and so on?

"Because of the then relatively limited resources of the Savings Banks Trust Company," Schwulst explained, "it could hardly serve as an effective central bank for its large members, especially in time of general emergency when all banks might simultaneously require loans."

For that reason, as a safety measure, Schwulst set up lines of credit with a number of leading commercial banks. With the consent of the board, The Bowery, like a number of other thrift institutions, also joined the Federal Home Loan Bank of New York—from which, it must be added, it withdrew in 1969, when it saw no further advantage in such membership. The lines of credit with commercial banks were designed to provide sources of "external liquidity" if it became necessary to meet abnormal periods of disintermediation. (By the end of 1973, these lines of credit amounted to $96 million. Since the Savings Banks Trust Company had meanwhile increased its own resources and had secured access to the open market for its short-term paper, The Bowery had an additional line of credit there of $65 million. Thus, in total it could if needed command $161 million from these two sources of external liquidity.)

Only once during Schwulst's administration did the thrift institutions have to contend with a threatening demand for heavy withdrawals. This occurred in 1959. The U.S. Treasury offered the public its "Magic Fives," an investment opportunity in government short-term securities that yielded 5 percent interest. At the time, this was more than the savings banks could pay. So depositors withdrew their savings in order to buy the higher-yielding Treasury notes.

I once suggested to a retired veteran of The Bowery that there are a number of financial analysts who discourage such disintermediation. In their writings they stress the *long-range* advantages of maintaining savings accounts. At this the retired officer smiled.

"Personally," he said, "I sometimes feel skeptical about some of these writers. Perhaps my skepticism is unfair, since it is based on a single flagrant case. Yet I keep remembering that case, and, unfair or not, it has always troubled me."

This, he said, occurred just before the Bank Holiday of 1933, in Bruère's era. Frightened depositors were withdrawing funds from all banks. A well-known columnist whose writings appeared daily in hundreds of newspapers won the gratitude of all bankers when he urged depositors not to touch their savings. He praised the security and the reliability of savings accounts. He was almost emotional in his plea to the American people not to abandon their confidence in the nation or their devotion to thrift, one of America's most admirable traits. It was a heart-warming column.

The morning after it appeared, the columnist himself joined the line at The Bowery. When he reached the teller he presented a withdrawal slip for all the thousands of dollars in his account.

The president was in his office when an incredulous head teller reported what was happening. The president walked out to the banking floor; and there, unmistakably, stood the noted columnist waiting for his money.

Such evidence of journalistic insincerity was more than the chief executive could bear. His lips tightened. He told the head teller, "Have the money paid out to him in one-dollar bills."

The teller stared. "*All* of it?"

"Every last dollar of it. And be sure the money is counted out dollar by dollar—*twice*."

Then President Bruère returned to his office. He was not surprised a few minutes later to hear the infuriated columnist uttering loud protestations in the outer office. But the dollar-by-dollar order was not rescinded. As my informant recalled, "If there was one thing Bruère could not stand, it was hypocrisy. And he knew how to deal with it."

247

During Schwulst's fourteen years as chief executive of The Bowery there were, of course, a number of changes in banking statutes and regulations. One such change, enacted in 1952, permitted savings banks to purchase preferred and common stocks. The state legislature, however, set strict limits on the quantity of stocks that could be purchased; the funds of depositors had to be safeguarded against sharp declines in stock values.

Schwulst and his associates were even more cautious than the legislature. It was not until six years after the legal power was granted that The Bowery's trustees, after long consideration, authorized such investments. In April 1958, a committee of trustees, headed by former Bank Superintendent William R. White, not only approved but recommended the purchase of certain common stocks.

The Schwulst administration then undertook a program of "dollar averaging"—that is, of limiting stock purchases to a specified amount of dollars per month—a common enough investment practice. By this means it was hoped that a larger number of shares would be bought when prices were low, and fewer when prices were high, thus increasing the likelihood of achieving a substantial market appreciation over a time span.

But no matter how cautious one may be, stock prices are always volatile, and The Bowery's common stock portfolio went through periods of sharp fluctuations in market value. At one time in 1968, the bank's common stock holdings had appreciated by more than $30 million. Within 18 months, the gain had collapsed to become a *de*preciation of *$10 million!* Contemplating such a swift change in value, a downward swing of $40 million, one can well understand Earl Schwulst's constant insistence on maintaining a strong net worth. The bank had to be able to withstand such changes.

He was not alone in stressing the importance of net worth. In 1970 the trustees' Equities Committee, of which

William White was chairman, adopted a policy statement which included these sentences: "A *sine qua non* of viability in savings banking, as in other business enterprises, is a strong net worth position. Strength in net worth provides the base for innovation and the ability to exploit unfolding opportunities to render greater public service."

The philosophy was soon vindicated. Within 30 months, the $10 million *de*preciation became a $50 million *appre*ciation.

In short, as Schwulst always maintained, if bigness has an advantage, it is the ability to offset asset depreciation or losses without being seriously shaken.

Many previous experiences had shaped Schwulst's concern for net worth and liquidity. One was his work, years earlier, with the Deposit Liquidation Board. There he had studied the plight of banks which had *not* given adequate attention to their fundamental soundness.

Another aspect of experience could be traced to his term as Superintendent of Banks in the Philippines. The mismanagement of some of the islands' financial institutions had been almost incredible—as in the case of the bank which had loans in a single enterprise equal to 90 percent of its deposits. The borrower was a bankrupt sugar plantation and mill. Schwulst had been forced to organize a consortium of other banks to rescue the threatened institution pending the raising of additional capital funds by its stockholders.

"Every sign of weakness in a bank must be treated in its own way," he has said. "Some banks are the victims of runs because of nothing more than unfounded rumors. Fears spread. People rush to get their money though there is no real reason for alarm. That happened to a certain Chinese-owned bank in the Philippines."

To save this quite solvent institution from having all its liquid resources depleted by frightened customers,

Schwulst, with the backing of the governor-general, persuaded the Insular Treasury to send money to the bank's assistance. The money was delivered, at his direction, in small-denomination bills—thousands upon thousands of them. They were carried into the bank in straw baskets just before its morning opening. Long lines of depositors, anxiously waiting to withdraw their funds, saw the money arrive, basketful after basketful. When the doors were opened for business, stacks of bills were visibly piled behind every teller's window. The first people to demand their funds received them without the slightest trouble. Those in the rear of the lines, seeing this and seeing more bills constantly being made available to tellers, finally decided that it was pointless to be worried about their money. Since the bank was obviously affluent, people began to turn away. Within an hour the lines had dissolved.

"And by noon," Schwulst recalled, "many who had withdrawn their money earlier were bringing it back for redeposit."

Such experiences, and there were others, had long ago convinced him that the primary responsibility of a bank's chief executive is to make certain that his institution at all times is strong enough to meet emergencies. "In addition," he once said, "every retiring bank head has the obligation of leaving to his successor an institution as sound or more sound than it was when he came to it."

This, in the judgment of his colleagues, Schwulst accomplished. Between 1951 and 1966 (when Schwulst retired after 30 years of service), the growth of The Bowery was steady and impressive. Indeed, one might call it spectacular, though in retrospect Schwulst has called it "probably excessive." This growth occurred in spite of the interval of disintermediation that marked the year 1959. The record is best described in figures:

Between 1951 and 1966, deposits expanded from $930

million to $2,349 million, an increase of 153 percent. Assets went from slightly over $1 billion to more than $2½ billion, a rise of 149 percent. And the bank's net worth increased from $114 million to $204 million, a leap of 79 percent. In those same fifteen years, *income* went from $27 million to $113 million, a plus of 319 percent. And finally, dividends paid to depositors, only $18 million in 1951, soared up to $107 million in 1966, an increase of 494 percent.

Throughout that period, the real estate operations of the bank were just as noteworthy. Independently in some cases, in joint action with sister banks in others, The Bowery financed home developments in those sections of New York that were in desperate need of rehabilitation, chiefly on the Lower East Side and in Harlem. This, of course, was in addition to its mortgage loans for thousands of smaller homes. And on 34th Street in Manhattan, opposite Penn Station, it purchased for $12 million a site contiguous to its own branch office, with its satellite, and offered the prospect of becoming one of the most profitable investments in the bank's history. What acquisition could be more promising in a long period of inflation than land in the very heart of New York?

Between a promise and its fulfillment, however, there can be a wide gap which forecasters cannot always predict. This depends on changes in a city, and no city changes as swiftly as New York. Moreover, no part of New York changes as rapidly as certain areas of Manhattan. In some neighborhoods this evolution is for the better, as on the rebuilt Avenue of the Americas. In others there is deterioration that appalls the observer, as in the vicinity of Times Square.

When the bank purchased the 34th Street property, it was the center of New York's thriving garment industry. The International Ladies' Garment Workers' Union estimated that 100,000 people worked in the area, a figure that rose to 130,000 at the height of every season. They produced 70 percent of all the feminine apparel manufactured in the United States. In monetary terms, this accounted for some $5 billion of annual revenue at the wholesale level.

Most of the workers in the area were exactly the kind of serious, frugal people whom thrift institutions had attracted from the earliest days of their existence. They were America's "little people"—immigrants from Europe and Puerto Rico.

They could be expected to patronize the bank, and they did. In addition—so the appraisers of the property believed—a fine new building in that centralized neighborhood would cater to important corporations which would be willing to pay substantial rental fees for so convenient a location. The future of the site seemed assured.

What nobody had foreseen was that the really big firms would, for the most part, turn to the great skyscrapers soon to rise farther uptown. What discouraged them here was that 34th Street, west of Sixth Avenue, was beginning to look frayed. Signs of deterioration were seeping in wherever one looked: a few sleazy shops, cheap eating places, crowds that appeared to be less than prosperous.

Nonetheless, the 34th Street property still constitutes a good source of revenue for the bank, and its prospects are still sound. The land which The Bowery owns is as valuable as ever. But the brilliant prospects that were held for it a decade ago may have to wait a while for realization. Meanwhile, the bank has not really suffered any loss.

As The Bowery's officers have been concerned about the welfare of depositors, so have its trustees. In 1961 any examination of the bank's records would have revealed that most of its mortgage holdings were in FHA and VA guaranteed loans. There was nothing wrong about this; on the contrary, it spelled security. But was there any reason to preclude increased investments in conventional mortgages *not* guaranteed by the government agencies?

A committee of trustees, under the chairmanship of Paul Windels, studied the pros and cons of moving in this direction. The committee concluded that the American economy, being sound, made it not only feasible but advisable to grant more conventional mortgage loans. The policy was adopted in 1962. It broadened The Bowery's sphere of operations considerably.

In general, depositors in mutual savings banks are unaware of such policy decisions. They take it for granted that trustees and officers will be alert to every opportunity to increase an institution's strength while augmenting its service to the public. And though they do not question the internal operations of their banks, I mention the deliberations of the Windels committee as an example of trustee activities that occur constantly, not only at The Bowery but also in other mutual savings banks.

August M. Strung, who was then vice president in charge of conventional mortgage lending, had for years been urging the bank to augment its investments in such loans. Now he had his way. Conventional mortgage lending—as differentiated from FHA and VA paper—became the bank's major investment activity.

Another thing that had long troubled Strung was The Bowery's payment of fees to mortgage companies for servicing (collecting payments on) Bowery loans. He wanted to retain such fees for the benefit of the bank's depositors. With the addition in 1971 of so-called "leeway" sections to the state banking law, he saw a way of achieving this: It was now possible, under the new authorization, for the bank to create its own subsidiary company to service its mortgage loans.

Called the Bowest Corporation, this company now has

principal offices in Los Angeles, in Orlando, Florida, and in Rochester, New York. It services not only The Bowery itself, but loans in excess of $1 billion for more than a hundred other institutional investors.

⌀⌀

"Earl Schwulst," one of his colleagues said, "had the faculty of making banking seem the most important and worthwhile occupation anyone could have. During his administration he set standards that other banks simply had to follow."

Perhaps the most extraordinary of his contributions were those which in their day set new standards for fringe benefits. He knew that employees of most firms, including banks, face four hazards: loss of jobs, disability, old age, and death. And he championed methods to cope with all of these. Today, insurance of every kind—health, life, accident, unemployment—protects all Bowery personnel; their benefits continue for life, even after retirement. Crawford has not only carried forward these benefits but has amplified them.

"I believe," said Jack Older, the bank's office counsel, "that we have a program of fringe benefits that is truly outstanding." And most bank officers concur.

As for Schwulst's concepts of the general duties of a Bowery chairman, he expressed them in language no one else ought to attempt to interpret for him. They are thoughts that apply to every corporate chief executive in the nation. Schwulst penned them on his retirement in 1966, when he was to be succeeded as chairman by Morris Crawford, Jr. and when John Larsen was to become president. The wisest thing a chronicler can do is allow the letter to speak for itself:

24

"DEAR RUSTY"

July 27, 1965

Dear Rusty,

As I bow out of the picture, I am going to give you just a few words of advice and that will be all the unsolicited advice that I shall ever give you as long as I am on the Board. You need little or no advice. You have the competency to be a great leader of the bank and you will be that on your own. However, I am constrained to pass on to you at this time a few little precepts based upon my experience which you may find useful. They are as follows:

1. Don't let yourself be diverted into outside activities, however worthy, to the neglect of your primary duty of running the bank. You are going to be under great pressure and under great temptation to become involved in many outside activities. I would suggest that you shove these things aside for at least the first year or two until you have a firm seat in the saddle and until you are entirely satisfied that your No. 2 man is able to carry on to your entire satisfaction. Even then, don't become too deeply involved in outside affairs. For failure to follow this precept, my predecessor, Bruère, narrowly escaped placing his career in great jeopardy. You cannot and should not, however, escape involvement entirely because a reasonable degree of involvement will be of advantage to the bank as the leading bank in its field.

2. Lead your Board. The Board cannot run the bank; that is your job. But the Board has the ultimate responsibility for the welfare of the bank. Therefore, you must not only lead the Board but you must also be the servant of the Board. Stand up to the Board on questions that you regard as important but stand up only to the point where you run into a serious difference of opinion and then lay the matter over for further consideration. I have been through this thing several times. If you find that, after laying over the matter for a while, you cannot persuade the doubters to go along with you, you would be well advised to drop the matter until some future time and perhaps altogether. It is possible that the doubters may be right. I know that they have been right more than once in my own experience.

3. You have earned, as you have deserved, the confidence, respect, loyalty, and affection of your fellow officers and employees. They know that you have a deep regard for their welfare and they know that you will continue to have it, even in a greater degree, as you take over the full responsibility for managing the bank. It is a part

of your nature to be absolutely fair and objective in dealing with the officers and employees. That is all they expect. They know that you will be as generous and liberal in your treatment of them as they deserve and as the bank can afford.

4. Keep on the sharp lookout from the very beginning for a man to succeed you when you are ready to retire. That was almost the very first thing I began to consider after I succeeded Bruère. You have in John Larsen an excellent understudy who will be able to pinch-hit for you during your periods of absence or if you should become ill. But John will probably retire before you do because of age. You should be giving very serious thought to whether you have anyone in the bank, with sufficient age differential, to be the man likely to take over upon your retirement. If you should find, after a reasonable time, that you do not have that man, you should be looking about to bring him in. He should probably be at least ten years younger than you are.

5. You have been diligent in visiting the branches. You have improved upon my own performance in that regard. I hope that you will continue to do this. The branch managers and their staffs may feel to be "a bit out of it," if the Chief Executive Officer does not get around to see them at least two or three times a year. I very much hope that you will keep this point in mind and do a much better job of it than I did.

6. Make full use of your officer staff. Consult with them frequently and solicit their advice. I have been surprised at how often incipient mistakes of judgment on my part have been brought to light through my conversations with my officers. This holds true particularly with respect to conversations I have had with you with regard to ideas that I thought were of great merit. You have checked me on more than one occasion when I would have made a mistake had I not asked your opinion. Your fellow officers

can be helpful to you just as you have been helpful to me in this regard and just as they have been helpful to me.

7. Never fail to keep your Trustees fully informed with regard to the affairs of the bank. Never hesitate to take your worries and your problems to them. They have a very high regard for you and they want to be helpful. Indeed, we have a rare Board in the fact that it is made up of unusually competent men of experience and judgment, men of affairs, men who have a sense of their responsibility as Trustees, and men who want to help management in every way possible without assuming the functions of management. I have been, and you are, very lucky in having such a Board. Don't fail to take advantage of it. Pick the brains of your Board members. Make them work. They want to work. To work effectively they must be kept informed, they must know what your problems are—otherwise, they cannot help you and, more importantly, they cannot discharge their overriding responsibility as Trustees for the safety and welfare of the bank and its depositors.

8. Always look at the bank's expenses with a very jaundiced eye. Only constant watchfulness will keep them under control. That is particularly important in the case of this bank because of the restrictions (which, on the whole, I believe to be sound) which we have imposed upon our investment policy. Our competing banks, generally, earn a higher rate of return than we do on our investments. We have only one way to counteract this, and that is to take advantage of the leverage which our size gives us, and that leverage can best be reflected in keeping a close rein upon expenses. This does not mean "penny pinching" necessarily, but perhaps that is not such a bad idea either.

9. Since I have some responsibility for having brought you to the attention of the Trustees and for your assumption of the high post of Chief Executive Officer of "by far" the largest savings bank in the country, I have every desire to see my judgment vindicated by your performance

as Chief Executive Officer. Of course, I have no doubt about the excellence of that performance or I would never have recommended you to be my successor. Nevertheless, I want you to know that I shall always be standing back of you and willing to help you in any way I can to the best of my ability. At the same time, you would not want or expect me to volunteer advice. That would be interference. You have the responsibility and you expect and intend to discharge it. My position is *simply* that I stand ready to help you whenever you think I can be helpful.

And now, may God be with you during the many years to come of your leadership of a great and noble institution. No one knows what problems you will face. They could be much more difficult than any that I have had to face. I think that in you we have the best man in the industry to lead the bank and to deal with such problems as may arise. I am certain that you will pass on to your successor not only a much bigger institution than I am passing on to you but one that will be enjoying an even greater degree of respect and regard in the community than it enjoys today. And that, my dear friend, is saying a great deal.

With affectionate regards and deepest gratitude from both Juanita and myself, I am

Ever yours,

Earl

To this, Morris Crawford, Jr. replied:

Dear Earl:

I have read and reread your letter several times. Although I am not much given to saving letters, I have saved a few important ones in my life. This is one that I shall always preserve and treasure, and from which I shall take guidance and strength over the years.

I think you know that I agree completely with the precepts which you have stated in your letter. It remains only to be seen whether I am able to interpret and apply them properly to situations as they arise in the future in our ever-changing environment. I shall do my best and will be supported in this effort by the knowledge that I can come to you, as I shall, for your help and counsel.

I am mindful that you have a great love and affection for, and a justifiable pride in, this fine institution, whose leadership you are passing on to me. It will always be my aim to preserve and enhance the usefulness and the importance of The Bowery, for I, too, love the old gal and take a deep pride in her.

May I repeat once more my deep thanks to you for your guidance over the past twelve years, for the opportunities you have given me, and for your warm friendship. I know that friendship will continue and grow for many years to come.

With affectionate regards,

Sincerely,
Rusty

25
IN QUEST
OF TRUTH

In 1953, the year Crawford joined The Bowery, Bank Superintendent William A. Lyon addressed an anniversary meeting of the Savings Bank Association of New York.

"Unbridled competition," he declared, "is out of place in banking. Banks handle ten or more dollars of other people's money for every dollar of their own. There can never be in banking such a thing as the right to fail. But this is not to say that competition is out of place in banking. Actually we should have just as much of it as possible, consistent with the preservation of the soundness and availability of our money supply."

The Superintendent did not have to stress the fact that *healthy* competition, the kind that has immemorially contributed to the prosperity of the United States, truly benefits everybody. It keeps costs down and it creates demand.

The questions that banks have not yet answered are: When does competition cease to be healthy? When does it become a consuming force that creates more harm than good? When does it threaten the economy?

Surely the kind of competition that makes it difficult, almost impossible, for the average citizen to obtain a mortgage loan can hardly be called beneficial. What, then, can be done to assure *sound* competitive practices?

The problem has confronted all savings banks as it has confronted The Bowery. Since the 1960s, it has concerned Crawford in two areas of responsibility—as chief executive of his bank and also, in 1964 and 1965, as president of the National Association of Mutual Savings Banks. His years in office have been years of crusading for the rights of the public as well as for the rights of savings banks.

Among the earliest reforms he and his associates sought was passage of the "Truth in Lending" bill. Introduced in 1960 by Senator Paul Douglas of Illinois, it had met instant opposition.

In retrospect one may marvel at the fact that anyone could have objected to so public-spirited a measure. The bill's moral principle was incontestable. It asked only that a borrower be told truthfully how much he must pay for the credit he receives. To tell a person his interest rate on a 12-month installment loan will be a simple 6 percent can be utterly misleading. By the time he has paid off half the indebtedness in six months, he will still be paying 6 percent interest on the entire original face amount of the loan. His true per annum rate will be closer to 12 percent.

In addition, he could be called on to pay extra charges which could raise the total cost of his credit above 20 percent. Some of these extra fees were described as "service charges," "investigation fees," "processing costs," "late penalties," and so on. The Douglas Truth-in-Lending bill insisted that all borrowers be informed of precisely how much they would be obligated to pay. This was to be expressed as a true percentage rate per annum on the money *of which the borrower had the actual use.*

Most savings banks, including The Bowery, had long been explicit in stating the terms of the loans they made. Crawford emphasized this in hearings before the Senate Banking and Currency Committee. He spoke as chairman of the National Savings Bank Association's Committee on Public Information, and he spoke with force.

Facing the senators, he was accompanied by a formidable panel of experts: Elmer Harmon, head of The Bowery's research and statistical department; Lawrence U. Costiglio, deputy director of the Savings Bank Association; James H. Kohlerman, a noted mathematician, and Professor Raymond Rodgers of New York University.

The opposition this group had to deal with came mainly from commercial banks, retail merchants who added interest charges to charge accounts, automobile dealers, finance companies that specialized in household loans, and several others who "sold" credit. One of the earliest protestations was that true interest rates would be far too difficult to calculate in ordinary transactions. Nobody could expect an average sales clerk to make such computations. The mathematics were too involved.

When Crawford heard this, he turned to Harmon. "Elmer," he said, "let's show the cards."

It happened that Harmon had worked with a few colleagues who had helped him devise what they called the "Quick Credit-Cost Computer." This was a card some seven inches long equipped with sliding scales. When the slide was moved to indicate the amount of money borrowed, the number of installments to be paid, and the rate of interest quoted, one could immediately read—in a small, window-like aperture—the true rate of interest payable on the entire loan. The computation could be made in a matter of seconds.

As the cards were passed to the committee's members, the senators experimented with them, chuckled over the results, leaned sideward to exchange whispered comments. The pasteboards effectively destroyed the contention that it would be difficult to calculate true interest charges. Senator Douglas put his card aside and said, "I want to praise the Savings Bank Association for its public spirit in developing this Quick Credit-Cost Computer. . . . You have rendered a great public service."

Senator Prescott Bush of Connecticut added, "It is a splendid thing you have done, an excellent thing. I congratulate you heartily on the development of this computer. I would like to see the savings banks all over the United States put this in the hands of every saver, because you are talking about something here that is important to our whole economy."

Acknowledging all these comments, and there were many more, Crawford said, "I would like to set forth the savings banks' full recognition that installment credit has become a way of life. We recognize that without credit, the economy of this nation would come to a standstill. In short, we believe that credit, when used advisedly, is healthy for Americans and for the American economy. But in this era of credit it is essential for the financial welfare of any family to know not only how to save and how to buy, but also how to borrow."

Indisputable as such philosophy might be, the Douglas bill encountered so much opposition that it was not then passed. Time after time it was again presented to the Senate Committee on Banking and Currency—in 1961, 1962, 1963, and 1964. The testimony, pro and con, eventually filled 5,078 printed pages.

Crawford and his associates tenaciously continued to argue their case. At one hearing, Senator Bennett leaned forward, peered hard at the thrift institutions' spokesman, and asked, "Do I understand, Mr. Crawford, that *your* bank's advertisements always indicate the actual and complete rate of interest you charge on loans?"

Crawford answered, "Yes, sir."

"Always?"

"Always. It is our undeviating policy."

"You are sure of that?"

"Absolutely."

"Then how do you explain this?" The senator suddenly waved a Bowery advertisement clipped from a newspaper. He had it carried to Crawford. The banker looked at it. If his face blanched, he could not be blamed. Whoever had been responsible for placing this particular advertisement had omitted the customary statement of true interest rates!

It had been an accidental oversight, the only case of its kind in all the hundreds of advertisements The Bowery had placed. The senators were wise enough to understand this, and Crawford's embarrassment brought sympathetic laughter rather than challenges. He was, after all, fighting for a just cause, and most senators appreciated this.

Yet so powerful were the lobbyists who opposed the measure that it was not enacted until 1968. That occurred after Senator William Proxmire of Wisconsin, rising on the Senate floor, made an historic plea for its adoption. Capping years of effort on the part of savings banks and other supporters of the Douglas act, Senator Proxmire helped at last to achieve congressional action. And Congress passed what was surely one of the great financial reforms of our times. It brought the kind of protection "little people" had never before been accorded.

Of course, one had to change one's concept of "little people." No longer was The Bowery Savings Bank visited by the bent and humble immigrant woman, a black shawl over her shoulders, who managed to put aside a dollar or two every few weeks; or by the sweatshop worker saving to send a son to college. These and others like them were as anachronistic as the horse-drawn trolley car. In the mid-1960s, more than 40 percent of all American families were earning over $7,000 a year. Moreover, the country had 90,000 millionaries and 23 million stockholders.

Nevertheless, there were still those millions of people who saved with worried eyes on the uncertain future. The fear of a rainy day was as pressing as ever—perhaps more so when one contemplated the incredibly high and ever increasing costs of hospitalization, food, living quarters, and everything else. Today's depositors might be thinking in terms of dollars instead of pennies, but they required protection for their savings as had their forebears a century earlier. And they were getting it.

❧

The name of The Bowery Savings Bank now appears among the patrons of many cultural enterprises. It was not always so. There was a time when state laws actually forbade philanthropy on the part of mutual savings banks. Legislators argued that trustees had no right to give away money which rightfully belonged to depositors. Little by little these regulations were eased, however. By the time Schwulst became president of The Bowery, it was recognized that such an institution ought to help support worthy projects in its community. The bank contributed independently to a number of causes, and Schwulst himself became head of the Greater New York Fund, through which The Bowery made some of its major gifts.

Then came 1966. A gala farewell performance was being given at the old Broadway home of the Metropolitan Opera Company. It was about to move to the modern new theater at Lincoln Center.

The farewell presentation was unforgettable. A census of the audience would have listed the social, artistic, financial, and political elite of New York—people who did not mind paying $150 for a ticket.

The venerable Maestro Leopold Stokowski launched the occasion by conducting the "Entrance of the Guests" march from *Tannhauser*. When he finished, to wild applause and a standing ovation, his baton was passed on throughout the evening to a dazzling succession of opera conductors—Zubin Mehta, Eric Leinsdorf, Fausto Cleva, Molinari-Pradelli, Joseph Rosenstock, and more. Forty internationally famed singers walked onto the stage, one at a time, each arousing applause and shouts of "Bravo!"

Many of them sang their favorite arias—sang, as one reviewer wrote, "from the heart." Some broke down in tears. One, Licia Albanese, knelt to kiss the boards of the stage in farewell. On this historic 1966 night, everyone present had to feel emotionally involved.

What was happening at the opera, in the theater, in the arts, and in every other phase of New York's cultural activities made Morris Crawford, Jr. place a new suggestion before the board of trustees. He argued that the bank, as an integral part of the city's life, ought more directly to support and participate in worthy civic activities. It ought to encourage them, to endow them.

The trustees agreed. As individuals, they had long been contributing to such causes. And so the bank expanded a policy of giving direct grants—but Crawford had his own rather unique way of doing this.

He went to the Metropolitan Museum of Art, to the Museum of Natural History, to the Metropolitan Opera, to the New York Philharmonic Society, and several other institutions. He gave each of them a Bowery passbook indicating that $500 had been deposited to that particular organization's credit. The bank planned to make additional contributions annually. Naturally, the money could be withdrawn at any time the recipients desired to use it— plus the dividends it had earned.

One need hardly say that the directors of these various institutions were astonished and delighted to have a bank president come in, unsolicited, with a contribution. Also, now that they had accounts at The Bowery, a number of the recipients deposited additional funds to draw dividends until the money was needed. Thus culture and banking shared in the benefits of what might be called Crawford's inspiration.

Today The Bowery's direct grants go to several dozen causes. At one time the bank even endowed a historic documentary television series, *The Silent Years,* for which it won an Emmy award. This desire to have the bank participate directly in public affairs was a reflection of Crawford's general philosophy. Once, when I asked Earl Schwulst to define the philosophy of his successor, he pondered a while, then said:

"Rusty goes much further than either Bruère or I, or any of our predecessors, in bringing to his job a sense of responsibility to the city and to the welfare of the people of New York. I do not mean only in a financial sense but, just as importantly, in a social sense. In this he is joined by John Larsen, who has the same dedication to public responsibility. Larsen's civic activities, combined with Crawford's, have made The Bowery more than a financial institution. They have made it, in my opinion, a vital force in every aspect of New York life."

These mid-1960s were years of extraordinary excitement for the nation. When Crawford was elected chairman of The Bowery in 1966 (on Schwulst's retirement), and John Larsen succeeded to the presidency, every banking and financial publication noted the events with generous space, pictures, and biographical data. But newspapers were more sparing in the space they allotted to it. That was hardly surprising. Nothing that happened in any bank could compete with other occurrences that preempted headlines.

For 1966 was the year when the first Soviet spacecraft, the unmanned Luna 9, landed on the moon. Four months later, the United States accomplished the same feat with its Surveyor 1. And in Europe France shocked her allies— and no doubt pleased the Politburo—by withdrawing her troops from NATO forces. In fact, wild events were shaking the whole world.

The 1966 race riots were erupting throughout America, with throngs screaming for "Black power!" and marching, arm in arm, to the strains of "We shall overcome!" These demonstrations continued through 1967, and in 1968 nobody could think about banks because, first, the U.S.S. *Pueblo's* plight off the coast of Korea threatened to draw the United States into a new conflict as grim as the one in Vietnam.

Hardly had this crisis been passed when, in a single year, both Robert F. Kennedy and Martin Luther King, Jr. were assassinated. And later, while Richard Milhous Nixon was being elected President by a skin-of-the-teeth plurality, Jacqueline Kennedy suddenly preempted international headlines by marrying Aristotle Onassis—an event which, despite the defense of her conduct by her friend Cardinal Cushing, brought her a considerable amount of criticism. The headlines of this marriage were just beginning to leave the front pages when another

Kennedy stunned the country. Senator Edward M. Kennedy plunged into a wildly dramatic misadventure destined to be labeled and remembered by a single word—Chappaquiddick.

With so many sensational things happening in the world, nobody could be interested in the internal affairs of banks—except, of course, the bankers. At The Bowery, Crawford and Larsen were quietly forging the kind of executive teamwork which resulted in some of the institution's most innovative years.

Not the least of their innovations was the creation of a marketing and public relations department (then under the supervision of Robert D. Pierson). Crawford was questioned about this when he attended an International Savings Bank Congress. To a foreign audience which had probably never considered marketing research as part of a thrift institution's operations, he explained:

"The annual report of any modern industrial enterprise discloses the huge sums devoted to research and development. I understand that the aggregate sum spent for that purpose last year by American industry was in excess of $17 billion. Have you ever seen any items called 'research and development' in the budget of *your* savings bank?"

Standing at a microphone, he saw only negative headshaking and perplexity. So he went on to report some of the benefits that had accrued to The Bowery from researching the needs of depositors and prospective depositors and from learning what competitors were doing.

"But just as we are constantly challenged by competitors," he added, "we must constantly challenge our *own* most cherished beliefs, traditions, and assumptions. We must at all times know who our competitors are. We must refine our investment techniques to meet new opportunities. To do this, we must use all the modern research and computer techniques available to study all areas of management concern."

Recalling that in America the savings banks had originally been founded to serve the poor, he maintained that these institutions were now serving all of society. "We must constantly define and redefine our business and our functions in the light of present-day reality rather than tradition. We must do our best to peer into the future and try to foresee how our society will look 10, 15, 25 years from today and plan our development to meet those conditions."

This venture into research has since been adopted by many banks. According to Robert Pierson, "It has affected every aspect of our service to the public, including our advertising. It has stimulated us to sponsor public seminars in which we invite questions on every feature of a family's financial concerns. These seminars, helpful as they may be to the audiences, are even more helpful to us. They tell us what services people desire and what we can and should do for them."

Another area to which the Crawford administration has given a considerable amount of energy is the vigorous promotion of Savings Bank Life Insurance. Though The Bowery has accounted for more life insurance sales than has any other savings bank, it at times had to move counter to the beliefs of many of its sister institutions. In 1966, Crawford analyzed this at a meeting in Hartford, Connecticut.

Some bankers, he said, "simply didn't feel that savings banks should be in the life insurance business. It's been said that if savings banks began to get into other types of business, the next thing you knew they would be running grocery stores. There might be some basis for this objection if, in entering the life insurance field, we were engaging in a business not related to thrift. Just the opposite is the case, for life insurance is a *form* of savings."

Another objection he noted was: "A handful of banks, all located in small towns, said that there was a public relations problem involved because they did not want to incur the ill will of life insurance agents in their communities." Refuting this, he reminded his audience that the amount of life insurance a bank could sell was limited by law. "Savings Bank Life Insurance cannot supply the *total* life insurance protection that the usual insurance buyer requires. Such a buyer, once exposed to life insurance through the medium of his local savings bank, is very likely to want to supplement his holdings and will thus become an easier prospect for life insurance agents."

It is impressive to note that Savings Bank Life Insurance —SBLI—is now a thriving part of the operations of most of the mutual savings banks in New York, Connecticut, and Massachussetts. By the end of 1973, more than $6 billion of such insurance had been written by 334 of these institutions. SBLI was a success.

Its popularity is further attested by the fact that within a year The Bowery averaged more than a million dollars in insurance sales every week. That was far more than any other savings bank managed to place. A significant thing about it was this: Whereas life insurance used to be bought almost exclusively by men, the traditional family breadwinners, by 1974 women accounted for 35.1 percent of all life insurance sold by the bank. (The national figure for women in 1974 was 25 percent.) What the change indicates is a revolutionary development in the American economy that has evolved even further since 1974: More women than ever are becoming either family breadwinners, or coworkers with their husbands in support of their families; or else, in the case of unmarried women, they now have heavy financial responsibilities to others.

Another comparatively new development, this one in the mortgage field, came with legislation that enabled savings banks to make mortgage loans in some states that had no such banks. This has been especially effective in California, Texas, Florida, and Virginia.

"All told," the National Association of Mutual Savings Banks reported at the end of 1974, "more than 1.3 million families in non-savings-bank states reside in housing currently financed by savings banks."

Since Bowery officers helped campaign for such developments, their gratification is natural. Still, not every goal for which Crawford and Larsen strived over the years has been attained.

One that has eluded them is the right of savings banks to make the kind of personal loans which commercial banks can grant. The enormous popularity of such consumer loans—based on no collateral beyond faith in the borrower's earning capacity and his integrity—has done much to change the image of banks and bankers. We have come a long way from the days when a sardonic cliché maintained, "You can always get a bank loan if you can prove you're rich enough not to need it."

For commercial banks, the personal loan is a highly profitable source of revenue. It offers a quick turnover of funds at attractive interest rates. Were all savings banks empowered to make such loans, as they are in some states, it would clearly enhance their earning potential while providing an essential service to their clients.

Crawford has been among the leaders of those crusading for this right. Testifying in Washington, he said: "There are periods in the lives of most individuals (usually the years when they are rearing children) when substantial saving is impossible. At this 'borrowing' age, these individuals should be able to obtain a reasonable amount of personal credit from savings institutions, thus cementing relations which will later result in savings. Our principal competitor today—the commercial bank—is serving this need and is, as a result, drawing off many of our potential customers, to say nothing of our present customers."

At another time, testifying before the New York State Legislature, Crawford adduced figures to show that a poll

273

had found 63 percent of the people questioned to be in favor of allowing savings banks to make personal loans. On this occasion he repeated, "We see a great opportunity to lend money to people at the time in their lives when they need to use normal credit, and to be entrusted with their savings accounts at another period in their lives when they become savers."

Nevertheless, the opposition to this, again led in the main by commercial banks, remained unyielding. Crawford, Larsen, and other savings bankers have continued the struggle for years. As recently as 1973, Larsen analyzed the conflict in an article he wrote for *The American Banker:*

"The only rationale that has been advanced for the withholding of such lending powers," he said, "is the fear in some quarters that mortgage funds may be diverted to consumer lending areas. This argument implicitly assumes that consumer lending is more profitable than mortgage lending and that an institution will, therefore, decrease its mortgage portfolio by the amount it commits to consumer credit operations. The net result of such an allocation, or so the argument goes, would be a decrease in funds available for the housing sector of our economy."

Having stated the charge, he refuted it. "Indeed," he said, "there is good reason to believe that the reverse may be true. Ability to offer personal loans may attract *more* deposits to savings banks and therefore result in *more* funds for the mortgage market." In support of this contention, Larsen cited the experience of savings banks in six states that permit them to make personal loans. Almost invariably, an increased ratio of such loans was accompanied by an increased ratio in mortgage loans.

"It is indeed an anomaly," Larsen concluded, "that savings banks, originally founded in the early nineteenth century to provide the working man with the major consumer service then needed—a safe place to keep his money to build financial security for his family—are today prevented by law from providing this universally used financial service, the personal loan."

Larsen's remarks reflected the convictions gained in a banking career begun in 1933 at the North River Savings Bank. A certified public accountant with a Bachelor of Science degree from New York University, John Larsen had left banking only once in his life—to serve in the wartime navy from 1943 to 1946. Immediately after World War II, he had returned to his financial career. At The Bowery he had steadily risen to the presidency. So he based his opinions on more than three decades of experience and knowledge.

But neither Crawford, Larsen, nor any other savings banker in New York State has so far been able to budge the forces that opposed them on the question of personal loans. Savings bankers averred that such a change would be in the public interest, and their hope for the future was sustained by the conviction that in a democracy, what is in the public interest must ultimately come to pass.

26
❧
ERA OF TURMOIL

On November 18, 1969, a riot occurred in the Grand Ballroom of the New York Hilton Hotel.

In his capacity as chairman of the Regional Plan Association—one of his many civic activities—Morris Crawford, Jr. was presiding at a luncheon of some 2,000 people. They had gathered to witness the granting of an award for public service to Governor Richard Hughes of New Jersey. On the dais the governor sat on one side of Crawford; on the other was Andrew Heiskell, board chairman of Time Inc., who was scheduled to deliver the principal address.

Crawford had just risen to launch the ceremonies after lunch when the main doors burst open with an explosive crash. A shouting mob rushed into the hall. According to later newspaper reports, the intruders were "black militants and white radicals." As they broke into the meeting they screamed, "Power to the people!" and "We want food!" and "We want jobs!"

Their leaders surged over the dais. Several men with bullhorns leaped up on the head table and roared their slogans to the stunned guests. Others released stink bombs, and with these a strong odor of marijuana. Coughing, eyes beginning to stream, guests rose from their seats and stumbled toward the doors.

Crawford had only one recourse. He called, "The meeting is adjourned!" The award ceremony ended before it had begun. Governor Hughes did not receive his tribute that day. The award was presented to him later.

Disruptive demonstrations of this sort had different meanings for different observers. Some felt they indicated a revival of ugly tribalism. Rapacious gangs, roaming the cities in behalf of this or that demand, brutally destroyed what they considered their opposition. Other people saw such activities as the emotional outbursts of minorities which knew no better means of self-expression. Some regarded them as symbols of a sick society, others of a healthy, self-asserting society.

Whatever they were, they reflected a frightening turbulence in America's urban life, much of it spurred by opposition to the Vietnam war. New York witnessed one of the most violent eruptions at Columbia University—a campus fracas that all but destroyed the office of President Grayson Kirk and brought hundreds of city police rushing to quell the disturbance with clubs, water hoses, and tear gas.

Because Bowery officers were involved in so many civic organizations, the rioting affected them almost as a personal challenge. "The welfare of a bank, any bank, is linked to the welfare of its community," one vice president said.

For years, Bowery officers had worked closely with the Regional Plan Association, the Citizens Budget Commission, and similar agencies dedicated to New York's welfare. Bruère, Schwulst, Larsen, and many of their colleagues had given civic organizations so much time and effort that serving the city did indeed seem to be part of banking.

Crawford's connection with the Regional Plan Association had begun during his first years with the bank. He had been asked to serve as co-chairman (with Andrew Heiskell) of a committee that studied the deteriorating affairs of New York's commuter railroads. Later he was asked to accept the chairmanship of a committee which was to review the proposed Second Regional Plan (the first having been offered decades earlier). The years of his chairmanship of this committee—and later of the Association itself—carried him into an era of riotous uprisings, like the one at the Hilton Hotel, that were striking at New York and other cities throughout the nation.

Bankers could not sally forth to quell riots with speeches or clubs. But they could do other things. They could try to uncover and remove the basic *causes* of minority discontent.

For this purpose, The Bowery had established a department of urban affairs whose principal duty was to help improve life in the city. This was done largely by financing the demolition of slums and the construction of modern housing—projects that created hundreds of jobs as well as hundreds of dwellings. With Vice President Pazel Jackson heading the Department of Urban Affairs, it has resulted in the building of modern, livable homes in districts that had become virtually unfit for human use.

While Crawford headed the Regional Plan Association,

John Larsen served—among other activities—as chairman of the Citizens Budget Commission. One of the most prestigious organizations in the city, supported by 365 outstanding business and civic leaders, it has since 1932 been the watchdog of New York's fiscal operations. Also, it has been a constant counselor for the solution of social problems.

"When John Larsen assumed the chairmanship of our Commission," a veteran staff member said, "he brought in a new spirit of efficiency, hard work, and vigilance. The result was that during his years in the executive post, our Commission accomplished more than in any other period I can remember."

Based on studies, the Commission recommended that the city stop bickering with the state over what it called "being short-changed" in monetary arrangements. It urged a more sensible method of cooperation among local, state, and federal authorities, a formula which has since been championed by a number of cities.

With equal energy, the Commission helped bring about a campaign against drug addiction. It opposed what it regarded as unreasonable borrowing by one city administration, persuading it to reduce its borrowing from a contemplated $400 million to $100 million. Thereby the citizens were spared an extra and needless $300 million of public indebtedness.

One could list a score of similar activities over which Larsen presided at the Citizens Budget Commission. All were aimed at making New York a better community. He was equally active, however, in the Boy Scout movement. Once, when asked if there was any connection between Boy Scouts and savings banks, he said, "If a Scout doesn't grow up with respect for thrift and self-reliance, we have failed in the training we gave him."

As a result of all such activities, the office walls of many Bowery executives are hung with plaques, citations, certificates of appreciation, and awards. Some are surprising. In 1972, for instance, Crawford was given the USO medal for his devotion to the needs of servicemen. And even on this occasion, as he made his acceptance speech, he concentrated on civic betterment.

What troubled him, he said, was that thousands of service men and women, returning to civilian life from Vietnam, could find no jobs in the cities. Before World War II, he recalled, "Cities were the centers of life all around them. The jobs and services were there. The major shopping was there."

Then, he reminded his audience, many of the cities' activities began being transferred to the suburbs. Offices, colleges, hotels, shopping centers—all were going out of the cities. "Urban life in America has lost its focus," he charged. "The cities are losing their historic function."

Crawford viewed the hegira to the suburbs as an attempt to *escape* from urban problems. "And the Regional Plan Association has tried to find a solution rather than an escape," he said. "We want to *save* the city instead of turning our backs on it."

No doubt many of his listeners thought that as head of The Bowery Savings Bank he had an obvious self-interest in the prosperity of New York. Only if its people were prosperous would they have the money to deposit in his institution. Crawford readily admitted the financial involvement of The Bowery, just as he pointed out the involvement of other banks, of insurance and real estate companies, of every source of investment in the building of New York and other cities.

"Unless we restore the cities' basic function," he declared, "their ability to bring people together for production, for stimulation, for enlightenment, for enjoyment, I don't see much future for the billions of dollars now invested in them."

Had he indulged in criticism without striking out for

remedial action, one might have accused him of giving mere lip service to a cause. But he had already tackled many urban problems with the same energy he had given to the challenges of the bank. In fact, he headed a group of more than 125 leaders of every segment, major and minor, of the city's population—industrialists, professional people, representatives of the arts, political figures, educators, and others.

In New York many civic leaders publicly called for a return to the businesslike integrity, the firmness of purpose, the dedication to the city's interests that had marked the administration of pugnacious little Mayor Fiorello LaGuardia. Stated another way, what Crawford and the Regional Plan Association sought was civic efficiency and humanitarianism.

Once I asked The Bowery's chairman how the trustees felt about the time and effort he gave to such causes outside the bank.

"If I didn't engage in these activities," he replied, "they'd probably say I wasn't doing my job as I should. The welfare of our bank depends on the welfare of our city. When I work for one, I work for both."

That becomes all the more understandable when one remembers that The Bowery now had more than $2¼ billion invested in mortgages, most of them in urban structures, both residential and business.

John Larsen had his own way of viewing the civic responsibilities inherent in the presidency of an institution like The Bowery. He was recently given the Annual Award of the National Jewish Hospital of Denver for his efforts in behalf of that institution. Rising to accept his plaque, he told an audience of some 1,500:

"As leaders in the business community, we have demonstrated in the past that we have the talents and the resources and the willingness to make dramatic improvements in many areas that affect large numbers of our fellow citizens. I see this as our *duty* to one another. As human beings we can do no less."

cＮo

Throughout the decade beginning in 1961, there were only two years, 1966 and 1969, when the receipts of the U.S. government were in excess of its expenditures. During the rest of the 1960s (principally because of the drain on the United States of its commitments in Vietnam), the Treasury spent far more than it collected. It plunged into the kind of indebtedness that would have been inconceivable even half a century earlier: a federal debt of over $300 billion, and more than $21 billion interest to be paid on it every year.

This was the period in American history when President Lyndon Johnson, despite all prior contrary assurances during his campaign against Barry Goldwater, was sending thousands of troops to Vietnam. William Manchester, in his chronicles, recalls the remark of a woman who said, "I was warned that if I voted for Goldwater the war would be escalated. I did vote for Goldwater— and it was." At any rate, together with half a million troops, billions of dollars went into the Vietnam struggle.

Yet the period was in many ways regarded as one of prosperity, as is always the case when the government spends billions on expendable war equipment. Such prosperity was actually a delusion. The country was sinking deeper and deeper into a morass of liabilities.

(Once, while watching naval maneuvers from the bridge of an aircraft carrier, I asked the captain how much it was costing in ammunition to have the anti-aircraft guns firing away at aerial targets hour after hour.

He answered, "About $53,000 per minute." That dramatized the price of military materiel, which is either quickly destroyed or, like aircraft, becomes obsolete even before its cost has been defrayed.)

How does all this affect savings banks? When hundreds of thousands of people are working to provide wartime needs, their pay is steady, and savings deposits presumably increase. Yet this is not an incontrovertible economic law. During the Vietnam "prosperous" years, Americans were paying out more than 35 percent of their earnings in federal, state, and local taxes. With living costs rising at the same time, many families had to make difficult sacrifices in order to save even a little.

"The truth is," a Bowery officer remarked, "one cannot repeat often enough that our bank is affected in one way or another by everything that happens in this country."

One can safely say that more of a dramatic nature has happened in the world during the administration of Rusty Crawford than in almost any other period. On an evening at the Overseas Press Club of New York, I sat with a group of pipe-smoking journalists who were evaluating the outstanding events of recent years. The majority agreed that Vietnam must be regarded as the salient American concern of the 1960s; and in the 1970s nothing of a political nature could overshadow the collapse of the Nixon Administration. Beyond this, however, there was little concurrence.

One man said, "Looking back, I'd place the progress of space travel, especially the landings on the moon, high on the list of recent historic events. This was the basis of scientific advancements which no other period has been able to match." (One visualizes the thousands of factories that have been constructed to manufacture products of these scientific developments—everything from solid-state television equipment to solar-heated homes, from supersonic rocketry to miniaturized electronic circuitry.

And one must speculate upon the billions in mortgage loans these new plants have required from banks like The Bowery.)

A British newspaperman asserted, "I would say the biggest and most important problem of recent times lies in the energy crisis and the actions of the Middle East oil countries. The price of oil, of gasoline, of related products has increased the price of everything from home-maintenance to travel. It has sapped away a great part of the buying capacity of the American public." (And a great part of its *saving* capacity, one had to add; this must inevitably affect savings banks.)

"What about Israel?" another journalist asked. "Until its security is guaranteed, I see no greater threat to world peace." (Many Americans who sympathized with the country's plight were withdrawing part of their savings to invest in Israeli bonds.)

So it went. Universal inflation, America's economic recession, the worldwide food shortage, the explosive increase in the price of gold, future relations with China and the Soviet Union—all these and other concerns, including the struggle for civil rights, had their spokesmen among the journalists. One had the impression that recent American history had been in the nature of a kaleidoscope, every glimpse of it revealing spectacular new aspects.

For The Bowery, there were the more immediate problems of community needs. These were social as well as physical and financial. Recent changes in legislation had made it possible for savings banks to *construct* dwellings, not simply to provide the mortgage money for such construction. The Bowery and the New York Bank for Savings were among the first to avail themselves of this opportunity. Recognizing the plight of slum areas, these two began to build where many others feared to go.

In the choice of sites, Crawford relied heavily on the

bank's newly established urban affairs department. Its head, Pazel G. Jackson, Jr.—formerly assistant commissioner of the Department of Buildings for the City of New York—knew the agonies of slum areas as few other men did. Within four years, his staff was able to report to the bank's board of trustees:

> The Bowery Savings Bank and the New York Bank for Savings have faced the housing problems of the City on an equal partnership basis. This partnership has set an example for the rest of the savings and commercial banks in the area, for private corporations of all types, and for the entire nation as to what two mutual savings banks can achieve working together. . . . They obtained approval from their respective Boards to build a Turnkey project on 123rd Street between Park and Lexington Avenues. Since that time two projects have been completed, four more are under construction, and many more are in planning.

As for Crawford and Larsen, they were able to report at the end of 1973 that: "Financing of city urban renewal projects remained a top priority in 1973. The Bowery was the lead bank in moving forward the construction of two major housing developments: the Hester Allen Project to provide living quarters for 107 underprivileged families on Manhattan's Lower East Side, and the Atlantic Terminal Project in Brooklyn, especially designed for the elderly and disabled."

These were in addition to many other programs for the rebuilding of desolate, often crumbling areas. The construction of such "Turnkey" buildings has never stopped. ("Turnkey" simply means that at the completion of a project, its keys are turned over to the city, which will own and manage it.) Today the Dry Dock, the Emigrant, the Dime, and other savings banks have joined the crusade to rehabilitate the slum areas.

In recognition of all these pioneering activities, the

city's Realty Board presented its award for outstanding service jointly to The Bowery and the New York Bank for Savings.

⌖

If one judges the decade of the 1960s solely by statistics, these were good years for the savings banks. Their assets almost doubled from $40.5 billion in 1960 to just under $79 billion in 1970.

Still, this gain was miniscule when compared to the increased assets of commercial banks during the same period—from $256 billion to $572.5 billion; or to the astonishing rise of savings and loan assets—from $71.5 billion to $176.5 billion. Considering such differentials, however, one must remember that there were only 506 mutual savings banks in existence at the time, while commercial banks and savings and loan associations could be counted in the thousands. Viewed in that perspective, the small number of mutual savings banks did very well indeed.

Over lunch some years ago, I discussed the increasing prosperity of banks with the then senior senator from New York, Irving M. Ives. He listened patiently before he said, "That's all very fine, and I'm glad to hear it. But what strikes me as being more important is that Americans are *saving* more than ever—or let me put it the other way around: More Americans than ever are saving, and that augers well for the future of the nation."

Basically his remarks reflected the feelings of men like Rusty Crawford and John Larsen. As savings bankers they necessarily were interested in the welfare of people, the only reason for which their institutions exist.

Today, one of the bank's deepest concerns relates to

unemployment. In a book published by the Regional Plan Association, *How to Save Urban America,* one reads:

> The main reason for persistent unemployment in New York City and the region, even in times of prosperity, is that most unemployed people lack the skills this specialized economy demands. . . . Only 10 percent of today's high school students receive any vocational training, and many of them are learning vocations for which there is little demand. . . . Students are told not to drop out, but many of those who listen receive diplomas that have been called passports to nowhere.

This has been even more poignantly true for veterans returning from Vietnam. Many of them went into the Armed Services when they were too young to have any vocational training at all. Where can they now offer themselves? The agony is even worse for those who were disabled.

True, there are agencies, private and governmental, that try to serve handicapped veterans. The Bowery has found a number of them fully able to fill office jobs. A one-armed man has no trouble in assorting bank mail; another with leg-paralysis is an expert accountant. And so the list grows. As another example of private endeavor, the Bulova Foundation maintains a school in Flushing, New York where scores of veterans in wheelchairs bend over work tables at which they learn the skills of watchmakers. Harry Henshel, chairman of the Foundation, spoke of this enterprise as "the gateway to self-support and self-respect for men who ask only to be given a chance to show what they can do."

Bankers of past generations were too often regarded, especially in novels and plays, as men obsessed by insatiable lust for financial power. Surely there have been such men, but there have also been those who have understood that *only people with jobs can become depositors.*

Today, virtually every savings banker makes this point. Crawford and Larsen have emphasized it in many speeches. But when they speak about the importance of creating jobs, one cannot help recalling the hostility expressed by conservatives to the "make-work" policies of Roosevelt's New Deal. "When you give people jobs which aren't really needed," they argued, "you reduce their self-respect and turn them into meaningless robots."

Yet today the Regional Plan Association, headed by a banker, points out: "The largest public job programs in U.S. history were the WPA (Works Progress Administration), the PWA (Public Works Administration), and the CCC (Civilian Conservation Corps) during the depression, which at their height put 4 million people to work. While there was some waste, work of value was accomplished. The building program alone produced 116,000 buildings, 28,000 bridges, 651,000 miles of roads, and improvements at 800 airports and at innumerable national, state, and local parks."

Viewing the enormous federal and local sums now being expended for unemployment benefits and for welfare payments, the Regional Plan Association argues: "If we are subsidizing anyhow, why not subsidize work in the public sector by creating public-service jobs?"

To ask men like Crawford what this has to do with banking is to elicit the reply: "Savings banks were founded to enhance the *general welfare* of wage earners and their families. If we ever forget that objective, we shall have lost our reason for existence."

27
TOWARD
A BETTER SYSTEM

The Bowery now had twelve offices. Ten were within the city limits. Two were in the Long Island suburbs of Westbury and Massapequa Park. The permanent office of the latter was inaugurated on February 17, 1974 in an atmosphere gay with flags, bunting, and an attending crowd. Local officials had warmly welcomed it as a stimulant to the community's growth.

But there were also those, as among the older residents of every town in the United States, who looked sadly upon "big-city intrusion" on small-town tranquillity. It inevitably alters the character of suburban areas, and not always for the better.

This became a vitally important consideration for The Bowery in 1976 when, by a new law, New York savings banks were permitted to open branches throughout New York state. Did small local banks resent the new law, or regard it as permitting unjustifiable competition? Were local residents resistant to the new branches?

Obviously it was important for the public relations department of The Bowery to do whatever it could to counter possible resentment in the communities where it was opening new branches. To achieve this, good will meetings were held before the opening of every branch, to assure members of the community that the quality of local life would be enhanced rather than threatened by the greater availability of banking services.

In the case of the Massapequa Park office, most local people were pleased by its advent. Chairman Crawford did not describe the new branch as a traditional savings institution. He foresaw it as becoming part of "a major economic force involved in a wide range of investment and banking services."

If he seemed optimistic, it was because the President of the United States himself had made it clear that he favored a liberalization of banking regulations. Nixon had appointed a commission to formulate such changes. Indications were that the President would press Congress for essential reforms.

At the time the Massapequa Park office was opened, Nixon was in China with Secretary of State Kissinger. The full impact of Watergate had not yet crashed upon the Nixon Administration. One could still hope that on his return the President would concentrate on domestic matters, including the improvement of the nation's banking system. Not that the American public was troubled about its banks; the public's attention was fixed on such things as the challenge for the Presidency by Senator George McGovern; on the eccentricities of international chess champion Bobby Fischer, who was playing the Russian champion, Boris Spassky. The spurious biography of Howard Hughes by Clifford Irving was also capturing the public interest.

The opening of the Massapequa branch could hardly overshadow such matters. Nonetheless, for Crawford it seemed to symbolize a coming era of broader opportunities for savings banks.

It was then a year and a half since President Nixon, in his concern for banks, had created the President's Commission on Financial Structure and Regulation. To its chairmanship he had appointed Reed O. Hunt, retired board chairman of the Crown Zellerbach Corporation. The Commission's objective, in bureaucratic terms, was "to review and study the structure, operation, and regulation of the private financial institutions in the United States, for the purpose of formulating recommendations that would improve the functioning of the private financial system."

Three of the Commission's twenty members represented thrift groups. They were J. Howard Edgerton, chairman of the California Federal Savings and Loan Association of Los Angeles; Richard C. Gilbert, president of the Citizens Savings Association of Canton, Ohio; and Morris D. Crawford, Jr. of The Bowery.

For eighteen months this Hunt Commission, as it came to be called, labored to produce its recommendations. It was aided by a staff of economists, lawyers, bankers, accountants, and other specialists. Its ultimate report was delivered at the White House on December 22, 1971. There the commissioners sat around a long conference table with the President, and Chairman Hunt began discussing his report.

"We propose," he said, "a number of fundamental changes in the nation's financial system."

It was like a warning of drastic suggestions to come. He made it clear, however, that though all the commissioners had signed the report, not every one of them agreed with every recommendation it made. Four men had filed dissenting opinions on specific points. But, Hunt added, "The signatures of the commissioners should be interpreted as an indication of their general agreement with the thrust of this report."

Hunt then proceeded to the body of his document. He reminded the President that the White House Council of Economic Advisers had predicted as far back as 1970 that:

> Financial services in tomorrow's economy will differ from those appropriate today. The demands on our flow of national savings . . . will be heavy in the years ahead, and our financial structure must have the flexibility that will permit a sensitive response to changing demands.

Thereupon the Hunt Report urged that "all institutions competing in the same markets do so on an equal basis." This was certainly in conformity with American principles. The commissioners made the prophecy that: "The public will be better served by such competition. Markets will work more efficiently in the allocation of funds, and total savings will expand to meet private and public needs."

Simultaneously the report emphasized some disturbing aspects of the American economy that could seriously disrupt the nation's welfare. It pointed out that:

> The recent period of sustained high interest rates [in commercial banks] had severe effects. Not only was the solvency

of a large number of firms threatened, but many borrowers who traditionally relied on financial institutions for loans found them unwilling or unable to lend adequate funds, even at historically high rates of interest. . . .

Corporations that normally would borrow from banks made it a common practice to issue commercial paper. Commercial paper outstanding rose from $8.4 billion at the end of 1964 to almost $39.2 billion by mid-1970.

In other words, more and more corporations were bypassing banks and going straight to the public in their quest for money.

(When the prime interest rate at leading commercial banks hovered around 11 percent in 1974, the treasurer of one large corporation told an interviewer: "Our company needs over $100 million to construct and equip several new plants we're building. Why should we pay a bank $11 million a year in interest charges when we can sell our own commercial paper at a 9 percent interest rate and pay only $9 million a year? Two million dollars saved is not an inconsiderable item.")

The Hunt Report also pointed to the dilemma of the small businessman who could *not* market his own commercial paper: "Small and medium-sized business did not have the alternatives to borrowing at banks, and therefore found their ability to acquire funds limited."

Limited? In many cases that was a euphemism for "impossible." Who would buy the paper of a small, unknown entrepreneur? Who would underwrite it?

Such circumstances were putting the small businessman in a precarious position. Unless he could compete fairly for the financing he required, he faced bankruptcy—as indeed did the entire American credo of equal freedom of opportunity for all.

Of course, the Hunt Commission concerned itself with the broad problems of every kind of financial institution—

savings banks, commercial banks, savings and loan associations, credit unions, life insurance companies, even private pension funds. But it placed special stress on the future of the thrift institutions. It endorsed the major reform for which Crawford and his savings bank colleagues had so long been crusading; namely, that "federal charters be made available to mutual savings banks."

The outcome of this White House meeting was that the Nixon Administration submitted legislation to Congress which would implement many of the Commission's long list of recommendations. It was reasonable to assume that thereafter the President might have pressed harder for congressional enactment if the Watergate debacle had not wrenched him away from affairs of state.

Early in his successor's administration, President Ford too expressed approval of the Hunt Report. By its terms, mutual savings banks would at last see their state-chartered status expanded to permit federal charters, and would thus come much closer to being full-service institutions—"a major economic force involved in a wide range of investment and banking services."

Because at the end of 1974 The Bowery was the biggest of all mutual savings banks with some 700,000 depositors and $3.5 billion in deposits, it had unique problems. It is not easy to adjust to such size if one hopes to retain the intimate person-to-person relationships that "family banks" want to preserve. Such relationships were part of their attractiveness when they were small, and undeniably there are some significant advantages to being small which a bank like The Bowery does not wish to sacrifice.

I remember discussing this matter of smallness with a

rural banker in Maine. I wondered how much business he lost to the large banks in Boston, only a few hours away.

"We don't lose *any* business to them," he said. "We get ours, and they get theirs."

Meaning?

"Well, for one thing," he explained, "if a man needed ten million dollars, he wouldn't come to us. We don't do business at that level. A few thousand is our average loan. The big Boston banks aren't interested in our kind of business, and we don't consider each other competitors.

"Besides, we offer our clients something the Boston boys are too big to offer—personal attention, personal interest, personal *understanding*. When a man comes into this bank, he knows he can talk directly to me, the president. He knows the three tellers by their first names. He feels at home. This is *his* bank. It's not like walking into one of those crowded multi-billion-dollar giants where the little man stands on line and feels like a nobody, where the only time he gets to meet a major officer is when he has to explain why he can't make a payment due on a loan. I think people feel happier and more at home in a small bank."

Can an organization like The Bowery make 700,000 depositors feel "happy and at home"? Can it assure its clients of ready access to the bank's officers? The only way is to have enough ranking officers to meet the need. By 1974, among its 900-plus employees, The Bowery Savings Bank now had—in addition to Chairman Crawford and President Larsen—approximately 80 other officers. There were four senior vice presidents: Peter J. André, Elmer M. Harmon (treasurer and chief investment officer), Theodore C. Jackson, and Christoph H. Schmidt. Schmidt, by the way, was formerly First Deputy State Superintendent of Banks.

And there were Jack S. Older, secretary and office counsel; Edward K. Smith, Jr., the controller; Robert D. Pierson, marketing director; Arthur H. Fuchs, general auditor; and William W. Johnson, personnel director. In fact, the roster of officers included 18 vice presidents, 17 assistant vice presidents, 19 assistant treasurers, 9 mortgage officers—and so on and on, with several women now among the vice presidents. When a customer wanted to see an officer, there was seldom a problem.

Moreover, the number has grown. Recent economic developments have often made it essential for depositors to consult officers. As instances: When advertisements informed the public that new regulations enabled them to earn 8.17 percent in savings dividends—provided they deposited a minimum of $1,000 for at least six years—hundreds of people asked for explanations. What if they needed their money during those six years? What if they needed *part* of it? They would accept assurances from no one but "somebody in charge."

The same was true when the Internal Revenue Service permitted self-employed people to put as much as $7,500, tax free, into a Keogh retirement fund. Depositors wanted clarification from responsible officers: Exactly what is meant by a self-employed person? Does it apply to the Avon door-to-door saleslady whose commissions depend entirely on the time and effort she gives her work? Is she employed by Avon or is she her own boss? What about the teacher who tutors on his own time and may be described as *partly* self-employed? Such people—and there are hundreds with similar problems, no two quite alike—request guidance only from those with official positions in the bank.

Not that all questions can be answered even by top-ranking executives. The uncertainty about whether or not to invest in gold was precisely such a matter.

"This was something about which I simply could not make recommendations," a vice president told me. "I tried to explain to questioners that, with gold selling at close to $200 an ounce when it became available, it was as likely to go down as up. Nobody knew. A depositor would have to make his own decision. We have to remember that when Andrew Jackson freed gold bullion for public purchase, its price quickly dropped. The same could happen in our time, and I did not want to be responsible for steering a depositor toward a serious loss.

"But I *could* remind him that the possession of a bar of gold yields no interest as does money in a savings account. I *could* warn him that a bar of gold will buy no food in a supermarket. It is not cash. Beyond that, I couldn't go on giving counsel." The bank official thought a moment, then added, "I guess it comes down to this: If you can't give the kind of advice you would give to yourself, it is better to give none at all."

In 1974, as it was a hundred and forty years earlier, the importance of maintaining forthright personal relations with depositors could not be overestimated. It was the spirit Joe DiMaggio conveyed in his television appearances for The Bowery. He dealt with people rather than with statistics. He appealed to basic needs and aspirations. It was an approach that made DiMaggio's commercials distinctive.

As Henry Bruère once put it, "The bank must maintain close contact with the millions of individuals whom it is meant to help in their quest for security." From that position, he said, "The bank may even come to lead in the effort to bring about stabilization in our national economic life."

Considering the state of the nation, one may add that there never was a more urgent need to strive for stabilization.

꧁

Efficient and able as an institution's managing officers may be, their activities require the understanding, the approval, and the cooperation of their trustees. One may indeed say that no mutual savings bank has any asset more important than its board of trustees. Those who serve in that capacity for the 486 mutual savings banks now in existence include some of the country's most distinguished citizens. Each brings unique experience and background to his position. Each understands that his primary responsibility is to safeguard the interests of all who deal with his bank, depositors and borrowers alike.

Over the years The Bowery has been most fortunate in the roster of its trustees. Their caliber has always been one of extraordinary distinction, and they served society as importantly as they served the bank. Thus Alan Greenspan left to become chairman of President Ford's Council of Economic Advisors; and James J. O'Leary left to fulfill his duties as vice chairman of the board of the U.S. Trust Company. Others on The Bowery's board included:

Francis T. P. Plimpton, formerly Ambassador and Deputy United States Representative to the United Nations; also former president of the Association of the Bar of the City of New York.

Joseph P. McMurray, former chairman of the Federal Home Loan Bank Board.

Alexander B. Trowbridge, president of The Conference Board, Inc., and former Secretary of Commerce; also former president of the American Management Associations.

Gustave L. Levy, senior partner of Goldman, Sachs & Company.

Walter B. Shaw, president of the Turner Construction Company.

Alger B. Chapman, chairman of the board of the Squibb Corporation.

Roger G. Kennedy, vice president of The Ford Foundation.

H. Adams Ashforth, chairman of the board of Albert B. Ashforth, Inc.

Walter N. Rothschild, Jr., chairman of the National Urban Coalition and former president of Abraham and Straus.

Robert C. Weaver, Distinguished Professor of the Department of Urban Affairs at Hunter College and former Secretary of Housing and Urban Development.

William R. White, former Superintendent of the Banking Department.

Martha R. Wallace, vice president and executive director of the Henry Luce Foundation, Inc.

Dr. James M. Hester, former president of New York University.

George S. Johnston, president of Scudder, Stevens, and Clark.

Richard R. Pivirotto, president of the Associated Dry Goods Corporation.

August M. Strung, former executive vice president of The Bowery Savings Bank.

George Faunce III, senior vice president, Marsh & McLennan Inc.

Of these, I am tempted to say, of course, that the bank is honored by their presence; but when you suggest this to a trustee, his reaction almost invariably is: "It's the other way around. I feel honored by being chosen."

One can only conclude that both appraisals are true.

28

THE VIEW FROM 1975

Among the challenges that confronted the mutual savings banks in 1974, one of the most urgent was the necessity of preserving adequate liquidity—the ability to meet deposit withdrawals on demand. In periods of prosperity, or even of normal stability, this was seldom a problem. The growth of deposits was generally accompanied by a sufficient increase in income from mortgages and other investments.

As for a bank's net worth, it could usually be maintained at a desired level. Should an unexpected drop in income threaten to destroy this balance, it was possible to reduce the dividend rate until such time as equilibrium was restored. Even when The Bowery's dividends were temporarily lowered, years ago, to 2 percent and less, the bank lost few depositors. There were not many competing investment opportunities that offered substantially greater returns on people's savings.

But today? Any attempt to reduce dividend rates in a savings bank, when others are not doing so, would probably cause thousands of depositors to withdraw their funds for investment in greater-yielding government bonds, or in commercial bank paper, or corporate securities, or even in competing thrift institutions that had not lowered their rates. So savings banks, their maximum dividend rates limited by the supervisory authorities, were locked into a position in which it was difficult to compete with others whose rates were not limited; or to pursue an independent course.

Another problem: Years ago, mortgages were issued for short terms, frequently for no more than three to five years. If their interest rates proved to be out of line with market charges, they could be adjusted upon the expiration and renewal of the mortgage. But consider the effect of a long-term mortgage which for 30 years returns interest of only 4 percent. If the bank must pay 5½ percent in dividends to match competition, that particular mortgage becomes a drain on resources. Nor can it be sold without incurring further loss. When the prevalent interest rate is 9 percent, no one will buy a mortgage or other investment yielding only 4 percent—unless he gets it at so drastic a discount that the bank is forced to accept a heavy loss. That is why thrift institutions have been seeking a feasible way to function with variable or adjustable mortgage interest rates—rates that jibe with current market levels.

Obviously, many of the current problems of thrift

institutions stem from the intense competition for money in a time of national inflation. So the question arose: Could mutual savings banks continue to survive *without* being given new means of competing with other financial institutions and with other investment opportunities?

Economists are hardly unanimous in the answers they offer. Some argue that thrift institutions now have greater deposits than ever, so why be concerned? The point is, of course, that their operating expenses have risen, as have those of every business; and at the same time, the proportion of earnings they have had to pay out in interest and dividends (because of intensified competition) has also steadily grown. As a result, the net-worth ratio of a bank like The Bowery dropped from 11.9 percent of deposits in 1945 to 6.39 percent in 1973. That is the predicament of many leading thrift institutions today in city after city.

"Back in 1945," Earl Schwulst has said, "only about one-half of net operating income was paid out. By 1972, the figure was up to nearly 94 percent." That left only 6 percent of net operating income to accrue to the bank's net worth.

That deposits of 482 savings banks (the number of mutuals in existence at the end of 1974) have been able to grow despite the energetic competition of the stock market, thousands of commercial banks, and savings and loan associations is in itself something of a financial miracle. Hampered by legal restrictions, limited to 17 states and Puerto Rico, they have appeared, as one banker put it, to be in the position of a prizefighter with one arm tied behind his back. "How much more efficiently we would be able to serve our communities and our depositors," he said, "if we were free to use all our potential strength!"

Yet even with one arm figuratively tied, the thrift institutions have done well. As impressive as anything else is the ingenuity with which they have found ways of expanding their services *within* the confines of existing legislation. Though innovations must in general earn the approval of the Banking Department, they have found Superintendents cooperative; and plans adopted by one bank are quickly put to use by others, so that they often become industrywide. In 1974 The Bowery and many of its sister institutions offered depositors a remarkably wide array of services. The very listing of them would have amazed savings bankers of the past, for they included such things as:

Education loans—enabling parents to borrow up to $20,000 for four years of educational costs. Such loans can be repaid over a seven-year period.

Profit-sharing retirement plans for corporations—through which corporate contributions to a retirement fund are held in trust and earn regular quarterly dividends.

Dividend check deposits—which enable a depositor who receives dividends from investments to have such dividend checks mailed directly to his savings account. There they instantly begin to earn interest. This obviates days of delays, and the consequent loss of interest, if such checks are mailed to a depositor and held until he finds it convenient to go to the bank.

Home improvement loans—permitting borrowers to receive up to $10,000, repayable over a ten-year period.

Savings payout plan—by which, as previously described, a depositor can arrange for periodic checks to be sent to him in his years of retirement.

Payroll savings—through which automatic savings are made possible by the deduction of stipulated amounts from paychecks, these amounts to be sent to the bank by employers in the same way that withheld taxes are paid to the government.

Packaged savings—whereby regularly-made deposits, even though small, are used to augment savings accounts, pay for life insurance, and purchase government bonds.

High-dividend accounts—which pay guaranteed dividend or interest rates that, when compounded, yield as much as 8.17 percent for funds left on deposit up to seven years.

Keogh plan—enabling self-employed people to create their own pension fund by making deposits that earn dividends. By the end of 1974, The Bowery had on deposit more than $40 million in its Keogh accounts.

Such a variety of services—and more are being added almost as quickly as they are conceived and approved—have helped the bank to remain a truly family-oriented institution. To the services already mentioned must be added the convenience of passbook loans (not only the most prompt but also the least costly of any bank loans available, since the funds on deposit continue to earn dividends while they function as collateral); the ease of banking by mail; depositor preference in granting mortgage loans; safety deposit boxes; "third party" payments through payment orders; FDIC insurance up to $100,000; low-cost life insurance.

Evaluating all these, one may say that current services have already gone a long way toward making The Bowery an institution concerned with many of the perceivable needs of the public. Most such services not only benefit its depositors; for the bank, they create additional channels for the inflow of money. One of the most obvious illustrations of this is the establishment of the popular Christmas and Hannukah Clubs. The public likes them because they are an effective incentive to saving. The bank likes them because they produce cash which in turn can be invested to earn dividends for depositors.

Yet several of the innovative plans adopted by the mutual savings banks, advantageous as they appeared to be, roused determined opposition. Some, like The Bowery's pioneering with payment orders, have led to legal battles. In December 1974, for example, two savings banks in New York State faced attempts on the part of commercial banks to *enjoin* them from issuing payment orders. The commercial banks argued that payment orders were nothing more than ordinary checks under an assumed name; and checking privileges had never been granted to thrift institutions. This was patently a test case. By the end of 1974 it had not been settled.

From the vantage point of 140 years of experience, the officials of The Bowery could certainly look back, as from a mountaintop, over long decades of service. Much of what they see is inspiring, for the bank has contributed to the welfare of millions of people—borrowers as well as depositors. It has helped countless "little people" to become "big people," prosperous and renowned. It has aided them to make the most of opportunity in a land rich in opportunity. Surely it has earned the right to be nostalgically sentimental and to refer to itself, as it occasionally does in publicity releases, as "the bank with a heart."

But when it turns to look toward the future, the scene is clouded by uncertainty. What will be the destiny not only of The Bowery but of all American savings banks?

Some economists advise, as did Leonard Lapidus, vice president of the Federal Reserve Bank of New York, that instead of continuing as they are, "mutual savings banks should be permitted to convert to stock commercial banks."

In the stress of modern times, there may concededly be reason to doubt the continued viability of the mutual savings bank in its old established form. Can it win in its efforts to become a federally chartered, full-service *mutual* institution? Or must it surrender to the "inevitability" of ownership by stockholders? In brief, are the mutuals prepared to abandon their traditional character?

Frederick C. Ober, chairman of the board of the Newton Savings Bank in Massachusetts, a past president of the National Association of Mutual Savings Banks, told a Senate committee that conversion to a stock bank could be most unfortunate. "The public," he said, "would clearly be the loser. The competitive presence of mutual institutions, oriented solely to the benefit of depositors and communities, insures maximum benefit to the public in terms of both interest rates to savers and the availability of mortgage funds to home owners."

He warned, too, that the very process of conversion would "in effect provide a covert windfall and, indeed, a potential bonanza for management insiders."

Not all savings bankers supported this opposition to stock status. A Maryland banker argued that all deposit-type financial institutions—thrift establishments, commercial banks, savings and loan associations, credit unions—are fundamentally alike. "They are all in the business of attracting capital from whatever source, and managing it profitably."

He went on to say, "Depositors will be attracted to those institutions that are able consistently to earn a higher rate of return on their depositors' money over what their competitors can earn. There is no economic difference in purpose," he concluded, "between a mutual and a stock financial institution."

This reasoning, I must say, appears to represent the thoughts of a minority among savings bankers. Most with whom I have met support the concept of mutuality. They tend to agree with the findings of Professors Lawrence D. Jones and R. Richardson Pettit, who supervised a profound and exhaustive study, "The Role and Viability of Mutual Banks," for the Rodney L. White Center for Financal Research of The Wharton School. Summarizing the report, Professor Irwin Friend said:

On balance, the Study concludes that there is relatively little difference between mutual and stock deposit institutions in terms of either their objectives or their ability to implement efficiently those objectives. Mutuality is seen as a viable and legitimate organizational form in the deposit service industries that can exist on a competitive basis.

In its own review of the report, the *Savings Bank Journal* recalled what Grover Ensley had said in 1971: "The relative merits of mutual and stock institutions should be determined by the action of free market forces. If equality of competitive opportunity is authorized for mutuals, the public will then be able to exercise an effective choice between the two types of institutions. In view of the historic role and continued prominence of mutual institutions in the financial structure, there is no reason to doubt that savings banks can compete effectively and serve a wider range of public needs efficiently."

Nevertheless, all bankers admit the future is uncertain. But then, at the end of 1974 nothing seemed predictable, nothing seemed stable. A *New York Times* editorial began with the words: "The year is ending with much of the nation in a state of deep anxiety over the course of the economy. There has been nothing like the present degree of apprehensiveness—or confusion—about the business outlook since 1930."

No financial institution was immune from the general uncertainty—and I include even Fort Knox. No seer could foretell what the value of Fort Knox bullion would be in a year, five years, ten years. Perhaps that was why there was no public rush to buy gold when it became available.

Moreover, it was sobering to remember that after World War II, when the United States owned seven-eighths of the world's gold bullion, the American dollar had perforce become the basis of international trade. There was no other comparable medium of exchange. To establish a universal standard of value, the United States pegged—and guaranteed—the price of gold at $35 an ounce. In any land (except the Soviet Union among Western states), gold and the dollar were joined in a solid foundation on which world trade could flourish.

It did flourish, and in flourishing it also shifted. So did wealth. Dollars flowed overseas and became "Eurodollars." The more Eurodollars the Europeans collected, the larger their lien became on America's gold. By the 1970s, the bullion owned by the United States had dwindled to such an extent that the country no longer had the power to *control* the price of gold.

Some head-shaking observers predicted that this heralded America's loss of leadership among nations. At the same time, the activities of the oil countries (which one congressman likened to the depradations of the Barbary Coast pirates) posed another threat to the American economy. Now the Arabs were draining away this country's wealth.

But were they really? Could any other country permanently undermine the American economy? Could the value of oil supplant the value of the dollar? Patriotic leaders in Washington were repeating Roosevelt's dictum: "The only thing we have to fear is fear itself." There was much logic on their side. At the end of 1974, the United States was still the greatest consumer and producer nation on earth. Its people, for the most part, were more prosperous than those of any other land. Eventually, the pundits assured everyone, stability would be restored as it always had been after American crises.

Historically, of course, the savings banks have been a symbol of stability. For a century and a half they have outlived every vicissitude the country has known. While thousands of commercial banks have collapsed in periods of depression, most savings banks have remained strongholds for the savings of "little people"; and more recently, for the savings of those not so little.

The average American, as his living standards rose,

might have become extremely sophisticated in matters of finance. His earning capacity steadily increased. Still, there were always new generations of young and "little" people who needed the kind of bank that welcomed, protected, and even paid for small deposits; the kind that cheerfully financed the modest requirements of home ownership. And institutions like The Bowery, though they may have grown to formidable size, have never stopped devoting their resources to the needs of "little people." They were created to meet the requirements of the American family, and that responsibility remains their primary concern.

But to fulfill that responsibility, change of operation is as inescapable, as inexorable, as the passage of time. No one would expect The Bowery of 1974 to conduct its affairs by the pen-and-ink, mental-arithmetic methods of a hundred years ago. In an age of electronic computers, of electronic ways of transferring funds from one account to another, new concepts of operation are the mandatory concomitants of progress. By any rule of logic, savings banks must be enabled to embrace new and broader concepts of service.

"Not because we want to grow for the sake of growth itself," said John Larsen. "The greater our resources are, the greater the services we can render."

And Chairman Crawford has said, "The first hundred and forty years of The Bowery's existence have given us the knowledge, the experience, and the means to serve the public more effectively. To do it we need new *tools*—the rights, granted by law, to compete fairly and equally in the financial world we inhabit. I am confident we will get them."

PART TWO

∽

The Decade
of Change
(1974 - 1984)

29

"GIVE US THE TOOLS"

It was a bold prophesy. In view of the problems that were assailing all banks and the nation itself, one might have considered the chairman's prediction too optimistic.

True, when you entered a Bowery office these days you found endless activity at the tellers' windows. You might conclude that this reflected a gratifying influx of funds, a proof of prosperity. It was an illusion. Many of those people were *withdrawing* their savings—a bleak situation that became more serious with every passing year of the 1970s.

It became so bad that at one Christmas season Crawford wrote a sober annual message to the bank's employees:

It has been a particularly trying year for savings banks. While The Bowery's problems have been less severe than many, we too have felt the effects of a significant outflow of deposits, the result of many customers' seeking relief from inflation in higher-yielding investments. Nor does it appear that the nation's serious economic problems are going to be solved in the near future. For a time there may be a worsening of present economic trends.

Given such a picture, it is comforting to look to The Bowery's history, which has spanned nearly one and one-half centuries, and to see that it has always been a fundamentally sound institution. It has not simply weathered economic adversity but has continued to grow and serve its customers well in spite of it.

In that way the past offered reassurance for the future. Yet in these trying 1970s banks like The Bowery were the victims of too many circumstances they could not change, circumstances rooted in the country's recession and in the high interest rates maintained by the Federal Reserve Board. I recall a day when The Bowery's legal counsel shook his head and told me, "The savings banks are being hit hard not only by their own misfortunes but by the misfortunes of their customers."

One illustration of what he meant was the new 54-floor skyscraper, One Astor Plaza. It had been built in the very heart of New York, on Times Square. Visitors to the city stared up at it in awe. They saw architectural beauty, but they could not see what that beauty masked.

The mortgage on this property, distributed among several banks, ran to $60 million. The Bowery's participation amounted to $17 million. Now the towering edifice was finding it impossible to meet its interest payments.

Nonetheless, it was an excellent property. It had distinguished tenants. It also housed two theaters, several street-level stores facing Broadway, a restaurant, and a huge garage.

What then was the problem?

"The building's cash deficit," Crawford explained to the bank's trustees, "is largely attributable to the bankruptcy of the building's major tenant, W. T. Grant & Co., and to escalating operating costs. It is also caused by the lack of income from the theaters and from disappointing returns from the restaurant and garage. Worst of all, it has an abundance of unleased space."

Since the immediate collection of interest was not possible, The Bowery joined the other mortgage holders in a Forbearance Agreement. Obviously, this step reduced The Bowery's income for the period of the forbearance—eventually a matter of several years.

Nor was this an isolated case. There were many in which forbearance rather than foreclosure was the wisest policy. (Ironically, at that very time Bowery advertising was lauding the economic vigor of New York, a public service campaign for which the bank won a civic award.)

These were indeed troubled times when trustees, seated around their oval conference table on the fifth floor of The Bowery headquarters, had to ponder tough problems. High among their concerns was the ever-increasing pressure of competition from commercial banks. These were attracting deposits to their money market funds, which were offering interest at 9 percent and higher. The savings institutions had not yet been granted the power to compete with such funds; *their* deposits were still yielding little more than half of such rates. So The Bowery customers could hardly be blamed for withdrawing their savings to invest in more lucrative ways. Day after day this increase in disintermediation (withdrawal of funds for investment elsewhere) was becoming more alarming.

To Crawford and his associates one thing was clear: If the savings institutions were to survive, they had to be granted

317

the legal means with which to compete effectively. They had to be empowered to pay more than 5¼ percent interest on the funds of depositors.

But securing such rights, if they could be secured at all, might take years of hearings and debate, and the officers of The Bowery felt they could not wait. Something had to be done quickly to stem the outflow of funds. But what? Could there be any legal means of offering depositors more than that law-stipulated 5½ percent?

The bank's counsel, Jack Older, closeted with Chairman Crawford and President John Larsen, believed there was a way; moreover, it was a way that could be taken at once without waiting for regulatory approval. The 5½ interest rate, he said, applied to the first $100,000 in deposits, the safety of which the Federal Deposit Insurance Corporation (FDIC) guaranteed. On sums of more than $100,000, Older maintained, the interest rate could legally be raised.

He was right, of course. Action came quickly in advertisements. The Bowery announced—one is tempted to say triumphantly—that its interest rates would rise on deposits in excess of $100,000.

Realizing that few people could rush up to a teller with $100,000 in their hands, the bank added that it would accept *pooled* deposits aggregating $100,000 if made by members of the same family.

The plan worked well—until it ran into trouble. It stumbled because of the mistaken zeal of some managers in The Bowery's suburban offices.

In those branches, when five or six members of a family pooled their resources to make a $100,000 deposit, *each member was given his own passbook*. This did not empower individual withdrawals or any other individual transactions. It was done so that each of the individuals involved could keep his own records.

When examiners for the Federal Deposit Insurance Corporation discovered this, they marched into The Bowery headquarters, as one man put it, "like a sheriff's posse". The examiners asserted that the individual passbooks represented so many *separate* accounts, each far less than $100,000. Therefore, the payment of increased interest rates was illegal when applied to such multiple small deposits.

Considering that some 176 such accounts totaling approximately $5 million were already on the books, the restraining order was so serious that officers of The Bowery immediately flew to Washington. Their objective was to reason with Frank Wille, chairman of the FDIC.

Meanwhile, to comply with the law, the bank stopped the issuance of individual passbooks for aggregate-type accounts. Still, Wille and his staff objected to the possibility of *strangers* pooling their funds to make a common deposit, thus illegally earning higher interst rates on small individual contributions.

Crawford flatly asserted that in every case The Bowery's aggregate-type accounts were strictly limited to family deposits. Unhappily, the timing was bad. The FDIC was in the process of investigating other pooled accounts being invited by certain brokerage firms. The case of The Bowery was therefore part of a "package" problem awaiting future determination.

In essense, of course, the bank's actions simply reflected its aggressive efforts to develop every possible way of increasing depositors' interest rates on their passbook accounts.

Throughout these weeks and months disintermediation not only continued but became steadily worse. In January 1976, the trustees stared at a chart Crawford placed on a tripod. It indicated that in the past 27 months the commercial banks had garnered *more than 50 percent of the growth of consumer savings*.

319

This erosion of The Bowery's assets had to be stopped, and the bank resorted to every legal means at its disposal. Branch managers and tellers were trained to persuade customers not to withdraw their funds. They became members of an Account Retention Club, which convinced a number of depositors not to withdraw savings. At the same time, advertisements in newspapers and in DiMaggio's television commercials stressed the wisdom and security of preserving savings accounts.

Strangely, throughout this trying period the spirits of The Bowery's employees seemed unaffected. No one had reason to fear the loss of his job. One had only to read the bank's in-house magazine, *The Chest,* to note the continuance of usual events such as the bowling team's victory in inter-bank competition. There were the usual employee picnics in summer and dances in winter, and in almost every issue of *The Chest* there were smiling pictures of Crawford or Larsen presenting awards for everything from outstanding services to longevity of employment.

No, hard times for the bank and the nation did not bring visible despondency to The Bowery employees. The perquisites they enjoyed were still at their command. They could go to the college of their choice and have The Bowery pay their tuition costs, a policy that every year brought higher education to more than 100 employees. They could have any sum between 1 percent and 11 percent of their salary automatically placed in a savings account, an amount instantly augmented by a bank contribution. They could still enjoy the benefits of health, dental, and other insurance.

As for Crawford and Larsen, they too had their brighter moments. Crawford, involved in many civic campaigns, received the Governor's Award for his sponsorship of "Choices for '76," a public service advertising campaign. Larsen was given a citation for his efforts in behalf of the National Jewish Hospital and Research Center in Denver.

In fact, no civic-minded activities were discontinued.

But when Chairman Morris D. Crawford, Jr. sat alone in his office, staring out of the window at the 42nd Street traffic, it is hard to believe he could think of anything but the bank's difficulties.

He had to face the harsh reality that the net outflow of funds now surpassed $100 million a year. This *had* to be stopped. In spite of all obstacles, most of them rooted in human indifference, the effort to obtain legislation that favored the savings banks had to be continued. If one felt frustrated, that had to be ignored.

Frustration resulted largely from the fact that in these late 1970s few officials in Washington were concerned about the lot of mutual savings banks. The nation was being harassed by too many other situations. There was the oil crisis precipitated by OPEC. There was the shocking decline of sales in the automobile industry, in the steel industry, in the housing industry. There was the calamitous spread of unemployment, the violence in Iran where 63 Americans were being imprisoned as hostages in the United States Embassy. These and countless other events, including the agonies of Watergate's aftermath, made it difficult for Washington to focus on the plight of thrift institutions. One high-ranking Treasury official was reported to have said, "The thrifts in trouble? So what?"

In short, while pressing for liberalized regulations—a cause to which Crawford was giving his heart, his mind, his strength—the banks had ample cause for gloom. Yet the people at The Bowery, although not exactly singing Mary Martin's "I'm A Cockeyed Optimist," still managed to keep their spirits high. In 1976 they celebrated the 200th anniversary of the nation's independence by stressing all that was good in America. They created a show of historic memorabilia, "Revolution in New York," which illustrated centuries of growth and increasing prosperity. After being shown at the Museum of the City of New York, the

Bicentennial exhibition went from one branch of The Bowery to another.

Behind all the pageantry and celebration, however, there was no change in the predicament of the thrift institutions. More than 10 million people who were out of work had no income to bring to savings banks. On the contrary, the unemployed were *withdrawing* funds to meet daily needs.

At the same time, soaring interest rates were making it impossible for small businessmen to borrow sufficient funds to pay expenses. Who could *afford* to pay almost 20 percent in interest charges? Small firms were collapsing for want of capital, leaving more and more people out of work. (Overseas, in the Soviet Union, *Tass* was reporting all this and rather smugly—or was it jubilantly?—predicting it presaged the end of capitalism.)

In the face of such undermining events, how could savings banks retain the *confidence* of depositors? This became all the more urgent on April 28, 1976. On that day, John Heimann, New York State's Superintendent of Banks, addressed the eighty-third annual meeting of the Savings Banks Association of New York State. He expressed the opinion—quickly reported by the press—that "two thirds of New York's savings banks have net worths which are less than the amounts considered necessary to operate with safety."

Crawford was shocked. He declared that such a statement was "ill considered and ill timed." Other bankers joined him in deploring the speech. The incident demanded instant reassurance for the public. It came in the form of strong advertisements and strong opinions voiced in newspaper interviews.

And as if there were not enough of such problems to occupy the head of a savings bank, Chairman Crawford was now confronted by still another challenge.

30

CHANGING
OF THE GUARD

Within the next few years, Crawford would reach the mandatory retirement age of 65. Following a widespread custom in American industry, he would be expected to recommend a successor to his post as chairman and chief executive officer.

Normally this would have been no problem. President John W. Larsen would step into the position. After more than 40 years of service to the bank, Larsen had all the attributes one could seek. But, unfortunately, he was a year older than Crawford. He would be the first to retire. So he joined Crawford and a committee of trustees in the search for the next chief executive officer.

They studied scores of resumés sent by headhunter firms. They interviewed more people than they could remember. Their eventual first choice, Clifford Whiteman, found himself unhappy in the restricted operations of a savings bank. His training had been in commercial banks. Within a year he departed, and the search had to be renewed.

"We need someone," Crawford wrote in a memorandum to the board, "who has had wide experience with mortgages plus experience in general finance and in public service." It was a combination of qualities not easy to find in any one person, either in or outside the bank.

By midsummer no selection had been made. At that time the officers of The Bowery Savings Bank held a mortgage meeting for their own executives and outside mortgage servicers. They met in the Thousand Islands. On the final afternoon the men took time off for rest and recreation, and Crawford played a round of golf with Ellis T. Gravette, Jr.

Gravette had flown from the West Coast where he had served as chairman of the Bowest Corporation, The Bowery's mortgage banking subsidiary. Now Crawford watched him tee off. His eyes followed the ball's flight over the middle of the fairway, and when he looked back at Gravette he was struck by inspiration.

"Bud" Gravette came from a banking family. Like his father and grandfather, he had been a successful banker long before joining Bowest. He had been induced to head that company because, in spite of a promising start, it was now losing money year after year, and he had a remarkable reputation for turning losses into profits. Under his leadership, Bowest had changed so dramatically that it was now showing more than $1 million a year in profits.

And before accepting the Bowest post, he had gained wide economic experience as chief executive officer of U.S. Financial, Inc., and as president of the Palomar Financial Corporation in San Diego. Earlier he had been vice president and a director of the Union Bank of Tucson and a special banking representative of the Burroughs Corporation's data processing division. Moreover, in addition to his business affiliations, he served on the boards of several philanthropic organizations.

To cap it all, Gravette was available. Recently he had left the chairmanship of Bowest to Arthur J. Damschen and the presidency to Dirk Brochema, Jr., both able executives. Gravette had preferred to retire to the Bowest board.

Where could wider experience and proven ability be found? As far as Crawford was concerned, the search for a successor could end here. But he remained silent, thinking, while they played the first three holes. By that time, Gravette, three up, seemed assured of winning the match. It was then, as they rode their golf cart toward the fourth tee, that Crawford made his proposal.

Gravette was stunned. "I was so surprised," he said, "that as far as golf went I lost all concentration. Rusty Crawford won the next three holes. He could not have picked a better way to even the match. At that point I asked, 'Now that we're even, do you want to withdraw your offer?' Rusty laughed and assured me he was serious."

Gravette was deeply appreciative. Obviously, no immediate decisions could be made. For his part, he would have to give it serious thought. Such an undertaking would involve his entire family. It would mean leaving their La Jolla home to move to the East, something he wanted before all else to discuss with his wife.

Crawford, in New York, described Gravette's extraordinary qualifications to each of the trustees. More than a month passed before he telephoned his candidate.

"I hope you're still interested," he said. "The board would like to meet you. They'd like you to come to New York."

Gravette came. His conversations with trustees revealed not only the lifelong knowledge of banking problems he had garnered but beyond that disclosed an almost passionate faith in the value of thorough specialized training—in banks or elsewhere—for the jobs people were intended to fill. (This reliance on proper training was something he was to stress year after year.)

As Gravette might well have anticipated, many a trustee wanted to hear his version of how he had converted Bowest's losses to profits. What he had accomplished there might suggest what he would do here. These were days when the board sought indications of the policies Gravette could be expected to pursue as chairman.

He explained, "Bowest had been purchasing mortgage loans from small, entrepreneurial-type businesses." In other words, he said, Bowest had acquired "an inventory of poor-quality mortgages that led to a loss of $1.8 million." Worse, the company suffered from disorganized, badly trained management, and it had failed dismally to comply with The Bowery's policies. These policies required commitments not only to *purchase* mortgages but to have comparable commitments to *sell*. Clearly, the fault for the bleak situation lay with management. Gravette's first corrective measure had been to make "essential management changes." Also, he had found that Bowest was heavily overstaffed. "We decreased the staff from 325 people to 197, with annual savings of $900,000 in salaries and an actual improvement in efficiency."

The trustees exchanged meaningful glances. It was evident that as chief executive Gravette would not hesitate to take whatever remedial steps were necessary to turn losses into profits.

In December 1977 he was unanimously elected president of The Bowery Savings Bank. To make the presidency available, John W. Larsen had been named vice chairman. So now Gravette was in a position that would enable him to sit on the board of trustees, thus giving its members an opportunity to come to know him before the time of Crawford's retirement.

Almost at the same time it became evident that the U.S. Savings and Loan League was fighting "to prevent some easement of regulations from becoming operational." This was shocking. Did it mean that the mutual savings banks would henceforth have to contend with the opposition of savings and loan associations as well as that of commercial banks?

The general opinion among the trustees was that the savings and loan associations would have to be shown that their future was *linked* with that of savings banks. "Better to have them as allies than as opponents."

It was, however, only one of the immediate problems with which the bank had to deal. The most pressing involved the need to strengthen The Bowery's financial position—its earnings, its net worth, its liquidity. One way was to continue investing in high-yielding bonds. As Dr. Elmer Harmon, executive vice president, put it, "The yields on our long-term bonds exceed yields obtainable in the mortgage market. They average 9.34 percent."

But even the best of bonds represented only one way to increase earnings. Another lay in opening new branches. Located in strategic areas, these could bring a rewarding response through new depositors. The Rego Park branch, opened in Long Island a year earlier, had already achieved deposits in excess of $100 million.

But launching a new branch usually called for music, entertainment, gifts for depositors; it also required the remodeling of a building and the installation of equipment. All this could be expensive. Sometimes it became theatrical. When an office was opened on the Avenue of the Americas in the heart of the city, one feature was "The Great Diamond Giveaway." Some 1,200 rhinestone rings were to be given to the first comers, and among those 1,200 there was hidden *one ring with a genuine diamond*. Thousands of people appeared for the opening ceremonies, and from there 1,200 women rushed off to have their new rings appraised.

So now, with happy memories of Rego Park, The Bowery turned to opening another Long Island branch in Bay Shore. Vice President Robert Pearson predicted it would acquire between 15,000 and 20,000 new accounts and deposits that would exceed $25 million. The branch was located, he said, in an area that would serve two Long Island counties, Nassau and Suffolk.

In June the office was opened with music, banners, and a gala reception for community leaders. From the start it outstripped all expectations for deposits, more than tripling Robert Pearson's predictions.

Spurred by this success, The Bowery opened still another branch, the Kings Plaza office in Brooklyn. This too was well received locally. All factors taken into consideration, however, the opening of new branches, no matter how rewarding, was a slow process, limited to a single new office per year.

Therefore one can appreciate the excitement among officers of The Bowery when the sudden opportunity arose to add *nine new branches in a single bold transaction*.

Those nine branches—four in Brooklyn, two in Queens, two in Long Island, and one in Manhattan—belonged to the 93-year-old Equitable Federal Savings and Loan Association. It had long enjoyed sound management, but now its executives were approaching the age of retirement.

Possibly they were weary. Possibly they had failed to train potential successors. In any event, they were amenable to the suggestion of a merger.

"As for us," Crawford said, "their offices would give us a presence in areas covered by our advertising, and they would bring us thousands of additional depositors."

But there was a formidable obstacle to be overcome. The Equitable was a federal thrift institution. It could not legally join forces with a state savings bank. Nevertheless, since both organizations were enthusiastic about the potentialities of a merger, they clung to the old adage of where there's a will there's a way. They plunged—I use the word advisedly—into efforts with federal and state authorities to make the plan a reality. Crawford, Gravette, and Counsel Jack Older met repeatedly with government representatives in Washington and Albany. They had to make it clear that such a merger would benefit the public as well as the two institutions.

In less than a year they succeeded, although success depended on some legal maneuvers in which they were inestimably helped by Stuart D. Root of Cadwallader, Wickersham, and Taft: First, Equitable had to become part of the New York State banking system. This change of charter opened the door to a formal merging of interests, and soon thereafter The Bowery was able to report:

> The merger which joins the two financial institutions that have served the New York area residents for many years (The Bowery 146 years; Equitable 94 years) has increased our position as the largest savings bank in New York State, with assets totaling more than $5.3 billion. The Bowery now has nearly half a million depositors being served in 26 offices in Manhattan, Brooklyn, Queens, Nassau and Suffolk Counties.

Naturally, Crawford was pleased. Everybody was pleased. Yet, one Bowery vice president sadly acknowledged, "We certainly didn't have the same kind of good luck with everything we tried. Take the matter of checking accounts, for instance."

What went wrong?

"Everything," the vice president said. "We had previously issued what we called Payment Orders. These served practically the same functions as checks. The commercial banks had immediately challenged our right to do so, claiming we were not authorized to provide checking services. Their complaint was sustained. Still, we wanted—in fact, we felt we *needed*—the right to offer checking privileges. We were sure they would bring in many new accounts. So we went through a series of legal hassles and hearings until, in 1976, we won the right to service checking accounts. Even so, when we had what we wanted the results were disappointing."

Disappointing? The better word was disillusioning.

Although several thousand customers took advantage of the new service, the average balance they maintained was only $308. This was hardly enough to make the operation profitable. The checking service was actually incurring a *loss*. Besides, 82 percent of those who opened checking accounts were Bowery depositors of long standing. They brought no new money into the bank.

(Four years later, as The Bowery approached its 150th anniversary, records indicated that only $35 million of the bank's $5.5 billion represented checking accounts—less than 1 percent of the total. Why, then, was the practice continued? Every officer had the same answer: "As a service to those who do want it. You don't have to make a profit every time you please a customer.")

To what degree the change of administration, from Rusty Crawford's to Bud Gravette's, would affect the operations of the bank, Crawford had predicted with unfailing accuracy. Even before he had proposed the name of his successor he had addressed an extraordinary memorandum to the trustees. When it was brought to Gravette's attention, he read and reread it with deepening interest. Crawford had begun by saying:

> When I came to this industry and to The Bowery in October 1953, the only important services we had to offer were regular savings accounts and savings bank life insurance. . . . Deposit growth was automatic and substantial. . . . Competition was virtually nonexistent. . . .
>
> The mood of savings bank leaders, with a few exceptions, was smug and complacent. Those of us who suggested the need for broader consumer-service powers were largely ignored. Those of us who urged federal legislation to put us in the dual banking system (federal as well as state) were tolerated but not supported by our industry as a whole.

Then Crawford had penned page after page of the problems the thrift institutions had to solve. And as Gravette read the document, nothing in it could have affected him as did its final passages. In these Crawford had predicted some of the challenges and situations his successor as chairman would encounter:

> He will face ever-increasing competition from existing sources and will undoubtedly encounter new and even more difficult forms of competition. He will have to cope with continuing cost escalation and constantly seek ways of reducing operating expenses and increasing gross income.
>
> This will involve aggressive and imaginative investment initiatives, if future growth is to be managed with due regard for a healthy net worth. He will probably have greater opportunities for expansion through merger. He will have to deal with an ever-deepening flood of federal and state regulations. He will undoubtedly be asked to serve on government commissions and industry committees, as I have, which will deal with the future of the industry. . . . He will face recurring questions such as Are mutuals an anachronism? Is conversion

331

to or merger with a commercial bank in the best interest of the bank, its depositors, and the community?

In general, I believe the decisions my successor will have to make will be bigger and tougher than those of the recent past, and wrong decisions will have a more serious impact on the bank.

In sum, Crawford's memorandum was a remarkably lucid prediction of changes to come. For Ellis T. Gravette, Jr., it indicated the challenges that awaited him.

31

❧

TOWARD
THE NEW ERA

March 12, 1980 was the day Morris D. Crawford, Jr. retired from the chairmanship of The Bowery Savings Bank. It was also the day Gravette became its chairman and chief executive officer.

The occasion was observed by a dinner for some 50 guests. Most were trustees and officers of the bank. Others represented the many state and community organizations that Crawford had served. They gathered in The Bowery's sixth-floor dining room "in a gala spirit of tribute rather than of farewell." Actually, there was no reason for a farewell because Crawford would continue his association with the bank as a member of its board of trustees.

Because no one wanted a mood of sadness to weigh upon the affair, the dinner became a good-humored "roast." Speaker after speaker rose to joke gently about Crawford's term in office, or about his golf game, or about the unfortunate "mistake" he had made years ago in leaving honest employment with Cadwallader, Wickersham, and Taft.

In the same vein, those who welcomed Bud Gravette to his new post commisserated with him. "He didn't know when he was well off in La Jolla," one man sighed with a doleful shake of his head. If, beneath the banter, they were all wondering what changes to expect from the new chairman, nobody spoke of such things. This evening belonged mainly to Rusty Crawford—a tribute to the truly remarkable growth of The Bowery under his long leadership.

Yet, changes, some drastic, were bound to come. Everybody knew that. As Crawford had prophesied, neither The Bowery nor any mutual savings bank could forever endure the restraints that prevented it from competing strongly in the financial world. Crawford testified at meetings in Washington and in Albany, urging deregulation. "I seemed to be devoting half of my life to arguing before legislators," he said, "and I seemed to be getting nowhere."

But he was wrong. The United States government at last recognized the validity of his arguments. Nineteen days after Gravette became chairman, on March 31, 1980, President Jimmy Carter signed The Depository Institutions Deregulation Monetary Control Act. Despite the President's happy smile as he handed out pens, it was by no means an ideal law. It made no pretense of granting *everything* the savings banks needed. It brought some disappointment as well as some relief.

What it did in a positive sense was broaden the sphere in which thrifts could invest their funds. And it created the Depository Institutions Deregulation Committee (DIDC).

334

This had the responsibility among its duties to supervise another concession—the savings banks' right to issue six-month money market certificates at interest rates that could compete with those of commercial banks. Although these rates might vary from week to week, they hovered at the outset around 8 percent to 9 percent.

New York newspapers immediately carried exciting advertisements of this new opportunity. The response was eager. In all savings institutions, lines formed to take advantage of this new chance for higher earnings.

"At The Bowery," said one officer, "we were suddenly *too* busy. And the lines grew longer and longer."

Was it, then, a glorious victory for the mutual savings banks, an occasion to cheer and hoist flags and rise out of the depths?

"Not at all," said Gravette, his voice grim. "What we had won turned out to be a Pyrrhic victory."

One trouble was that those eager people at tellers' windows were in large numbers the bank's own customers. They were rushing to transfer their deposits to the higher-paying six-month certificates. These transactions accounted for no new inflow of cash. They merely transferred $5\frac{1}{2}$ percent passbook deposits to 8 percent and $9\frac{1}{2}$ percent certificates. So The Bowery was in the position, as were the other savings banks, of paying far more interest on money it already had.

As for *new* funds that soon poured in, Gravette put it bluntly, "It was a case of the more money you had coming in, the more you lost. A financial paradox."

The explanation lay in simple arithmetic: Several hundred millions of dollars did pour in, and on these new funds the bank was obligated to pay an average of 8 percent to $9\frac{1}{2}$ percent in interest. To *earn* money on this seeming bonanza, The Bowery had to invest it for returns considerably greater than $9\frac{1}{2}$ percent. But where invest it? Who was offering such terms?

One man said, "As these six-month certificates became due, we were paying larger and larger sums in interest, and losing more and more money in the process. Figure it out. Even at 8 percent, to sell $500 million in certificates would cost us $40 million a year in interest. How long could we keep that up?"

To stem this ruinous outflow of cash, the bank discontinued the kind of advertising that had caused the phenomenon. It also deliberately trimmed its offer of interest to a figure *below* that of the market. This had its effect. The influx of new money dropped off. Some of the "old" money drifted away to other banks. Before long the trustees learned (with hosannas of relief) that the six-month obligations had been reduced by some $200 million a year.

Gravette said, "The trouble was that the government had put the cart before the horse. It should have granted us broader *investment* rights before giving us the right to pay out high interest rates. For the thrifts it was a case of piecemeal legislation that backfired."

❧

These were days when Eleanor Gallagher, Gravette's secretary, would glance into his office to see him frowning in thought, tapping a pencil on his desk. At such times she never interrupted. He had a good deal to consider.

For one thing, he realized it could be ruinous to await rescue by government agencies. That might not come for years if it came at all. The Bowery would have to take steps to rescue *itself*. It would have to alter the course it had been following. And that could involve some drastic changes in plans and operations.

He knew there was a right way and a wrong way to change the course an institution had followed for a century and a half. The wrong way was to be impetuous, to upset procedures with impulsive, panic-driven orders. The right

336

way was to adopt a strong, carefully planned course that would make the most of future opportunities. Even in these early days of his administration he recognized the need of lifting the bank out of its narrow, government-regulated limits of operation and of shaping it into a veritable "financial supermarket"—a bank that supplied its customers with every important financial need.

But Gravette did not rush into an immediate spate of changes. He had no wish to sacrifice the fundamental strength of Rusty Crawford's policies, which had lifted the bank to heights it had never before attained. If recent years had brought The Bowery a tidal wave of setbacks, the cause lay with inflation, with government fiscal policies, with unemployment, and other forces beyond Gravette's control.

"I did, however, have to take *some* drastic actions in those early days," Gravette said. "The bank was in a pretty desperate situation as far as its dwindling net worth went. The truth is we were struggling for survival. Although we had to take measures that seemed tough—like letting a number of people go—we wouldn't have survived if we had hesitated. Believe me, it was not easy for me to cut costs when it meant cutting personnel, but I had no choice if the bank was to be saved."

The trustees strongly supported what he did. One of them bluntly put it this way:

Consider the mortgage division as an example. We had a hundred or so employees waiting for the mortgage business to pick up when it was at its lowest ebb. Men were sitting at their desks, drawing salaries, with no customers in sight. Gravette transferred as many of them as he could to other jobs. The rest had to be let go. For the welfare of the bank it was the only choice. Certainly those who lost their jobs were not happy. Neither was Gravette. But a chairman's duty is to keep the bank solvent for the sake of depositors *and* employees. He did what was essential, painful as it might be.

337

In another move to reduce costs, the new chairman encouraged early retirement on the part of employees nearing the mandatory retirement age. The monetary inducements offered were generous. Many employees welcomed them. In a single year 70 men and women took advantage of the opportunity.

Measures such as these saved the bank several million dollars. Also, to discourage passbook depositors from moving their funds to other banks, Gravette insisted on intensifying customer courtesy. "Nothing wins customer loyalty as well as a genuine, friendly show of concern for their problems."

A lady needed information about her savings account, but it was Saturday, and the bank was closed. She nevertheless decided to telephone The Bowery on the chance that somebody might be there, someone trying to catch up with office work. She was right. Her call was answered. The man who listened to her query said, "I'll try to find out what you want, madam. If you'll give me your number, I'll call you as soon as I can."

Within ten minutes the woman got the information she needed. She was enthusiastically grateful. "Please give me your name," she said. "You've been so kind I'd like to write to the chairman to tell him how helpful you were."

"That's very kind of you," the man said, "but you needn't do that. This is part of The Bowery's service."

"Maybe so, but it's service that deserves appreciation. Do give me your name so that I can write to the chairman."

"I can save you the trouble," the man said. "This *is* the chairman."

⚬⚬⚬

One may feel that the government was remiss in failing for so long a time to act on the needs of savings banks. Yet, when one remembers the problems and events that assailed the country in 1980, one can scarcely blame federal legislators for giving their attention to other matters.

What were the nation's *primary* concerns that year?

☐ In January the United States indignantly reacted to the Soviet Union's invasion of Afghanistan. It placed an embargo on the sale of grain and technology to the Russians. This heightened the strain between the two powers, and such strain inevitably threatened world peace.

☐ In April, some 7,000 miles from Washington, there was a misconceived, badly planned military attempt to rescue the American hostages imprisoned in the American Embassy in Teheran. The tragic collapse of the venture caused the deaths of eight American soldiers and sent five others, badly wounded, back to military hospitals. Newspaper accounts, editorials, broadcasts, and some congressmen bitterly castigated this debacle, and nobody could think about savings banks.

☐ Soon these headlines were preempted by the blastlike eruption of Mount St. Helens, inflicting death and devastation over wide areas of Oregon and Washington.

☐ On the political front Ronald Wilson Reagan won an overwhelming victory over Jimmy Carter to become the fortieth President of the United States. One can understand that nothing interested the country's lawmakers more than what the new administration would do to strengthen the economy and to ease world tensions.

☐ In New York City, the home of so many savings banks, a madman drew attention away from all other events when he raised a weapon in front of the Dakota apartments and shot John Lennon to death.

With such things as these happening, and there were many more, it was hardly surprising that the average legislator, when asked about mutual savings banks, brushed the question aside with a hurried, "Not now, please, not now."

So Gravette felt that most of The Bowery's help must

come from its own ingenuity. If the bank was to survive, its heavy losses of recent years must somehow be converted to profits.

This was a matter to which he gave long thought. Others with whom he conferred added ideas of their own. In time—roughly by late 1981 and 1982—Gravette formulated a five-year plan. That was the approximate time, he believed, it would take The Bowery to climb from its depressed state to a level of profitability.

The plan was designed to shape the bank into an institution quite different from any which past Bowery generations had been able to conceive. Gravette's inspired way to describe it was as "a financial supermarket" because the innovations he foresaw were bound to lead the bank into a score of new financial ventures and services.

It would begin by offering customers a broad new range of consumer aids—everything from help in the preparation of income taxes to professional counseling on investments.

To complement these services for individuals, The Bowery would offer commercial services to corporations and small businesses. Payroll programs, relocation assistance to corporate personnel assigned to posts in other cities, group insurance of all kinds—these and others would serve as a strong entree to the commercial market.

At the same time the bank would expand its geographical base by finding ways to serve customers in Florida. Gravette chose that state because an astonishing number of Bowery depositors moved to Florida in their years of retirement. Why lose them? Why not follow them—if legal means could be found?

Next, a revolutionary way of raising the bank's capital needs would be through the sale of stock. Again, this would depend on receiving regulatory permission from the government to become a stock-issuing corporation. The value of funds raised in such a manner was that they entailed no payments of interest; purchasers of stock shared only in

340

profits. ("Depositors are the bank's creditors; stockholders are its partners.")

Nor did the five-year plan stop there. It envisioned offering tax shelters of all available kinds to consumers; handling investment forms such as mutual funds, equities, tax-exempts; investing in joint ventures, especially in real estate developments; making the kind of loans to businesses and consumers that traditionally had not been offered through The Bowery's usual channels.

It was a far-sighted, exciting plan, a step into an entirely new concept of banking for The Bowery. But at the outset it lacked one vital ingredient—*the right people to manage so many new undertakings*. How could the bank develop an efficient staff to operate so diverse a program?

32

"TRAINING PEOPLE IS OUR TOP PRIORITY"

The management group with whom I so frequently had luncheon in the bank's dining room all agreed on one thing: Bud Gravette's primary aim was to have people trained to the utmost level of their capabilities. That applied to every executive as well as to newly hired employees.

"It applied even to Bud himself," one man asserted. "Believe it or not, while he was chairman he took time out to attend a management course sponsored by IBM. He wanted to learn how IBM's executives were trained. You might say that the training and development of people was almost a passion with him."

Yet the passion was nurtured in an organized manner. At the start Gravette brought in a team of A. T. Hudson & Co. analysts, better described as efficiency experts, to study The Bowery operations and to suggest areas that could be improved and made more cost-effective. Their studies involved not only methods but people. And it became evident that certain personnel lacked the resilience and even the desire to cope with innovations. They would never adjust to a changed environment. Regrettably, they would have to be let go.

In inaugurating an overall training program, Gravette found two able officers to head it, Diane Tracy and Grace Pichardo. They not only shared his ideas but enriched the program with enthusiastic plans of their own.

Both young women knew The Bowery well. Diane Tracy had spent three years on the bank's account at Creamer Dickson Basford Public Relations. At the bank, Grace Pichardo had risen from assistant teller to executive posts in marketing, advertising, and communications. The two made an efficient, imaginative team. When they gave Gravette a comprehensive outline of what they would like to do, he found it excellent.

"You've got the ball," he said. "Run with it."

Run, they did.

They devised a program aimed at training not only new employees but prospective managers and even senior management personnel. Its description filled more than 100 typewritten pages. It was founded on a tersely worded philosophy:

Our first responsibility is providing excellent customer service. Without the customer there would be no jobs, for the customer is the one who ultimately pays our salaries and keeps us in business. In order to keep our customers satisfied we must give top priority to the training, development, appraisal, and counseling of our employees.

344

Explaining why even *top management* required certain aspects of training, the statement continued:

> The Bowery's success, to a large extent, rests on your ability to develop and manage the talents and abilities of the people you supervise.

It took several months to prepare the curriculum to be followed by each group, together with the necessary equipment—charts, slides, screens, and the rest, including lecture rooms. It became the most proficient training program any bank had to offer.

For senior management personnel there was an eight-week course in executive procedures. At the outset professional experts were retained to lead the discussions. Later, 36 carefully selected managers were given special training so that they might become trainers of others. The program was intensive in every detail. Twice it included two weeks of concentrated study and problem solving at a retreat away from New York. Usually, this focused on 18 people at a time, and Hilton Head was typical of the places that afforded the privacy needed for such conferences. Gravette made a point of attending these seminars.

The most unusual program, however, was the one designed for "management trainees"—people with attributes that marked them as able candidates for management jobs. These were usually recruited on college campuses among outstanding graduates, and also among Bowery employees who demonstrated unusual capabilities.

"We hire only six in a group," said Senior Vice President Diane Tracy, "so each one receives individual attention. Each goes through his training on the full salary of an employee. Each is from the start assigned to an advisor, generally a senior manager to whom he can go for counsel and guidance. In addition to classroom instruction, every

345

trainee is given on-the-job-training in a number of fields. It's a thorough, comprehensive course that takes 43 weeks to complete. Our investment in each such person is about $30,000. And because we want to be sure to retain him—or her—he is assigned to a position in which he will be paid more than he could receive at any other bank."

Both Miss Tracy and Miss Pichardo quickly add that training is just as important and carefully planned for newly hired people who will fill nonmanagement positions— tellers, secretaries, and all the rest.

"We wrote this curriculum," explained Vice President Pichardo, "with the conviction that all newcomers who start work for the bank ought, before all else, to be indoctrinated in the deep-rooted principles, the long history, and the *spirit* of the institution. They ought to be given reason to share its pride. That isn't pretentious. It's a matter of making them glad they came to The Bowery. Their training begins with a day of orientation. They hear the history of the bank and they see it illustrated with slides. Then they're given an idea of the various departments in the institution. They spend several weeks in classroom instruction before being assigned to their jobs."

For those who will be tellers there is a truly extraordinary bit of training "equipment." On the eighth floor of the 42nd Street office, there is a modified replica of the banking floor. Here a long line of tellers' windows has been installed. Computer readouts and every other piece of apparatus have been provided—everything needed to serve customers. The new employee is confronted with every conceivable problem that may arise at a teller's window. (Incidentally, tellers will now be known as customer service representatives—if ever the public can be trained to stop calling them tellers.)

This particular course for newcomers runs for 15 weeks. Each participant is required to take a written test, and *only*

346

100 percent is considered a passing grade. Candidates who score less are reluctantly "released from employment."

Of course, instruction, especially at the management level, can never end. In these days of rapid technological developments, new methods, new services, and new products are constantly being put to use. To keep the managers of the 26 branches instantly informed of all innovations, The Bowery instituted its own video network as the best and quickest means of communication. Gravette said of it:

> At the 42nd Street office we now have a fully equipped video studio in which we produce programs completely in-house. All of our 26 branches are equipped with video monitors to allow instantaneous playback of tapes. Programs can be produced and viewed by all employees within 24 hours. And new branches, as they are opened, can easily be equipped with monitors at a relatively low cost.

Apart from Diane Tracy and Grace Pichardo, no one gives more attention to the training program than does Bud Gravette. His active participation in it is marked by repeated meetings and discussions with management groups as well as with newly hired trainees. "Regardless of how ambitious our plans for the future may be," he said, "they won't work unless they're managed by competent, fully trained men and women. That's why I give top priority to efficient training."

Gravette had to give thought to his own efficiency, too. For some time he had realized that he could not give the bank his best efforts while he combined the offices of chairman and president, as he had been doing. The two positions demanded too much of a man's time and energy. The bank ought to have a president.

347

The truth was he had already begun a search for someone capable of sharing his duties, someone who could become president. And he did not have to look far.

A senior partner in the renowned law firm of Cadwallader, Wickersham, and Taft had for some years represented The Bowery in litigation and in conferences with federal and state banking officials. No one was in a better position to understand The Bowery's problems than was Stuart D. Root. Even now Root was pleading the need for further deregulations for thrift institutions. In Albany, as in Washington, he was welcomed as an authority on the subject, and in both places he had friends among influential legislators.

Gravette regarded him as the ideal choice for the presidency. But would he be willing to leave his law firm?

Root now smiles at the recollection of what happened. Pacing his office, he said, "Bud Gravette asked me to come to lunch, and I found myself listening to one of the quietest, most persuasive, most logical, most irresistible men I had ever met. Of course, he knew how deeply I felt about the welfare of The Bowery. It had been one of my primary interests for more than a decade. And now, as I saw it, he was giving me an opportunity to make the most of my interest. I couldn't help remembering that another partner of Cadwallader, Wickersham, and Taft had set an example in leaving the law firm to join the bank. That had been Rusty Crawford. I was being invited to follow in his steps. Yes, I accepted the offer. It was one of the best decisions I ever made."

As for Gravette, he told the trustees he could not have enlisted the skill of a more qualified man.

Stuart D. Root walked into his new office on January 15, 1981, and brought with him a philosophy that viewed present savings as a guarantee of the nation's future prosperity, for those savings would eventually be spent. Surely

348

it was an appropriate creed for the president of a savings institution.

❧

To lend power to the savings banks' campaign for greater freedom of operations, The Bowery commissioned the Wharton School's Economic Forecasting Associates to make a thorough survey of thrift institutions and to recommend ways of rescuing them from their trials. An unbiased professional study, Gravette believed, must influence the Washington agencies.

Other banks quickly recognized the value of the undertaking. Four of them—Manhattan Savings Bank, Emigrant Savings Bank, American Savings Bank, and Seamen's Savings Bank—hurried to cosponsor the study on what Gravette called "a reimbursement basis."

When the Wharton Report was issued it dealt with five principal ways in which the government could help the thrifts. The one that seemed to win most favor in Washington involved "assisted mergers." It described the value of having weak banks merged under the supervision of the FDIC, with that agency's financial help. The word "assisted," however, made The Bowery executives like Gravette and Root scoff. "Assisted means *forced!*"

Five such "assisted" mergers had already occurred in New York City's savings banks. By pooling their dwindling assets they appeared to strengthen their combined net worths, especially when they were backed by FDIC financial support. As examples, the merging of the Greenwich Savings Bank with the Metropolitan was expected to cost the FDIC some $465 million. The Central-Harlem merger would cost the agency $160 million in support. So it went.

At any rate, the Wharton Report was so important that it went to the White House, and it brought quick reaction. A

349

meeting of bankers, economists, agency heads, and Cabinet members was called by President Reagan. Stuart Root was invited to attend as president of The Bowery.

At the conference table he sat beside Vice President Bush, facing President Reagan. For a time he listened in silence. What appalled him was the attitude of some powerful officials who maintained, "The thrifts can't be in trouble. They have a steady cash flow of deposits." This attitude was incredibly blind to the *outflow* of funds.

Every person at the conference was asked to voice an opinion. When the President of the United States called upon Root for his views, The Bowery's representative read from a prepared statement:

> Mr. President, I echo the great thanks we have for your seeing us this morning.
>
> For 150 years The Bowery Savings Bank has survived depressions, numerous wars, financial panics, and earlier inflations. It has grown to over $5 billion and well over 700,000 accounts.
>
> Today The Bowery is staring at the prospect of an assisted or *forced* merger—a term that is a euphemism in the eyes of the press for *failure*. Apparently, this is to occur around November 1 of this year. The economic cost (FDIC insured) will exceed $1 billion and will be borne by the budget and by the commercial banking system, itself showing signs of strain. The forced merger policy will claim within one year banks having over $20 billion in assets *in New York alone*.
>
> In meetings with your representatives I have been told that this is not a problem because the cash flow of these banks is strong. I say, Mr. President, that such a view is highly simplistic. In New York it actually collides with the law which makes it a *felony* for a teller or clerk to receive a deposit when the bank has run out of reserves.
>
> Last year The Bowery lost over 50,000 accounts and lost $722 million in deposits. This is more than the assets of almost 19,000 banks and savings associations in the nation.
>
> When I return to New York today I expect to see a report showing our loss for this year so far to be nearly $40 million in the first quarter alone.

Let me repeat, sir, each new *forced* merger is seen by the press and the public as a new failure. The Bowery is a national institution. Further undermining of the public's confidence must be avoided. I believe we can avoid it with no budget consequence while we await the positive impact of your entire economic recovery program.

It was a direct and effective statement that helped, at least for the moment, to scotch the threat of having The Bowery compelled to merge with another bank.

And it was not the only legalistic battle in which Root was engaged. With all the energy he could summon, he tried to win permission for The Bowery, for all savings banks, to issue tax-free certificates. This would free a part of earned interest from federal taxation. It would enhance a healthy cash flow for the bank by attracting deposits at a reasonable interest rate; the tax-free stipulation would presumably make up for the higher interest paid by money market accounts.

"It was a good idea, and we made a strong bid for it," Root said, "but it was approved for only one year."

He tried other ways of "climbing out of the doldrums," often aided and accompanied by the bank's counsel, or they appeared together with representatives of other banks. It was a campaign for deregulation that never stopped. "I was constantly commuting between New York and Washington and between New York and Albany," Root said. He not only pleaded his case in person; he wrote letters and pamphlets to the appropriate legislators and to the regulatory agencies.

One of the most effective facts stressed by The Bowery, one that Root had pointed out to President Reagan, was this:

The United States Government is the underwriter of the security of the $22.5 billion of depositors' funds in the ten leading New York City-based savings banks. Virtually all these

351

deposit liabilities are insured by the Federal Deposit Insurance Corporation. Closing troubled thrifts and paying off their depositors is unquestionably the least desirable and most expensive alternative to deregulation.

The thought of having the FDIC pay out $22.5 billion must have jolted a number of legislators, for suddenly they showed new interest in the plight of the thrifts, and new anxiety, too. The regulatory agencies began to draft "emergency powers" for the Congress to consider.

Even more heartening was the reaction of the Congress itself. The chairmen of the finance committee in both the House and the Senate spoke of scheduling new hearings on behalf of the thrifts. In Albany, added support came from State Superintendent of Banks Muriel Siebert and her deputy, Alan Cohen. There was ferment everywhere, a sense of rising excitement and achievement.

But at noon on March 30, 1981 something happened that made Washington and the rest of the country forget the thrifts and, for that matter, almost everything else.

President Reagan came out of a meeting at Washington's Hilton Hotel and, as usual, waved a cheerful greeting to those who applauded as he walked to his car. Before he could step into it, a demented young man in the crowd pulled a gun out of his pocket and began firing. One bullet struck the President's chest. He staggered. Instantly Secret Service protectors threw themselves around him. Some were wounded. James Brady, the White House press secretary, fell to the ground with a bullet in his head. And although the would-be assassin was instantly felled and overpowered, Washington burst into pandemonium. The President was rushed to a hospital behind speeding motorcycles.

For days thereafter the nation was more concerned about hospital reports than about the ailments of the economy or the problems of banks. It was a time when every church and synagogue in America offered prayers for the President's recovery, for James Brady, and for the Secret Service men who had been wounded.

In ensuing days, as the President's condition improved, the sense of relief and thankfulness which spread through the nation brought reassurance to Washington, too, and slowly, very slowly, legislators tried to concentrate again on those concerns that had occupied them before the assassination attempt. Among them, though not a major issue, was the worsening condition of thrift institutions.

Two months after the President left the hospital, in May, the federal regulatory agencies at last drafted a bill that would give the savings banks some emergency powers. "By no means everything we wanted," said Stuart Root, "but it was a forward step." For a while the future did seem brighter—until the White House announced its opposition to the measure. It was summarily dropped.

Not to be defeated, the savings banks' lobbyists again intensified their efforts. And again they made progress. In July of 1981 the leadership of the House Banking Committee introduced its own bill intended to help the thrifts. But individual legislators pounced upon it with revisions, restrictions, additions, deletions, and the entire bill had to be rewritten.

Meanwhile, the chairman of the Senate Banking Committee, Senator Jake Garn, Republican of Utah, announced that he would introduce a deregulation bill.

The occurrence of such legislative events, although far from being conclusive, were important for two reasons: First, they indicated that Washington was indeed giving serious, if intermittent, attention to the exhortations of the thrifts; and second, they explained the increasing impatience of Gravette and the heads of other New York savings banks. With their funds steadily being drained away, how long could they afford to wait for rescue through the on-again-off-again tactics of the government?

Fearing that legislative wrangling and indecision might continue for years, the chairman of The Bowery sought relief in another area—*voluntary* mergers. (Voluntary as opposed to forced.)

After conferences with many banks, Gravette proposed merging with four of them—the East River, the Dry Dock, the Emigrant, and the United Mutual. A single organization created out of all these could bring profitability to them all. It would do away with the cost of maintaining redundant branches, often facing each other at a corner where one bank could serve the purpose of two. It could establish a single, centralized main office for overall administration. It would reduce the total work force by 1,136. It would add billions in deposits to a common fund and to a common net worth. By adopting such economies, it would save more than $68 million a year in operating costs.

Truly, it was a dramatic and feasible rescue plan. Superintendent Muriel Siebert praised it and heartily recommended it to federal officials. So did her deputy, Alan Cohen. Why, then, was it so abruptly abandoned?

The answer came out of Washington.

33

THANKS TO JAKE AND FERNAND

In spite of all other pressing business, both houses of Congress were roused, by 1981, to the dangers of ignoring the thrifts. This was not only because of the $22.5 billion involvement of the FDIC in New York's mutual savings banks. There was another consideration, one that impinged on the very reputation of the United States, on its image before the world: If the Congress allowed some of the nation's largest savings banks to collapse, would it not suggest the bankruptcy of the American economy itself?

It was a crisis that had to be faced.

Senator Jake Garn announced that the bill he was about to present to his Senate Banking Committee would, unlike his previous attempts, grant the thrifts all the liberalized rights they needed to survive. That welcome news came in September. Within a month his committee held hearings on the proposals—and, as always, encountered the delays of amendments.

Those representatives of New York savings banks who attended the hearings squirmed in their seats. Would all these proposed amendments eviscerate the benefits of the legislation?

A few months later, in February of 1982, Congressman Fernand St. Germain, Democrat of Rhode Island and chairman of the House Banking Committee, introduced his own bill "to provide emergency aid to the thrift institutions."

If one wonders why so many months elapsed, from September to February, in the preparation of this legislation, one has only to reflect on other matters that were demanding the attention of the Congress and of the nation:

☐ President Reagan presented an urgent, yet controversial, tax-cutting bill that would reduce taxes by $37 billion while the country's deficits were soaring; he telephoned almost every member of Congress in his effort to have it passed.

☐ The country's air industry was being harassed by a strike of air traffic controllers—a strike branded illegal by the President.

☐ The country was gambling a multibillion-dollar stake in launching the reusable space ship Columbia.

☐ In the area of foreign affairs, The White House was announcing sanctions against the Soviet-imposed military government in Poland.

☐ Israel, Lebanon, and Syria were embroiled in crisis after crisis while Philip Habib and Secretary of State George Schultz poured their energies into seeking a solution.

356

□ On this side of the Atlantic, El Salvador and Nicaragua were causing ever-increasing concern in Washington.

Taking all such events into account—and there were others too—one might have marveled at the fact that at so trying a time the problems of the thrifts remained high on legislative agendas. Certainly much credit for this must be attributed to the determined and skillful persistence of the savings banks' lobbyists.

At any rate, with deregulating legislation at last "in the works," Gravette consulted with Crawford, Larsen, and other trustees. All agreed this was no time to press the plan for a five-bank voluntary merger. It was wiser to await congressional action that might provide all the relief the thrifts sought.

Even the state's champions of the consolidation idea, Bank Superintendant Muriel Siebert and Deputy Alan Cohen, acknowledged that it was prudent to wait and see what Congress would do. So the waiting period continued.

It was not a time of idleness. Gravette was implementing the five-year plan by adding whatever services the law permitted him to undertake. An example was the introduction of H & R Block, Inc., to the banking floor. Depositors could now have income tax returns prepared at The Bowery.

Not that Gravette forgot the consolidation plan; far from it. Much of the bank's management training was intended to make The Bowery's staff ready for new challenges. The prospect of consolidation, however, piqued the curiosity of William Isaac, new chairman of the FDIC. He telephoned Gravette to ask if he might come to The Bowery for a personal indoctrination in what the bank was aiming to achieve.

"By all means," Gravette replied. "Come at your earliest convenience."

Isaac came. It was the first time that the head of the

357

FDIC had visited The Bowery. At six o'clock that evening he was given a demonstration, among other things, of the training program devised largely by Diane Tracy and Grace Pichardo. It impressed him so profoundly that he asked, "Could I bring my staff to see all this? Would you repeat it for them?"

Gravette naturally welcomed the opportunity. It was the highest kind of flattery. Exactly one week later, on June 22, 1982, William Isaac was back with members of his staff.

In greeting them, Gravette said, "Our program today is designed to show you the strength of our management team, how we train and develop people, the innovative ways by which we are improving service to our customers, our new investment programs, and our plans for the future. We will highlight some of the creative things which we believe will once again make us a profitable leader in the financial marketplace."

For the next hour and forty minutes, in that eighth-floor classroom, Gravette, Stuart Root, Diane Tracy, Grace Pichardo, and nine members of the management staff explained not only the details of the unique Bowery consolidation plan but indicated how specialized training would help the bank's five-year plan once it was freed of restrictions.

"Many of our key managers are new to the bank," Gravette told the visitors, "Stuart Root and myself included. We recognized the need to bring other new people into the organization since we needed broader experience and more specialized skills if we were to meet the challenges of the rapidly changing financial industry."

What followed was a series of crisp talks by management personnel, illustrated with slides.

"That evening," Grace Pichardo said in recollecting the event, "we not only made friends at the FDIC. We won their respect and the backing we so sorely needed."

But all the praise and admiration of the Washington

guests could not check the continuing deterioration of the bank's mortgage business, any more than it could change the nation's economy. The outflow of funds at The Bowery still exceeded the inflow. It became so bad that, to stave off the threat of ruin, the trustees even considered selling the 18-floor headquarters building on 42nd Street. That would have been tragic. Apart from the emotional trauma it would have caused Bowery veterans, it would have advertised the bank's difficult situation, probably impelling many depositors to withdraw their funds.

Gravette found an ingenious alternative. Some of the building's upper floors, no longer needed for bank operations, were sold as business condominiums. This brought some $16 million in cash, yet preserved the ownership of "the most beautiful bank in the nation," as it has been described.

Thus passed another crisis.

◈

And finally—people at the bank must have wanted to raise their arms and shout "Eureka!"—Congress made its decisive move. Both houses passed the Garn–St. Germain Depository Institutions Act. In October of 1982 President Reagan signed it into law. It is no exaggeration to say that it saved many members of the thrift industry from collapse.

Among its most important clauses, the Act phased out many of the differentials between the interest rates that savings and commercial banks could pay (under Regulation Q). Of outstanding significance, it permitted state banks to convert to federal charters without losing the benefits of FDIC insurance. And, something for which Crawford had long campaigned, it granted mutual savings banks the option of becoming *stock* institutions. Of this, *The New York Times* later said:

359

For an industry devastated in recent years by high interest rates, billions of dollars in losses and hundreds of failures, the chance to go public represents hope for a new burst of prosperity.

Another of the Act's stipulations was destined to save 15 New York savings banks, including The Bowery, from collapse. This was a clause that empowered the FDIC "to provide non-cash assistance to thrift institutions." Though the transfer of cash was explicitly forbidden, the FDIC nevertheless retained the right to issue *promissory notes* to banks that showed a sagging net worth.

When Dolores J. Morrissey, the bank's treasurer, read this in the bill, she took immediate action. Arms laden with bank records, she flew to Washington. It was a trip repeated again and again. As a result of her efforts, the FDIC gave The Bowery Savings Bank a seven-year promissory note in the amount of $58 million. In exchange, the bank gave the FDIC its own seven-year note carrying the same interest rate. The transaction, adding $58 million to The Bowery's book assets, helped lift it out of the danger zone.

(Actually, not one cent had changed hands. Yet, there was that $58 million entry on the assets side of the books— an entry guaranteed by the United States of America. Somewhere, I recall, a British journalist wrote that he could not understand American ways of doing business. "In the United States," he said, "when dealing in non-existent millions, human genius for creating wealth knows no limits.")

Another feature of the new legislation was that federal-chartered savings banks were no longer confined to dealing almost exclusively in mortgages. Unlike commercial banks, however, they could make commercial loans only up to 10 percent of their assets, and consumer loans up to 30 percent.

In short, Garn and St. Germain had truly opened the

gates of a new era. Morris D. Crawford, Jr., emerging from a trustees' meeting, said with a triumphant smile, "At last we're getting the right to do what we should have done twenty years ago!"

Gravette, for his part, seized upon the new freedom to give his five-year plan full sway. New excitement permeated the bank, a sense of full speed ahead. In the mortgage division, adjustable rate mortgages (the ARM program) would now be offered on luxury-class homes in amounts up to—and even exceeding—$1 million. Personal loans would be augmented by automobile loans, even boat loans. The innovations came as if they had been pent up for years.

But Gravette had to confront another problem. Were The Bowery's officers really equipped by experience to compete in the open financial market with such commercial giants as Citibank, Chase, Chemical, and the rest? To trustees who came in to see him, Gravette said, "We need someone who is thoroughly familiar with all commercial bank activities; someone experienced in the field of large commercial loans, consumer loans, securities, investments, trust funds, international exchange, and all the other functions of a financial institution."

Once again, then, The Bowery had to launch a search for someone with specific, proven abilities of the kind this new era required, someone able to grasp a multitude of new opportunities. The search passed over many highly qualified people before it focused on Jerald C. Newman.

One has only to consider his record to understand why the trustees unanimously endorsed his selection. He had amassed a good deal of banking experience before becoming executive vice president of the Bank Leumi Trust Company of New York. When he joined that institution it had three New York branches. Largely as a result of his energetic efforts, Leumi grew to 25 city and suburban offices. His executive duties had encompassed all the operations of a large commercial bank—corporate planning, marketing, management analysis, and the unending drive to attract new big-business clients.

The Bowery trustees were impressed, too, by the fact that Newman had earlier in life taught business courses at New York University. Even now, in the evenings, he was lecturing to master of business administration (MBA) classes at Long Island University. In recognition of his academic work he had recently received the University Medal from the State University at Stony Brook for his decade of devotion to the institution's growth. His cultural interests had been recognized by the White House when President Reagan appointed him to serve on the National Commission of Libraries and Science Information Centers.

Jerald Newman was inducted as The Bowery's president on October 21, 1982—a position opened for him by having Stuart Root elevated to the office of vice chairman. Hardly had the new president settled behind his desk when he glanced up to see a hesitant young lady in the door.

"I'm on the staff of *The Chest*, the bank's magazine," she explained. "Could I ask a few questions for the story we're going to run?"

Newman smiled. Tall, dark-haired, he adjusted his glasses, wondering what kind of questions he could answer before learning more about Bowery procedures. But he waved to a chair and said, "Sit down and go ahead."

The girl sat with a pad on her knee and a poised pencil. "First," she said, "could I ask why you chose to come to The Bowery at this particular time?"

Newman promptly replied, "Because this is a *challenging* time. As a result of the Garn–St. Germain legislation I foresee a complete turnaround in banking. Look at Mr. Gravette's five-year plan, and you know The Bowery isn't going to be simply a savings bank any more. Now we're going to have to change people's *perception* of what we are. They'll have to see us as a full-service financial institution.

Savings banks that don't evolve in that direction are going to have a problem to survive."

The girl had many more questions, but in that first answer Newman indicated the course he planned to follow. It was the course on which Ellis T. Gravette, Jr. had himself embarked years earlier—to change the traditional "little man's" repository for savings to a financial institution that would serve the little man and big men, too, *in every possible way*. The analogy to a financial supermarket was becoming a reality.

And there would be an emotional satisfaction in achieving such a change in time to commemorate The Bowery's 150th birthday in 1984.

34

FULL SERVICE BY 150?

On an autumnal morning in 1982 early customers of the 42nd Street branch abruptly stopped as they entered the doors. They tilted their heads back and gaped. What they saw was unbelievable—a magician's trick, an optical illusion, something never before seen in an American bank. How had this thing come into the building? And why?

They were staring at a fully inflated, multicolored balloon five floors high and some 45 feet in diameter.

Within minutes the bewildered customers were joined by reporters, cameramen, and a massing of

Bowery employees. A number of young women, gaily attired in the costumes of foreign lands, circulated in the crowd, distributing pamphlets about the joys of travel.

By the time Bud Gravette, Stuart Root, Joe DiMaggio, and other bank people joined the spectators, the news had spread that the balloon symbolized a new Bowery enterprise. The rumor was validated when Gravette raised an arm for attention and made a brief speech of explanation.

"We're here," he said, "to introduce an exciting new service—*Bowery Travel*." He might have added that this was the first time in the annals of American banking that such an innovation had been offered to the public. But, instead, he went on, "This is really the kickoff of a comprehensive program which will provide customers with a broad range of additional personal services."

Somebody whispered, "What if this balloon explodes?"

Gravette seemed not to hear the interruption. "Our customers," he said, "are much more sophisticated today than they were ten years ago. They expect more from financial institutions. We are going to prove that a savings bank can meet and exceed those expectations."

"What if it collapses?" the low voice persisted.

Gravette still appeared not to hear the question. "When we decided to offer travel services," he continued, "we looked at a number of travel agencies. We selected the Fugazy International Travel organization to be our joint-venture partner because of its outstanding reputation as a well-established and highly respected travel organization. Both The Bowery and Fugazy have served the people of New York since the 1800s, and both have been leaders in their respective industries. We will do well together. And I'm delighted to introduce Bill Fugazy."

The crowd applauded, and William D. Fugazy, chairman of the board of his company, responded with an expression of his pleasure in joining The Bowery in the new enterprise.

Then Gravette resumed, "Bowery Travel now offers services provided by any first-class travel agency—airline reservations and tickets, hotel accommodations, car rentals, tours, cruises, business travel, limousine service, all these as well as assistance with letters of credit, insurance, passport applications, and customs."

With a wave of his hand he indicated where, on the banking floor, travel representatives would have their desks. "They will tell you," he said, "about our newly formed Bowery Travel Club in which savings plans will help save for trips, while the deposit normally required by travel agencies will be waived. These, as you know, are challenging times for savings banks. You can see we're meeting those challenges with optimism and innovation."

Then he turned to someone in the audience. "In answer to your questions, sir, this balloon is perfectly safe. It will neither explode nor collapse." He paused and motioned to Joe DiMaggio. "All right, Joe. All yours."

Thereupon, to conclude the ceremonies, Joe DiMaggio banged a bottle of champagne on the balloon's gondola and christened the inflated giant "The Bowery."

Almost daily now innovations took astonishing forms. In developing its five-year plan the bank was quickly becoming a pioneer in providing imaginative services, and quite often one type of service logically led to another.

For instance, travel service customers who planned to go abroad would need foreign currencies. The Bowery therefore entered into a joint venture with the foreign exchange firm of Deak–Perera and gave it space on the banking floor.

In its first month hardly 100 customers availed themselves of its presence. In the second month the number grew to 250; in the third to 650—"and we were clearly on the way to a successful, profitable operation."

In the latter half of 1983 new customer services and commercial banking activities multiplied so fast that even The Bowery's own employees found it hard to keep abreast of all that was happening. Lunchtime conversation generally began with, "Say, have you heard the latest?"

Realizing that the cooperation of all branch managers would be needed to make the most of the programs, Gravette decided to indoctrinate them all in a single session. He would do it through the newly installed video communications system—the pride of Diane Tracy and Grace Pichardo. Moreover, here was an opportunity to introduce the bank's new president, Jerald Newman, to the officers of the 26 branches.

So the chairman arranged for Newman to speak to the entire organization through the medium of videotapes; he would report all recent developments in banking services. Thus it was that, after business hours, the officers of the 26 branch offices sat in front of their video screens, studying the new president's face and listening to every word he told them.

He began by stressing the fact that had often before been heard, "We plan to become a financial supermarket, dealing in every quality service that will benefit our customers and ourselves." Perhaps the branch people had already heard of the automobile loans that were being made, and the boat loans, and the adjustable rate mortgages in amounts up to $1 million. But many of these officers may well have been astonished to hear Newman tell them, "Chairman Gravette has developed a system of lending funds to other institutions *within our own industry*—that is, to healthy savings and loan associations." He spoke too of the COBRE program, COBRE being an acronym for Commercial Bank Real Estate.

"In COBRE," he said, "we offer companies—those that give us substantially *all of their commercial banking busi-*

ness—the opportunity to obtain favorable loans as well as mortgages for company-related real estate."

One of the most exciting and gratifying features of Newman's talk was that the bank had recently raised cash by offering a $147 million mortgage-backed bond issue. The details, and there had been many, had been masterfully handled by Treasurer Dolores Morrissey. Rated Triple A, the issue had been completely sold out at the offering. According to The Bowery's general counsel, Lee Rassnick, the bonds carried the strongest security any bonds could provide—mortgages that represented $1.80 for every dollar in bonds.

The videotape went from one innovation to another. Never in the history of the bank had so many changes occurred in so short a time. As further examples, Newman reported that The Bowery would soon have clearing facilities for credit card charges made on Visa, Mastercard, and American Express. And the commercial banking division (just formed) was prepared to make business loans anywhere in the United States in the range of $25,000 to $1 million.

"In the short time the commercial banking division has been in existence," the videotaped report continued, "we have made about 30 such commercial loans, creating a new portfolio of approximately $5 million. And we have gained some 250 corporate checking accounts that we never had before."

In all, it was a stunning recital of change. What had been a $70 million quarter loss a year earlier had been reduced to $47 million, and The Bowery was well on its way to earning healthy profits in its 150th anniversary year.

With so many rapid changes being made in the operations of the bank, Gravette wanted to be sure that all his associates understood what was happening—and *why* it was happening. He summoned them to a meeting in one of the classrooms reserved for lectures to trainees.

Some 30 people attended. Gravette set a mood for easy informality; he took off his jacket, invited others to do the same, and sank comfortably into a deep chair. Legs crossed, he glanced around not only at his own management group but at representatives of Ogilvie & Mather, the bank's advertising agency, and at Howard J. Rubenstein, its public relations counselor.

After the exchange of a few pleasantries, he said, "I'd like you all to understand why we are undertaking to provide so many varied services."

"This," said a voice, "is something I've been waiting to hear."

"The answer is really simple," Gravette continued, "once you consider it this way: When a person has just one interest binding him to the bank—say a savings account—it's very easy for him to move that account to another bank, and we've lost a customer.

"*But*—" Now he raised a finger for emphasis. "Suppose he also has a safety deposit box here, and he has a personal loan on our books, and an automobile loan, and he can write checks on his Bowery account, and his business trips are arranged by our travel agency, and his mortgage payments are made here, and he has a money market account with us, and he has tax shelters in either Keogh or IRA deposits, and he has various types of insurance bought through us, and we give him relocation services if his firm sends him to another city. I could go on and on. The point is, if he has *many* ties to The Bowery, he is not likely to leave us. And that—apart from the fact that we profit from the services we render—is one rationale for what we are doing. Another is that if we are to compete successfully with commercial banks, we have to match them or outdo them in the services we offer."

One man raised his hand to pose a question, "Won't all these changes require new training for our managers?"

"Absolutely," Gravette agreed. "We have arranged for such training. It will be given on a volunteer basis by The New York Institute of Credit. They expect to start with a class of 26. Eventually, we hope, some of these 26 will be able to train others."

There was silence before a low voice said, "Now that we're bidding for big business, what happend to The Bowery's historic concern for the welfare of the 'little man'?"

"That will never change," Gravette replied. "Remember this: If we prosper, we'll be *able* to help the little man prosper. If we don't prosper, there isn't much we can do for him. And let me point out that most of our loans have gone to small firms owned by the so-called little man. So I repeat—in this respect The Bowery will never change."

ᘯᕁᘗ

In the latter half of 1983 a remarkable new feeling of confidence suddenly permeated the bank. I could feel it in the very lilt of conversation among officers. What had been an atmosphere of uncertainty, often of downright worry, was dispelled as if by a burst of sunshine after a storm. People joked again, laughed again.

The reasons were evident. For one, the mortgage business was having a revival. Loans were being granted on an almost unlimited variety of real estate undertakings— private homes, apartment dwellings, business buildings, factories, warehouses, large residential developments, hotels, all the rest. New regulations—or deregulations— would allow mortgage rates to remain fixed for four or five years, with the option of thereafter being changed to variable rates. In other words, the interest rates would match economic trends.

And day after day commercial loans were being made to businesses not only in New York but in other states. With so many new services being inaugurated, there was actual talk of changing the venerable name of The Bowery Savings Bank to the broader, more inclusive designation of The Bowery Bank.

"Someday it will come," Gravette predicted.

There was also increasing expectation of altering the institution's charter from a mutual bank to a stock corporation. By the laws of New York State, two successive sessions of the legislature would have to sanction such a change, and the past two sessions had already done so. All that remained was for the state's voters to ratify the amendment at the next general election in November. If they did so, the bank could at once offer its stock to the public. To ensure passage of the act, an informative campaign would have to be launched to publicize the need, and the Rubinstein agency was given the task.

Meanwhile, Gravette continued to surround himself with the kind of staff needed to manage a full-service financial institution. First there had been Vice Chairman Stuart D. Root, unexcelled as a spokesman for deregulation; he had in truth been serving the entire savings bank industry. Next had come Jerald C. Newman, backed by the right experience to lead The Bowery into vigorous competition with commercial banks.

Then Gravette had brought in Leopold S. Rassnick as senior vice president and general counsel, a man who had previously served not only the Federal Reserve Bank of New York but also the state's Association of Savings Banks. In his case, The Bowery gained priceless and unique legal experience of the kind it would need more and more urgently as it expanded its activities.

And as an outstanding achievement, Gravette had recently induced Alan R. Cohen, Muriel Siebert's successor as State Superintendant of Banks, and his associate, Gary Brody, to join The Bowery. Among the bank's officers and trustees this was regarded as a triumph. Who could command greater public respect among consumers, and more earnest attention among legislators, than those who had been responsible at the very highest level of state government for overseeing the activities of the state's banks? They brought to The Bowery not only experience but distinction.

"I came to know Alan Cohen well when he was Superintendant of Banks," Gravette said. "What deeply impressed me was his ability as an administrator. He ran his office firmly, with clear knowledge of a bank's problems. And The Bowery, with its many new interests, is going to need a strong, overall administrator. In Cohen and Brody we got the best administrative team we could find."

They very soon proved themselves by helping to add another new service to the bank's activities. This was InVest, an advisory function in which Bowery experts would offer investment counseling. These experts would not *sell* stocks and bonds. Working on a salary basis rather than on brokerage commissions (the practice in most commercial banks), they would limit themselves to analyzing individual needs and offering professional guidance.

With the addition of Cohen and Brody, The Bowery now had what was probably the most efficient and diversified managerial team in its history. "I can't think of a more ideal setup," one executive declared, "for seeing us into our 150th year."

35
ᘒᘒ
SALUTE TO
TOMORROW

How does one observe a 150th anniversary?

Surely in the case of The Bowery it should be an occasion glowing with a spirit of joy, achievement, pride, especially since it marked a time of exhilarating financial recovery. But could the bank's celebration—at best, a local event in New York—be wholly unrestrained when the nation was being beset by international tragedies and bitter uncertainties about the future?

For it was then, just four months before the 1984 anniversary, that the Soviet Union blasted a Korean commercial plane out of the night skies, killing 269 people, of whom 61 were Americans. The country was outraged. Its flags, flown at half-staff, symbolized fury as much as mourning. Outside the United Nations building, scarcely a half mile from The Bowery, crowds were shouting their horror of the Russian act. There were cries of "Throw them out of the country! Close their embassies and their consulates! Have done with them!"

Even while this was happening, American marines, on a peacekeeping mission in Lebanon, were suddenly bombarded by terrorist shells. Within two days, five Americans were killed and others wounded. It was hardly surprising that editorials and even some congressmen were demanding, "Either blast the hell out of those terrorists or bring our boys home! We can't let our troops be sitting ducks for a cause that isn't even theirs!"

Nor was that all. One almost forgot that the American Navy was holding maneuvers off both coasts of Central America, its presence warning the communist forces of Cuba and Russia to stay away from that part of the world. Almost too many things, all of them bad, were embroiling the United States. It was a difficult time to concentrate on plans for a cheerful, carefree celebration.

Nevertheless, a small committee of six people met regularly to formulate a year-long observance of the anniversary. After all, it had become almost axiomatic in America that historic moments were not to be ignored. And The Bowery Savings Bank certainly had distinctions that *ought* to be honored.

For instance, of the 50 largest corporations in the United States, not one was as old as The Bowery. True, there were smaller companies, even a few banks, that had attained the age of 150. Their number could be listed on a single page of a small notebook. But they offered no guidance for planning a large-scale celebration.

Of course, there were suggestions in what the bank had

done to mark its 100th anniversary in 1934. There had been flags bearing the number 100, a trademark also featuring 100, newspaper clippings of interviews with President Henry Bruère and other notables. There had been concerts and other forms of entertainment at all branch offices. In a commemorative book, author William Dana Orcutt had written:

> The Bowery Savings Bank, at the moment of its centennial, has been far more vital to the progress of the individual and the community than the recorded history *of any single institution.*

That was indeed flattering. Yet, Orcutt had added with keen foresight:

> None of the functions for which mutual savings banks were founded have yet been fully served. There is still room for higher developments, and there are abundant opportunities for progress.

He made it seem that Gravette's five-year plan had long ago been preordained. Now, fifty years later, The Bowery was at last making the most of "abundant opportunities." One member of the planning committee said of the contemplated celebration, "We wanted to focus on *achievement,* not merely old age."

Barbara J. Edler, another member, pointed out, "If you consider only the affairs of the bank, not of the nation, we were extremely lucky in the matter of timing. Two or three years earlier it would have been impossible to be cheerful about The Bowery's financial condition. We simply couldn't have held a happy pose while our resources were being drained away."

But now, as Grace Pichardo put it, "We could plan with confidence. The bank would enter its 150th year with renewed strength."

Some 1984 activities were almost ritualistic. There would be visualizations of The Bowery's endless contributions to the growth of New York. Someone suggested that if every building that owed its existence to a Bowery mortgage—from homes to skyscrapers—could be concentrated in a single, vast composite photograph, it would be like the view of a major world city with a towering skyline.

But physical memorabilia, the committee realized, were only one phase of the bank's service to society. It had actively participated in virtually every philanthropic and social undertaking New York City had sponsored, and in every nationwide charitable campaign.

These were some of the aspects of history the anniversary committee decided to emphasize. Historical exhibits would travel from branch to branch. Every office would be decorated with pennants bearing the number 150, and employees would wear buttons exhibiting the 150 figure. As for the opening day of the celebration, it would witness a gathering of civic, industrial, financial, and political leaders at a gala dinner.

The theme of that dinner? Nothing, it seemed to me, could be more appropriate than a repetition of something Morris D. Crawford, Jr. had said some years earlier: "In the extraordinary record of its past and in the bold initiatives of its present lies the brilliant promise of The Bowery's future."

Epilogue

ぐ～〉

It seemed appropriate, at this historic moment in banking annals, to ask how veteran Bowery leaders viewed all that was happening. The stifling regulations they had for so long been trying to nullify had at last been removed. On October 1, 1983, deregulation won a long-delayed victory. Savings banks—indeed, all banks—could henceforth set their own interest rates for the funds they sought to attract.

As if to celebrate this triumph of deregulation came a kind of banking hysteria. All banks, commercial as well as savings, advertised in full-page and even double-page spreads the generous interest rates they were prepared to pay, usually around 11 percent. Chase Manhattan even offered $10 to those who came in to seek information on renewing their Certificates of Deposit (CDs).

Surrounded by such competing inducements, The Bowery ran its own full-page advertisements. They were headed, "Have Our Banks Gone Mad?" The average newspaper reader would probably have answered, "Mad is too mild a word for it."

Actually, The Bowery's publicity proved to be the least hysterical of all. It analyzed the many choices offered to depositors in this dawn of an unregulated age. And its banking floors were crowded with customers eager to get the highest possible returns on their money.

This, then, was the excited atmosphere in which I asked former leaders of The Bowery to appraise the future of their institution as it entered its 150th year. The first reply came from former Chairman Morris D. Crawford, Jr. He wrote

This bank and this industry have just passed through the most difficult three years in savings bank history. The trauma has been greatest in the large Eastern money centers—especially in Manhattan where the competition has always been fiercest.

Legislators (state and federal) and some regulators were finally faced by events—reason having failed—to broaden savings bank powers and make them equivalent in most respects to commercial bank powers.

This came after decades of pious declarations that thrifts had a unique, important, albeit narrow, social function to serve the "little man" and to provide the housing market with long-term, fixed-rate loans. The rate explosion at the outset of this decade, with its devastating impact on many thrifts, finally overcame the political bias of the lawmakers who did, at last, what they should have done in the public interest twenty years ago.

Now, armed with full powers, the thrifts are engaged in a desperate game of catch up. The swift and the innovative will survive and prosper. This may be—together with many other contemporary developments in the financial world—the penultimate step in the irreversible march to a single form of full-service financial institutions.

Shortly after the arrival of Crawford's letter came John Larsen's. With 50 years of service to the bank—40 as an employee who rose to the presidency, and 10 additional years as a trustee—Larsen had an unequaled background for his analysis of the bank's situation in 1984. He wrote

In appraising the future of The Bowery one must reflect on the courses which are now open to all savings banks.

Many, but by no means all, will probably convert to *stock* savings banks (a course recently made available to them) in order to increase their net worth much more rapidly than would be possible solely through the retention of earnings. The buyers of such issues of (savings bank) capital stock, of which there have already been a number, will have a reasonably safe investment provided short-term interest rates do not again escalate in the near future.

If they do, most thrift institutions will once more drop into the red as far as earnings are concerned; there still exists a serious mismatch between maturities of their assets and deposit liabilities.

Some savings banks, both mutuals and stock, and particularly the largest ones, will strongly emphasize the new powers they have and will try to attain a service mix similar to that of a commercial bank.

I think this will be a very difficult undertaking. Some that try will not succeed, and there will be consequent mergers with existing commercial banks.

Many others will continue to concentrate on serving their communities, making primarily local mortgage and other loans. They will operate in much the same fashion as savings and loans associations, and some of the savings and loans will join those savings banks which emphasize traditional commercial bank functions.

The stock institutions (both savings banks and savings and loans) will no longer be trying to obtain the best possible return for depositors, but rather for the stockholders. Is there a difference? In my opinion there is (although with rate regulation and other controls and restraints that have existed for many years, the difference has been more theoretical than real.)

What course will The Bowery follow? Probably conversion to stock. But whether or not conversion takes place, I believe there will be a strong emphasis on what, for a savings bank, must be regarded as new and innovative services and investments.

This venerable institution, "the bank with a social conscience," which for so long was dedicated to serving the consumer, the "little man," and to encouraging thrift and community betterment, will have evolved—not entirely of its own volition—into a bank competing in the marketplace (effectively, I hope) to make as much profit as it possibly can for the benefit of its stockholders.

Oh, what changes high interest rates have wrought! The Bowery may even become eligible to rejoin the American Bankers Association.

The third response came from former Chairman Earl B. Schwulst whose service to the bank dated back to 1936. From 1949 to 1952 he was The Bowery's president; from 1952 to 1962 he was its chairman as well as president; and from 1962 to 1966 he was chairman of the board. Thus, for almost half a century, he had shared all of the institution's vicissitudes.

Now he summed up his feelings about the future by quoting Shelley's "If winter comes, can spring be far behind?" And he began his letter with a summation of The Bowery's most recent trials:

For two years or more prior to the current 1983, The Bowery Savings Bank, along with the other major thrift institutions in the principal financial centers, has been struggling to survive the effects of inflation—an inflation resulting from government deficit financing and the price and wage policies of big business and big labor. The government for many years has been spending far more than its revenues from taxation. It has been

382

financing its deficits largely by borrowing heavily from the commercial banking system, including the Federal Reserve Banks; such borrowings are the equivalent of printing the money to cover the deficits.

Meanwhile, management and labor have often permitted production costs to rise more than productivity gains (if any) would justify. The commercial banking system, including the Federal Reserve, validated these costs and prices by their willingness to finance the process in all its stages—production, marketing, and consumption. High prices resulted in a rising demand for credit, and steadily increasing interest rates followed, some rates exceeding 20 percent.

Mr. Paul Volker, chairman of the Federal Reserve Board, recently stated to a congressional committee that the Fed would not again be a party to such a situation if inflation again threatens to raise its head.

The thrifts were caught in this high interest tide with little means to combat it. As was so often pointed out to investigating committees, most of the thrifts' assets (sometimes referred to as "imbedded" assets) were long-term mortgages and bonds carrying low interest rates. Moreover, the investing powers of the thrifts and their general field of operations were severely restricted by law and regulation.

I am proud of the fact that the management of The Bowery, with the active help and support of its trustees, took the lead in securing needed changes in the law. They were active in securing the legislation which enabled those governmental agencies that insured deposits to strengthen the net worth positions of their thrift institutions whose assets were essentially sound.

And when the Fed, with the concurrence of the Treasury, finally took the step of severely tightening credit, the inflationary trend was stopped; prices fell and the level of interest rates also fell. For a time there was a severe economic slump, with rising unemployment. But the tightening of credit worked. The recession has been easing, production and productivity have been improving, and unemployment has been receding.

And the thrifts have at last turned the corner. The Bowery, as an example, has substantially cut operating expenses. The hemorrhaging of deposits has virtually stopped. Bank borrowings and their heavy cost have been materially reduced. The cash flow position has improved to the point where the bank is, after many months, again entering the mortgage and bond markets in a very substantial way.

So the long winter of discontent has given way to the hope and promise of the new spring which seems to be not far behind.

Yet now, as I look into the crystal ball, I see some clouds on the horizon. At the moment they are not ominous, but they could become so. They are

1. *The foreign situation.* It is full of risks. However, it is hard to believe that the political leaders of our country and of Russia will not have the will, the wisdom, and the determination to avoid nuclear confrontation. In spite of the mutual repugnance each country has for the political and social system of the other, the leaders, if they are the sensible men I believe them to be, will find some way of accommodation, some means of avoiding this final madness.

2. *Deficit financing by the government.* Over the past half century we have had very few years when the federal budget was in surplus. The deficit in the fiscal year just ended was a record breaker, and heavy deficits are forecast for the next several years. If our government cannot live within its income (as you and I and our businesses have to do if we are to avoid bankruptcy), what escape is there from inflation? In its effect inflation is the most regressive and insidious tax. It is regressive because it erodes the value of incomes and falls especially hard upon the laborer and upon those who live on modest and fixed incomes. It is insidious because the poor devil who is hit hardest by it cannot identify the author of it. He probably blames the grocer or the butcher. He does not realize that the principal culprit is his own government.

If and when inflation should again begin to signal serious trouble, the first remedy to be applied will probably be that of tightening credit—that is, raising interest rates. Should that happen before the thrifts have made sufficient headway in converting their "imbedded" assets into higher yielding assets, they could be in trouble again. We can only trust that our President and the Congress will have the fortitude to forestall the revival of inflation by, at least, *moving* toward balancing the budget. They can best do this by cutting spending throughout the government. If that is not sufficient, our taxes should be raised. The imperative thing is to get the budget under control.

3. *Adversary relations between business management and labor.* Let us hope that business management and labor have learned from the recent recession that their relationship is not (or should not be) basically that of adversaries. They seemed during the recession to have made some progress in that direction. After all, both are dependent on the success and profitability of business. Their combined effort should be focused on maximum productivity per unit of production cost. That is the only sane road to higher salaries for management, higher wages and benefits for labor, higher dividends for stockholders, and—last but not least—lower rather than higher prices for the consumer. In short, it is the best way to serve the public interest.

4. *Changed character of major thrifts.* Their deposit structure has radically changed in the past few years, as have their investment powers and the general scope of their operations. Small-saver passbook deposits are shrinking, being supplanted by fixed interest and fixed maturity Certificates of Deposit (CDs) and by high-rate open-market accounts. In these, balances are generally higher than in regular passbook accounts. And depositors are far more sophisticated. They move readily from one bank to another and in and out of open-market investments.

The thrifts have learned from their recent bitter experience that "borrowing short and lending long" is hazardous. There must be a better synchronization of maturities between investments and deposits. The ready mobility of the new type of deposits has created the necessity of maintaining a strong secondary reserve of liquid, short-term investments to deal with unexpected deposit movements and other emergencies. *Flexible* interest rates on investments may be expected to play an increasing role in the portfolios of the thrifts.

And if they are to grow they will require access to the open market to raise capital. We can therefore anticipate a substantial movement of those institutions away from their traditional concept of mutuality into a stock type of organization. Before many years have passed we may see that these institutions have become more and more like commercial banks and possibly indistinguishable from them.

In conclusion let me say that I see this change coming to The Bowery. It does not dismay me. The bank will not forget its origin 150 years ago, nor the motivation which inspired its public-spirited founders to serve the "little fellow." The Bowery will merely be entering a field of broader scope in its service to the public. If The Bowery can continue to have the kind of management and direction that have brought it through the recent crisis, it will hold its own against all competition. And spring will at last have succeeded the winter of near despair.

Of course, I had asked Chairman Ellis T. Gravette, Jr. to add *his* views of the bank's future. Before all else he expressed deep regret for the departure of Vice Chairman Stuart Root. Root had decided to return to the private practice of law, though he would—at Gravette's urging— retain his seat on the board of trustees. Having lauded the vigorous and invaluable services Root had rendered, Gravette continued

> At the writing of this letter, The Bowery Savings Bank is on the edge of one of the most exciting eras in its history. The last four years have been a time of great soul searching. As we have striven for broader powers that would allow us to compete more effectively, we have also been preparing ourselves to take advantage of those powers once they were attained.
>
> The powers have been granted and now we are putting them to work, consequently becoming a new and different institution. The challenge before us is to put these powers to work as quickly and efficiently as possible, so that we can compete with the Wall Street brokerage firms, commercial banks, and large retail organizations which are now our direct competitors.
>
> In addition to offering a broader range of consumer services and commercial services, The Bowery is entering into the international banking market. Our competition has for many years provided international services to its customers and if we are to compete effectively, we must do the same. In September 1983, The Bowery became affiliated with an international holding company which owns an international bank and an asset management company. In the very near future, The Bowery will therefore be able to provide international services to its customers. Through the asset management company,

The Bowery will provide management services for foreign investors in the United States. This has the potential of providing great benefits to the bank, since a large majority of funds invested in foreign countries by Europeans are invested in the United States.

In response to recent changes in the New York State Constitution which permit thrift institutions to convert to a stock form of ownership, The Bowery is putting together plans to recapitalize the bank. In order to be competitive, The Bowery and other mutual institutions must be able to raise capital from other sources besides earnings. Without this ability to raise capital, savings banks have no protection against high interest rate cycles such as those we've recently experienced; mutual institutions would be at the mercy of government subsidy forever. Raising capital is key to the future growth and diversification of The Bowery and other mutual institutions.

In the years ahead, The Bowery will in all likelihood diversify geographically. Repeal of legislation prohibiting interstate banking will happen in the near future. But even without repeal, we are witnessing the transition to interstate banking because of forced or required mergers. This may well mean that The Bowery will merge or become affiliated with other financial institutions across state lines. Some of these financial institutions may not even be banks.

We, of course, can't talk about The Bowery's future without talking about people, because our employees are our future. All the new opportunities we've been granted are meaningless unless our employees are prepared to take advantage of them. In fact, from 1980 to the present, our major focus has been on the development of our people. We've spent considerable resources in providing employees with educational programs that will enable them to meet the challenges of this rapidly changing financial environment. The development of employees is a long process; the rewards are not immediate. We believe, however, that all great achievements are made by first planting a seed and then tending to it and caring for it, until it has grown to maturity.

At The Bowery we're striving for perfection. We want to deliver the most competitive products and the finest services to be found in the financial industries. Well-trained, competent employees are the key to arriving at this goal. There is simply no other way.

Three generations of Bowery Chairmen: Earl B. Schwulst (seated), Morris D. Crawford, Jr. (left), and Ellis T. Gravette, Jr. (right).

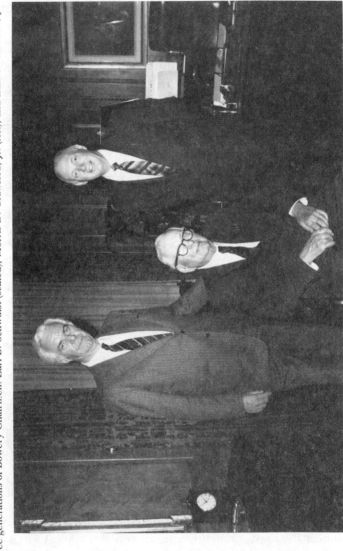

We must attract the most qualified employees. And then we must pay them better than anyone else and provide them with opportunity for development and the finest working conditions. The costs involved are minimal compared to the benefits the Bank will receive in terms of efficiencies and increased margins of profit. In other words, we must meet the needs of our employees if we expect them to help us meet our standard of excellence. If we do, no one will be able to compete with us. *We* will be the competition.

Inevitably one comes to realize that 1984, the 150th year of The Bowery's existence, promises to be the most extraordinary in its history.

What began a century and a half ago as a repository for the nickels and dimes of frugal, hard-working immigrants—and later became New York's leading source of mortgage loans—has reached a wholly new stage of growth. Call today's bank "a financial supermarket" or "a financial department store"; whatever description one favors, The Bowery has become a financial institution that serves virtually every monetary need of those who enter its doors.

Moreover, it has not only expanded domestically but also, as Chairman Gravette has indicated, its services are becoming international.

Never in all the years of its existence has the bank's future been as exciting or as richly diversified as in the flourishing year of 1984. A chronicler of the institution's history can appraise this milestone only by repeating the ancient observation, "All that is past is but prologue."

Appendix

❧

Edward W. Lowry, Jr., 1945 to 1960
Robert J. McKim, 1945 to 1973
Francis F. Randolph, 1946 to 1973
Murray Shields, 1947 to 1968
Cedric A. Major, 1948 to 1961
Francis T. P. Plimpton, 1948 to 1983
Morris D. Crawford, Jr., since 1961
Eugene R. Black, 1963 to 1973
Gustave L. Levy, 1964 to 1976
Alger B. Chapman, 1964 to 1979
Joseph P. McMurray, since 1966
John W. Larsen, since 1966
William H. Donaldson, 1968 to 1973
Robert C. Weaver, 1969 to 1980
James J. O'Leary, 1969 to 1974
Alexander Trowbridge, 1969 to 1976
Walter N. Rothschild, Jr., since 1970
Martha R. Wallace, 1972 to 1981
August M. Strung, 1973 to 1982
Alan Greenspan, 1973 to 1974
James M. Hester, 1973 to 1975
George S. Johnston, since 1973
Roger G. Kennedy, 1973 to 1979
Richard R. Pivirotto, since 1973
Walter B. Shaw, since 1973
George Faunce III, since 1975
Roswell B. Perkins, 1975 to 1982
H. Clifton Whiteman, 1976 to 1977
Edgar R. Fiedler, since 1976
Richard Ravitch, 1977 to 1982
Ralph F. Leach, since 1978
Ellis T. Gravette, Jr., since 1978
Eugene H. Luntey, since 1980
Christopher F. Edley, since 1980
Stuart D. Root, since 1980
Jerald C. Newman, since 1982

OFFICERS

Chairman of the Board
ELLIS T. GRAVETTE, JR.

President
JERALD C. NEWMAN

Executive Vice President
ALAN R. COHEN

Senior Vice Presidents
GARY BRODY
ROBERT DiSALLE
ANTHONY M. GALLENO,
Controller
PAZEL G. JACKSON, JR.,
Mortgage Loans
MICHAEL J. MENDITTO,
Operations Division
DOLORES J. MORRISSEY,
Treasurer
EUGENE A. PAULSEN,
Data Processing Director
LEOPOLD S. RASSNICK,
Secretary and General Counsel
DIANE A. TRACY,
Communications Director

Vice Presidents
JEFFREY S. ASHENDORF,
Deputy General Counsel and
Assistant Secretary
JOSEPH P. BEHAN
BERNARD P. CANNON,
General Auditor
BARBARA J. EDLER,
Marketing Director
SAMUEL FELDMAN
RICHARD H. FREUND
WAYNE GOTTLIEB,
Administrative Assistant
to Vice-Chairman
THOMAS GRANT
RONALD M. HILLERY,
Consumer Loans

LOUIS J. MAGRENE
JACK L. MOLLIN,
Commercial Services
RICHARD T. MORRIN
CLARKE A. MURPHY, JR.
JOHN OLBETER
JOHN M. PANOPOULOS
GRACE PICHARDO,
Associate Communications
Director
ROBERT O. RICHARDS
JACK SCHWARTZ
ALFRED G. WALLACE
J. ROBERT WATTS

Assistant Vice Presidents
EUGENE C. ALCAIDE
RUTH M. BOWMAN
JOSEPH P. BOYLE
KATHARINE B. BROWN,
Deputy General Counsel
KENNETH J. COOPER
RODEINA DAVIS
SANDRA DORFMAN
ANTHONY C. GRIMMER
GRANT H. LIANG
MARION S. MAINO,
Consumer Affairs Director
GERALD P. MAJOR,
Security Officer
EDWARD E. McKINLEY
KATHLEEN MURPHY,
Personnel Director
VINCENT J. PALADINO,
Chief Appraiser
PARVEL A. ROYALE,
Deputy Consumer Loan Officer
MYRNA SOCOL,
Training and
Development Director
JOHN P. WILLIAMS,
Deputy Controller

Index

399

400